Psychologists
Defying
the
Crowd

Psychologists Defying the Crowd

Stories of Those Who Battled the Establishment and Won

Edited by
Robert J. Sternberg

American Psychological Association
Washington, DC

First Printing, July 2002
Second Printing, October 2004

Published by
American Psychological Association
750 First Street, NE
Washington, DC 20002
www.apa.org

To order
APA Order Department
P.O. Box 92984
Washington, DC 20090-2984
Tel: (800) 374-2721; Direct: (202) 336-5510
Fax: (202) 336-5502; TDD/TTY: (202) 336-6123
Online: www.apa.org/books/
Email: order@apa.org

In the U.K., Europe, Africa, and the Middle East, copies may be ordered from
American Psychological Association
3 Henrietta Street
Covent Garden, London
WC2E 8LU England

Typeset in Meridien by EPS Group Inc., Easton, MD

Printer: Port City Press, Baltimore, MD
Cover Designer: NiDesign, Baltimore, MD
Technical/Production Editor: Jennifer L. Zale

The opinions and statements published are the responsibility of the authors, and such opinions and statements do not necessarily represent the policies of the American Psychological Association.

Library of Congress Cataloging-in-Publication Data
Psychologists defying the crowd: stories of those who battled the
establishment and won / edited by Robert J. Sternberg.
    p. cm.
Includes bibliographical references and index.
ISBN 1-55798-919-2 (alk. paper)
1. Psychology—Practice. 2. Psychotherapy—Practice. 3.
Psychologists. 4. Dissenters. I. Sternberg, Robert J.
BF75 .P747 2002
150'.92'2—dc21
                                                    2002018559

British Library Cataloguing-in-Publication Data
A CIP record is available from the British Library.

Printed in the United States of America
First Edition

Contents

Contributors

Elliot Aronson, PhD, Professor Emeritus, Department of Psychology, University of California, Santa Cruz

Ellen Berscheid, PhD, Department of Psychology, University of Minnesota, Minneapolis

Kelly D. Brownell, PhD, Department of Psychology, Yale University, New Haven, CT

John Garcia, MD, PhD, Professor Emeritus, Department of Psychology, Psychiatry, and Biobehavioral Science, University of California, Los Angeles

Howard Gardner, PhD, Graduate School of Education, Harvard University, Cambridge, MA

Jerome Kagan, PhD, Department of Psychology, Harvard University, Cambridge, MA

Elizabeth F. Loftus, PhD, Department of Psychology, University of Washington, Seattle

William J. McGuire, PhD, Department of Psychology, Yale University, New Haven, CT

Walter Mischel, PhD, Department of Psychology, Columbia University, New York

Ulric Neisser, PhD, Department of Psychology, Cornell University, Ithaca, NY

Robert Perloff, PhD, The Joseph M. Katz Graduate School of Business, University of Pittsburgh, Pittsburgh, PA

Paul Rozin, PhD, Department of Psychology, University of Pennsylvania, Philadelphia

Roger N. Shepard, PhD, Professor Emeritus, Department of Psychology, Stanford University, Stanford, CA

Dean Keith Simonton, PhD, Department of Psychology, University of California, Davis

Robert J. Sternberg, PhD, Department of Psychology, Yale University, New Haven, CT

Edward Zigler, PhD, Department of Psychology, Yale University, New Haven, CT

Preface

Today, if you are a graduate student on the job market who has training and published research in cognitive–neuroscientific approaches to the study of memory, and you have half a brain, you will have several good job offers and maybe quite a few such offers. If, however, you are a graduate student combining techniques of personality research with those of cognitive research to study creativity, your job pickings may be slim or nonexistent, even with a whole brain (and a good one at that). There is nothing intrinsically right or wrong with either the problems or methodologies studied by these two hypothetical graduate students. Rather, one of the students has followed the crowd, and the other defied it. And in psychology as in other sciences and other fields, those who follow the crowd generally find the rewards—at least the more immediate ones—to come much more easily and rapidly than do those who defy the crowd.

Creative scientists often defy the scientific establishment (Sternberg, 1999; Sternberg & Lubart, 1995). Such scientists may choose to go their own way with respect to theory, research paradigm, philosophical orientation, or subject matter studied. The risks can be great, because the cost of such defiance can be rejected articles, unfunded grant proposals, and, in extreme cases, scientific oblivion. Yet, these scientists—individuals such as Wilhelm Wundt, Sigmund Freud, and Alfred Binet—are often and perhaps usually the ones whose work lives on, whereas the work of those scientists who conformed to existing scientific tastes may have a shorter life span.

Of course, many conforming psychologists have done great and significant work. But the question is this: Can a scientist not conform and still win? The pressure to conform on young scientists, in general, and psychologists, in particular, is great. Rejection rates of journals and granting agencies in psychology are among the highest of any field, reviews by referees sometimes the most vicious. Radically nonconforming work is less likely to be accepted. Young scientists typically have only 5 to 7 years before they reach an "up or out" decision for tenure, and even graduate students may find that working within the research paradigms of their mentors is substantially safer than finding their own way when they seek a letter of recommendation.

Scientists who defy the crowd are rare because there is so much pressure to conform. In the short term, the rewards of conformity are great: easier job placement or promotion, better funding, easier acceptance of journal submissions and book proposals, approbation of colleagues, and a sense of affiliation with the crowd. In the long run, however, the rewards of creative nonconformity may be substantially greater.

The goal of this book is to show young (and even older) investigators in psychology that defying the crowd can pay off in science and in a scientific career. The book presents brief, first-person accounts from eminent psychologists who have defied powerful establishment forces to find their own way in the face of opposition.

Each contributor to the book was asked to address, to the extent possible, the following eight questions:

1. How have you defied the scientific, clinical, or political establishment in your work?
2. Why did you do this?
3. What kinds of opposition did you encounter?
4. How did you respond to this opposition?
5. What, if anything, would you do differently now?
6. What were the costs to you, professionally and personally, of defying the establishment?
7. What were the benefits of your defiance?
8. What advice would you give other scientists who consider following a similar path of defying the establishment?

The book shows firsthand the trials and tribulations, as well as the joys, of scientists who have chosen their own paths. It also provides positive role models for young (and older) scientists and encourages psychological scientists to stay true to their mission in the field. I hope this book provides inspiration to the many psychologists who have wondered whether standing for principle has been or will be worthwhile.

My efforts in preparation of this book were supported in part by National Science Foundation Grant REC-9979843 and by Javits Act Program Grant R206R000001 as administered by the Office of Educational Research and Improvement, U.S. Department of Education.

Grantees undertaking such projects are encouraged to express freely their professional judgment. This book, therefore, does not necessarily represent the position or policies of the Office of Educational Research and Improvement or the U.S. Department of Education, and no official endorsement should be inferred.

References

Sternberg, R. J. (1999). A propulsion model of creative contributions. *Review of General Psychology, 3,* 83–100.

Sternberg, R. J., & Lubart, T. I. (1995). *Defying the crowd: Cultivating creativity in a culture of conformity.* New York: Free Press.

Psychologists Defying the Crowd

Elliot Aronson, author of *The Social Animal* and inventor of the jigsaw classroom, has been described as a frustrated playwright and director, a popularizer, and a renegade experimental researcher, among other things. None of those titles bothers Aronson, who sees himself as a combination of tough scientist and soft humanist. Defying the establishment has allowed Aronson to make extraordinary headway in the areas of communication, education, and public health. He has combined theory and practice to advance knowledge and to make an impact on the lives of those he studies. His real-world achievements have fostered cooperation in the classroom, increased the use of condoms among college students, and addressed from a causal standpoint the hot-button issue of school violence.

Drifting My Own Way: Following My Nose and My Heart | 1

And something ignited in my soul
fever or unremembered wings.
and I went my own way,
deciphering
that burning fire
and I wrote the first bare line,
bare, without substance, pure
foolishness,
pure wisdom
of one who knows nothing,
and suddenly I saw
the heavens
unfastened
and open.
—Pablo Neruda, *La Poesia* (D. Whyte, Trans.)

After years of writing mediocre poetry, Pablo Neruda (1992) made a momentous decision: He decided to stop trying to imitate other poets and go his own way. And, as beautifully stated in his poem, then, and only then, did he become a true poet. Don't get me wrong. I am not trying to compare myself to Neruda. Far from it. I didn't sit myself down one fine day to make a conscious decision to go my own way at all costs. Nor was it ever my intention or desire to "battle the establishment" or to "defy the crowd" (as suggested by the title of this book).

So what am I doing here? I accepted an invitation to write a chapter for this book because I found the assignment interesting and provocative on two counts: First, it provided me with the opportunity to take a good hard look at what I have been up to in and out of the laboratory over always meant spending a considerable amount of time debriefing participants after collecting their data—to make certain that they left the experiment in at least as good shape as they were in when they entered. It sometimes meant taking the time and trouble to fight it out with human subjects committees—which often consisted of academicians who knew nothing about social psychology, who seemed to feel that human beings were as fragile as soap bubbles, and who were dead set against any procedure that contained the least bit of deception or discomfort. Over the past two decades I watched with dismay as many of my colleagues, faced with these real challenges, retreated from testing interesting hypotheses in a meaningful way. In reading the journals, it struck me that a major concern with many of the experimenters was how to design an experiment that was benign and boring enough to slide, unscathed, past human subjects committees.

Getting Started in This Business

When I was graduating from college in the mid-1950s, it was not my intention to do graduate work in social psychology. I was thinking more in terms of developmental or personality psychology. I thought that social psychology was a fairly pedestrian area. The approach that most social psychologists seemed to be taking was perhaps best exemplified by the Yale research on communication and persuasion. The centerpiece of this line of research was the demonstration that, if you present people with a message indicating that nuclear submarines are feasible, it is more effective if you attribute it to a respected physicist like J. Robert Oppenheimer than if you attribute it to an unreliable source like the Soviet propaganda sheet *Pravda* (Hovland & Weiss, 1951). Needless to say, to a more sophisticated observer, this research probably would be considered an important building block in the foundation of communication research. It did succeed in demonstrating the importance of source credibility. But to a young man just entering graduate school, it was so obvious that it hardly seemed necessary to perform an elaborate experiment to demonstrate that it was true.

Indeed, in those days, almost everything done in social psychology was inspired by a rather simplistic derivation from reinforcement theory. Thus, in the Oppenheimer–*Pravda* example, it is clearly more rewarding (in the sense that it is more likely that one's opinions are correct) to be in agreement with a trustworthy expert than to be in agreement with a biased newspaper run by a totalitarian government. Even classic experiments that weren't specifically inspired by reinforcement theory (e.g., Lewin, Lippitt, & White's, 1939, work on democratic and autocratic leadership and the Asch, 1951, experiment on conformity) could easily be recast and explained in terms of that simple and ubiquitous concept. The problem wasn't that there weren't other theories around. The problem was that there weren't other theories around that could make predictions that couldn't somehow be subsumed under the dominant and apparently more parsimonious wings of reinforcement theory. For example, in the Asch experiment, because it was dealing with something as trivial as the size of a line, a reinforcement theorist might suggest that it is simply more rewarding to go along with the unanimous judgment of four other people than to defy that opinion and brave their scorn and ridicule.

Because the field was so thoroughly dominated by reward–reinforcement theory, whenever an individual performed a behavior it had to be because there was a concrete reward lurking somewhere in the background, so the name of the game, in those days, was let's find the reinforcer. It goes without saying that there are many situations in which reinforcement works well as a way of increasing the frequency of a response. But I kept asking myself, Is that all there is to social behavior? After all, I had lived for 22 years as a social being; I knew that, in my everyday life, there were a lot of things I felt and did that could not be accounted for by simple reinforcement. I strongly suspected that the human heart and mind were more interesting than that. How could I find a way to tap into that complexity, to demonstrate that human beings do not ordinarily live by reinforcement alone?

Then, in 1957, in the spring quarter of my first year as a graduate student at Stanford University, I enrolled in a seminar taught by Leon Festinger. It was a very small seminar. It appears that most graduate students made the conscious decision to keep away from Festinger because he had the reputation of being very tough on students. I soon learned that the rumors were true. Festinger did not suffer fools gladly. (Actually, he didn't suffer smart people gladly either!) He had a rapierlike wit and was fully capable of using it on anyone who tried his patience. Festinger also had the reputation of being brilliant. That was enough to entice me to sign up for his seminar, although I must admit, it was with no small amount of trepidation. In those days, I was not very confident of my own abilities. Indeed, I wasn't sure that I would be able to make it through graduate school. The last thing I needed was to study under a professor who was almost certain to tear me apart. But I wanted to experience his alleged brilliance firsthand.

I was soon to discover that he was more than brilliant. I have known a great many brilliant people; Festinger is the only person I would call an outright genius. And, although he could be (and often was) devastatingly cruel, he also had a surfeit of personal warmth, which I found to be very attractive. Not only did I become his advisee, but he and I also eventually became close personal friends, a friendship that remained close until his death in 1989. But I am getting ahead of my story.

As luck would have it, in the seminar, Festinger was in the process of developing the theory of cognitive dissonance (1957). It is a very simple theory. Basically, all it says is that if an individual simultaneously holds two cognitions that, taken alone, tend to contradict each other, he or she experiences dissonance. *Dissonance* is defined as a negative drive state, not unlike hunger or thirst. Accordingly, a person experiencing dissonance will try to change one or both cognitions to make them more consonant with each other. The way in which people changed their cognitions led to some very interesting predictions.

In those 10 weeks, a whole new world opened up for me—a world of exciting hypotheses, some of which were the direct opposite of predictions made by reinforcement theory. It was in that seminar that social psychology came alive for me. Let me give you one example.

Near the end of that quarter, one of my fellow students (Judson Mills) and I were sitting around drinking coffee and chatting about some of the implications of this brand new theory. We speculated that if people were to go through an unpleasant, painful, or humiliating experience to attain something, they would like that thing better than if the experience they went through to attain it was benign. This would be especially true if the thing they obtained turned out to be unattractive. Theoretically, the cognition "I went through all that unpleasant effort to get this thing" would be dissonant with any aspect of the thing that was less than attractive. To reduce the dissonance, I would downplay the negative aspects of the item and emphasize the positive aspects of the item, rendering it more attractive. Now, that struck me as an interesting and exciting idea to test.

When Mills and I presented our hypothesis and design to our fellow graduate students, they could not conceal their incredulous amusement. In other words, they laughed at us. They were convinced that our hypothesis was utter nonsense because it went against common sense. By common sense, of course, they meant reinforcement theory. Reinforcement theory suggests that stimuli associated with pleasant events (not unpleasant events) would be liked better. But Mills and I followed our curiosity, went our own way, ran the experiment (Aronson & Mills, 1959), and (to steal that powerful last line from Neruda) the heavens unfastened and opened! For me, designing and conducting experiments is hard work. But it is more than hard work; to invent a design and procedure that is exactly right is also an exciting process. It is particularly exciting when, at the end of the experiment, the data are in line with my predictions, open up new avenues of research, and challenge the traditional explanations for phenomena. All that came about in my very first experiment. I felt as though I had come home.

It wasn't me, it was the theory. Dissonance theory proved to be a particularly fruitful vehicle for generating hypotheses that challenged the established way of looking at things. My colleagues and I confirmed the following predictions:

- If people are paid only $1 for telling a lie, they come to believe that lie to a greater extent than if they are paid $20 for doing it (Festinger & Carlsmith, 1959).
- If children are threatened with mild punishment to prevent them from playing with an attractive toy, they devalue the toy to a greater extent than if they are threatened with severe punishment (Aronson & Carlsmith, 1963a).
- If a stranger induces army reservists to eat disgusting food, they come to like it better after eating it than if a friend had induced them to eat it (Zimbardo, Weisenberg, Firestone, & Levy, 1965).

Because the early dissonance researchers were breaking new ground and challenging old assumptions, it is not surprising that we aroused some animosity. It is an understatement to say that our work received a great deal of criticism (much of it hostile; some of it downright derisive) from those psychologists who seemed reluctant to give up their belief in a monolithic reward reinforcement theory (see, e.g., Chapanis & Chapanis, 1964; Lott, 1963a, 1963b).

Criticism notwithstanding, almost all of the early experiments have stood the test of time and have been replicated over and over again by unbiased researchers. On a personal level, I did not experience the criticism—even the hostile criticism—as a deterrent. On the contrary, I have found that the best way to answer critics is not with argument and debate but with more convincing research. Over the next few years, I was so excited by the implications of the theory that I designed and conducted a great many experiments testing a wide variety of its derivations (Aronson, 1961, 1963, 1966a, 1966b, 1966c; Aronson & Carlsmith, 1963a; Aronson, Carlsmith, & Darley, 1963; Aronson & Festinger, 1957; Aronson, Turner, & Carlsmith, 1963; Festinger & Aronson, 1960).

It didn't take very long, however, before my curiosity led me to realize that dissonance theory, as Festinger originally stated it, had some important weaknesses around the edges. Although I always considered dissonance theory to have great heuristic value as a generator of interesting hypotheses, the seeds of my major concerns were sown early on, while I was still in graduate school. Festinger was not very receptive to my concerns. He loved the parsimony and breadth of his theory and didn't want it tampered with. Indeed, he was fond of telling me that he thought the theory was perfect as originally stated. As a graduate student, however, I kept coming up with hypothetical situations in which it wasn't entirely clear to me what the theory would predict—or whether it would make a prediction at all. In short, it was becoming increasingly clear to me that the theory needed its boundaries tightened a bit.

What comes to mind most specifically are two strenuous running arguments that Festinger and I had about two vivid examples he used in his initial book on dissonance theory (Festinger, 1957). The first involved a person stepping out of doors in a rainstorm and not getting wet. Festinger was convinced this would arouse a great deal of dissonance, whereas I had considerable difficulty seeing it. My disagreement went something like this: "What's that got to do with him? It's a strange phenomenon, all right, but unless he feared he was losing his mind, I don't see the dissonance."

The second was Festinger's example of a situation in which dissonance theory didn't apply. This was the case of a man driving, late at night, on a lonely country road and getting a flat tire. When he opened the trunk of his car, he discovered he didn't have a jack. In his book, Festinger maintained that, although the person would experience frustration, disappointment, perhaps even fear, there are no dissonant cognitions in that situation. My argument was succinct: "Of course there is dissonance! What kind of idiot would go driving late at night on a lonely country road without a jack in his car?" "But," Festinger countered, "where are the dissonant cognitions?"

It took me a couple of years, but it gradually dawned on me that what was at the heart of my argument in both of those situations was the self-concept. Thus, in the raindrop situation, as far as I could judge, the self-concept was not involved; no self-concept, little or no dissonance. In the flat tire situation, the self-concept was involved; for me, what was dissonant was (a) the driver's cognition about his idiotic behavior with (b) his self-concept of being a reasonably smart guy. Accordingly, just 3 years after the publication of *A Theory of Cognitive Dissonance* (Festinger, 1957), in a grant proposal to the National Science Foundation, I suggested that dissonance theory makes its strongest and clearest predictions when the self-concept of the individual is engaged (Aronson, 1960). That is, in my judgment, dissonance is greatest and clearest when what is involved is not just any two cognitions but, rather, a cognition about the self and a piece of our behavior that violates that self-concept.

Festinger was not pleased. To defy the crowd is never easy. But, as I implied earlier, to defy Festinger could be downright suicidal! I loved Festinger (harshness and all), and I was not being intentionally defiant. I simply had an idea and wanted to follow it. Indeed, I never intended this theoretical "adjustment" to be a major modification of the theory.

In my opinion this "tightening" retained the core notion of inconsistency but simply shifted the emphasis to the self-concept, thus clarifying more precisely when the theory did or did not apply. However, this apparently minor modification of dissonance theory turned out to have far-reaching heuristic and theoretical ramifications.

In addition, this modification uncovered a hidden assumption contained in the original theory. Festinger's original statement (and all of the early experiments) rested on the implicit assumption that individuals have a reasonably positive self-concept. But if an individual considered himself to be a "schnook," he might expect himself to do schnooky things, like go through a severe initiation to get into a group or say things that he didn't quite believe. For such individuals, dissonance would not be aroused under the same conditions as for people with a favorable view of themselves. Rather, dissonance would occur when negative self-expectancies were violated—that is, when the person with a poor self-concept engaged in a behavior that reflected positively on the self.

To test this hypothesis, Merrill Carlsmith and I (Aronson & Carlsmith, 1962) conducted a simple little experiment that demonstrated that, under certain conditions, college students would be made uncomfortable with success; that they would prefer to be accurate in predicting their own behavior, even if it meant setting themselves up for failure. Specifically, we found that students who had developed negative self-expectancies regarding their performance on a task showed evidence of dissonance arousal when faced with success on that task. That is, after repeated failure at the task, participants who later achieved a successful performance actually changed their responses from accurate to inaccurate ones, to preserve a consistent, although negative, self-concept (see also Aronson & Carlsmith, 1963b).

Over the next several years, I carried this line of thinking a step further (Aronson, 1968; Aronson, Chase, Helmreich, & Ruhnke, 1974), elaborating on the centrality of the self-concept and dissonance processes and suggesting that, in this regard, people generally strive to maintain a sense of self that is both consistent and positive. That is, because most people have relatively favorable views of themselves, they want to see themselves as (a) competent, (b) moral, and (c) able to predict their own behavior.

Briefly, my reasoning goes something like this: Efforts to reduce dissonance involve a process of self-justification because dissonance is almost always experienced after engaging in an action that leaves one feeling stupid or immoral (see Aronson et al., 1974). Moreover, the greater the personal commitment or self-involvement implied by the action, the greater the dissonance and, therefore, the more powerful the attitude change. For example, in the initiation study that Mills and I conducted (Aronson & Mills, 1959), the two dissonant cognitions are as follows: I am a smart person *and* I did a stupid thing by putting all this effort into getting admitted to a lousy group. People's view of themselves as competent, smart people would be threatened unless they justified their having gone through a severe initiation by believing that the group they had joined was worthy of their effort.

As I indicated earlier, Festinger was not pleased with my modification. Indeed, for several years he expressed considerable annoyance to me for what he considered an unwarranted limitation on the scope of the theory. Eventually, however, he came around to my way of thinking. Perhaps he was simply mellowing a bit. At any rate, he conceded that by combining dissonance theory with the notion of the self-concept, I had succeeded in clarifying the predictive power of the theory, enriching its domain and creating linkages to what was to become an emerging body of research on the self (see Aronson, 1999, for an elaboration of this issue).

Studying Interpersonal Attraction

As indicated above, it was dissonance theory that first led me to challenge the monolithic simplicity of reward/reinforcement theory as an explanation of all social behavior. When I turned my interest away from dissonance theory, my curiosity continued to lead me to challenge the simplicity of that notion into domains far removed from dissonance theory. I was convinced that thinking human beings were much more exciting creatures than B. F. Skinner and the other radical behaviorists ever gave us credit for being—and, in the back of my mind, I guess that I was looking for additional domains in which to challenge that way of thinking.

It didn't take long. When I started to become interested in the antecedents of interpersonal attraction, I was struck (but hardly surprised) by the fact that reward/reinforcement theory was once again the dominant way of looking at the world. In the early 1960s, research on liking was still very sparse—and quite boring. Almost all the researchers and commentators at the time seemed content with the notion that we tend to like people best who provide us with an endless supply of tangible rewards; do us favors; shower us with love; agree with us on all opinions and attitudes; and are generally attractive, graceful, wonderful people (Byrne, 1961; Homans, 1961). It stands to reason that we frequently do like people who reward us, like us, and agree with our opinions. But is that all there is to interpersonal attraction? Are more liking, more agreement, and more rewards always better? I seriously doubted it—and I was curious to investigate the exceptions to this general law.

The unifying premise of my research in this area was and is that human beings are cognitive animals. As such, we do more than react to the number and intensity of rewards; we also interpret the meaning of rewards. Thus, sometimes more is less, depending on the sequence and the meaning we attribute to that sequence. For example, although we might like people who like us and dislike people who dislike us, my students and I demonstrated that the people we like best are those that begin by disliking us and gradually come to like us more over time. And the people we dislike most are those that seem to like us early on and, over time, gradually come to dislike us (Aronson & Linder, 1965; Aronson & Sigall, 1967; Berscheid, Brothen, & Graziano, 1976; Mettee, 1971; Mettee, Taylor, & Friedman, 1973). We also showed that, under certain specified conditions, committing unattractive actions (like clumsily spilling a cup of coffee all over oneself) can actually increase a person's attractiveness (Aronson, Helmreich, & LeFan, 1970; Aronson, Willerman, & Floyd, 1966).

Taking Some Time Off to Learn What Kurt Lewin Had Up His Other Sleeve

In those days, our experiments on interpersonal attraction were about as realistic as one could make them—in the laboratory. Gradually, however, I began to realize that something was missing from my experiments in this domain. No matter how realistic we tried to make the laboratory situations, they were a far cry from the way real people met in the real world and became attracted to one another. It was a dilemma. On the one hand, I didn't want to limit myself to observing people in close relationships because I wanted to know what causes what, and only an experiment could give me precise data on causation. On the other hand, the laboratory seemed too sterile a place to study something as intimate as interpersonal attraction. My search for a better way was motivated by my desire to "do things right," as stated near the beginning of this chapter. In this instance this translated into a strong need to study interpersonal attraction in a manner that combined the precision of the laboratory with the intimacy of the real world.

At that time, a friend of mine was leading T-groups for professional psychologists. He suggested that I join his group, partly as a way for me to find what might be missing from my research and partly simply to experience the phenomenon. Basically, a T-group is a group of 10–20 people who meet in a situation in which they are committed to speak openly and honestly about their feelings and impressions of one another and of what is happening in the group. As such, it is a place where people often form strong positive or negative feelings about one another. It is not a therapy group and is usually not led by a therapist but by a social psychologist who knows something about group dynamics and interpersonal communication. The *T* in T-group stands for *training*, which is short for *sensitivity training*.

It is interesting to note that the invention of the T-group came about by accident. But it was an accident that occurred in the presence of a brilliant scientist who was quick to appreciate the importance and potential utility of what he had stumbled upon. In 1946, Kurt Lewin, perhaps the greatest innovator and theorist in the history of experimental social psychology, was asked to conduct a workshop to explore the use of small group discussions as a way of addressing some of the social problems of the day. The participants were educators, public officials, and social scientists. They met during the day in small groups.

But Lewin was also interested in studying group dynamics. So he brought along five or six of his graduate students who closely observed the groups during the day and took extensive notes. The observers then met every evening to discuss their interpretation of the dynamics of the group discussions they had observed that day.

One evening, a few of the participants asked if they could sit in and listen while the graduate students discussed their observations. Lewin granted them permission to attend. As it happened, one of the educators entered the room just as the observers were discussing and interpreting an episode that she had participated in the preceding morning. As she listened she became increasingly agitated. Finally, she interrupted and said that the observers' interpretation was all wrong. She then proceeded to give her version of the episode. The ensuing discussion proved to be interesting and instructive. The next night, all 50 of the participants showed up and eagerly participated in the discussion, frequently disagreeing with the observations and interpretations of the trained observers. The session was both lively and illuminating.

Lewin and his students were quick to grasp the significance of that event: A group engaged in a problem-solving discussion can benefit enormously by taking time out to discuss its own dynamics or "group process" without special training as observers. Indeed, the participants themselves are much better observers of their own processes because each is privy to his or her own intentions, which are not directly available to outside observers, no matter how astute and well trained they may be. After a time, what evolved was the agendaless group: The group could meet with maximum benefit if it had no formal agenda and no problems to discuss other than its own dynamics. By giving and receiving feedback to one another in an honest and nonjudgmental manner, the members of a T-group were, in effect, creating a safe atmosphere for learning to improve their skills at interpersonal communication and for gaining insight into the impact their behavior has on other people.

Lewin was a great teacher, and many of his graduate students went on to become productive social psychologists. Most became adept at conducting laboratory experiments to test social psychological hypotheses. Some preferred to lead T-groups, eschewing the pursuit of basic research in favor of helping individuals gain insight into their own lives. To most T-group leaders, the laboratory seemed pallid and uninteresting. To most experimental social psychologists, T-groups seemed much too vague and impressionistic to be of much scientific value. The evaluation of the effectiveness of T-groups consisted mostly of testimonials from participants which, understandably, was unsatisfying to a scientist.

I refer to these two directions as the two sleeves of Lewin's coat: You shake one sleeve and out pops the hard scientists; you shake the other, and out pops the soft humanists. As a student of Festinger's I was very much in the scientist sleeve.

But once I attended my first T-group, I was hooked. I was thrilled by the atmosphere of openness, honesty, and straight talk that prevailed. Because of the unique process of the T-group, I got to know more about those 14 strangers in 4 hours than I did about most of the colleagues that I had known for more than 4 years. After participating in a few T-groups, I decided to learn more. So I spent a few summers at Bethel Maine (the mecca of T-groups) and eventually, went back to school, becoming an intern at the National Training Laboratory, where I learned to lead T-groups. I am convinced that the T-group is an important tool for self-understanding. I have always enjoyed the process of leading groups and the good feelings that come from being of use to the participants.

For the next several years, there was a sense in which I was leading a double life. During the week I would be conducting rigorous laboratory experiments at the university. On weekends, my wife and I would lead intensive T-groups in the community. My scientific colleagues on campus could not understand why I was "wasting my time" leading T-groups; most of the T-group participants from the broader community could not believe how I could be doing something as sterile as trying to understand the rich complexity of human behavior by conducting laboratory experiments. However, I myself saw no disconnect: In the course of leading T-groups I also learned a lot about interpersonal attraction, social influence, and communication skills that I could not possibly have learned in the social psychological laboratory alone. It is clear to me that my experience as a T-group leader enriched my understanding and skills as an experimental social psychologist. Moreover, my ability to bring the clarity and logic of a scientist into the T-group allowed me to cut through the rhetoric to get to the core of an issue. This particular talent proved to be an important asset for the participants in the groups I led.

Writing The Social Animal

In many ways, writing *The Social Animal* (Aronson, 1972) is the most gratifying thing I have ever done. But it didn't come about because I had an overwhelming desire to write a textbook. Far from it. In the mid-1960s, I was so deeply immersed in doing experiments that writing a textbook was the furthest thing from my mind. The beginnings of *The Social Animal* were actually an outgrowth of the joy I derived from teaching undergraduates.

My favorite course has always been introductory social psychology. I am passionate about the things we know about social psychology, and I get a great kick out of being first—that is, I enjoy the process of awakening college freshmen and sophomores to the excitement and promise of this discipline. But by the mid-1960s, I was growing increasingly impatient with the existing textbooks in our field. It's not that they weren't scholarly enough; it's not that they were inaccurate; it's not that they didn't have enough graphs, tables, charts, or references. If anything, they had too much of that stuff. But it seemed to me that these books were not addressing the problems that our students were most concerned about. For example, in that era, our country was being torn apart by the war in Vietnam, by the racial divide, by political assassinations, and by numerous other events that were taking place in the world. Our existing textbooks did a pretty good job of ignoring those issues. As a result, my students found the texts dull, nonengaging, and, well, too academic. If social psychology was supposed to be about anything, it should be about our insights into the important events and problems that are affecting our daily lives. Something was definitely wrong.

In those days, I'm afraid I did a fair amount of public griping and kvetching about the limitations of existing textbooks. One day, one of my teaching assistants, probably having grown weary of my constant complaining, challenged me by saying, "Why don't you write one of your own?" I dismissed the idea out of hand. It embarrasses me to admit it, but my response was somewhat snobbish. It went something like this:

> I'm a scientist. We scientists shouldn't be wasting our time
> writing textbooks. There are hundreds of social psychologists who

are fully capable of writing a decent textbook. A scientist's time is much better spent doing experiments that shed light on how the human mind works. Let's leave the textbooks to textbook writers.

Yet, I desperately wanted my students to read something that would attempt to relate our scientific research in social psychology with the important events taking place in the world. These things were happening all around us. Let me give you an example of what I was experiencing.

Earlier that year, I had hired a young man to help me paint my house. The painter was a gentle and sweet-natured person who had graduated from high school, joined the army, and fought in Vietnam. After leaving the army, he took up house painting and was a good and reliable craftsman and an honest businessman. I enjoyed working with him. One day while we were taking a coffee break, we began to discuss the war and the intense opposition to it, especially at the local university. It soon became apparent that he and I were in sharp disagreement on this issue. He felt that the American intervention was reasonable and just and would "make the world safe for democracy." I argued that it was a terribly dirty war, that we were killing, maiming, and napalming thousands of innocent people—old people, women, children—people who had no interest in war or politics. He looked at me for a long time; then he smiled sweetly and said, "Hell, Doc, those aren't people; those are Vietnamese! They're gooks." He said it matter-of-factly, without obvious rancor or vehemence. I was astonished and chilled by his response. I wondered how it could be that this apparently good-natured, sane, and gentle young man could develop that kind of attitude. How could he dismiss an entire national group from the human race? Over the next several days, as we continued our dialogue I got to know more about him. It turned out that during the war he had participated in actions in which innocent Vietnamese civilians had been killed.

What gradually emerged was that initially he had been wracked by guilt—and it dawned on me that he might have developed this attitude toward the Vietnamese people as a way of assuaging his guilt. That is, if he could convince himself that the Vietnamese were not fully human, it would make him feel less awful about having hurt them and he could retain his self-concept as a decent person.

I felt strongly that my students deserved to read something that could tell that kind of story from a social psychological perspective. To fill this need, as a supplement to the formal textbook we were using, I prepared a few rough essays on my favorite topics in social psychology and laced them with examples like the one above—examples that served to beg for a social psychological analysis. I mimeographed these essays and gave them away to the students in my course. The essays were hurriedly put together, somewhat sloppy, and certainly incomplete

—but they succeeded in capturing some of my own passion for the field and its relevance to society. A few publishers got wind of the project and asked to see what I had written. They urged me to flesh the essays out a little for possible publication as a textbook.

Once again, I backed away. I told the publishers that I wasn't interested in doing that. I explained that I saw the essays as primarily a teaching tool—not as a textbook. In retrospect, I think I feared that if I ever actually sat down with the idea in mind to write a textbook, I would become "a textbook writer," and that would take me away from my beloved laboratory.

As luck would have it, a short time later I was invited to spend a year as a fellow at the Center for Advanced Study in the Behavioral Sciences in Palo Alto, California, with nothing to do but think and write. Without really planning to, I threw those essays into a carton along with other books, papers, and notes and had them shipped to Palo Alto. So there I was, in my study at the center, without any teaching or administrative responsibilities, and without any research assistants with whom to plan and conduct experiments. I had plenty of time on my hands, and so, between other writing projects, I picked up that collection of sloppy essays and began to play with them. Before I knew it, they began to emerge as actual chapters. After a few months, I had written about half a book.

I was writing it as a very personal statement. In a sense it felt like I was shamelessly opening my family photo album and sharing it with my readers. For example, in opening the chapter on aggression, instead of doing the usual thing like defining *aggression*, I told a true story of a conversation I once had with my young son. It went like this:

> A few years ago, I was watching Walter Cronkite broadcast the news on television. In the course of his newscast, he reported an incident in which U.S. planes dropped napalm on a village in South Vietnam believed to be a Vietcong stronghold. My oldest son, who was about ten at the time, asked brightly, "Hey, Dad, what's napalm?" "Oh," I answered casually, "as I understand it, it's a chemical that burns people; it also sticks so that if it gets on your skin, you can't remove it." And I continued to watch the news.
>
> A few minutes later, I happened to glance at my son and saw tears streaming down his face. Struck by my son's pain and grief, I grew dismayed as I began to wonder what had happened to me. Had I become so brutalized that I could answer my son's question so matter-of-factly—as if he had asked me how a baseball is made or how a leaf functions? Had I become so accustomed to human brutality that I could be casual in its presence? (Aronson, 1972, pp. 141–142)

When the book was about half finished, I showed what I had written to some of the major publishers. They had three basic criticisms:

1. The writing style was far too casual, too chummy, too personal, too intimate.
2. There weren't enough references. (I had committed the grave error of failing to cite 11 experiments to illustrate a point when 1 or 2 would do!)
3. My outline called for only 9 chapters, whereas every fool knows that all textbooks in social psychology "require" 14 or 15 chapters.

I told the publishers that I was writing for college freshmen, not professionals. Accordingly, I refused to formalize my style or turn the book into an encyclopedia of references. Furthermore, my decision to write only 9 chapters was deliberate and nonnegotiable. I would write only about those areas of social psychology that I was truly passionate about. If that left me with only 9 chapters, so be it.

When they heard that, they dropped me like the proverbial hot potato. They told me that it was all well and good to "write for college freshmen," but it was not college freshmen who ordered textbooks—it was professors. And most college professors would not adopt a book like this. They went on to say that because my book could not possibly compete with "real textbooks" and was too scholarly to be a trade book, it would fall between the cracks and perhaps sell a few thousand copies and quickly go out of print. As one publisher put it, "It will sink without a trace!"

One editor (Haywood "Buck" Rogers of the W. H. Freeman Co.) was undaunted. He liked the book. All it takes is one publisher; Freeman published the book in 1972. Much to my surprise and delight, it was an instant success. Undergraduates seem to enjoy it precisely because of its personal style and its relevance to their lives. One reviewer, writing in *Contemporary Psychology*, called it "a masterpiece." Another reviewer, writing in *Contemporary Sociology* called it "a rare gem of a book." The American Psychological Association gave it its National Media Award for books. Thirty years later, it is in its 8th edition and still going strong. It has been translated into 16 foreign languages. During the Cold War, it was particularly popular in Eastern European countries such as Poland and Hungary. My subsequent travels behind the Iron Curtain revealed that the book provided many people with a clearer understanding of what they were experiencing in terms of propaganda, self-justification, and the dynamics of power. This was all wonderful. But most gratifying of all for me has been that whenever I attend a psychology convention, I am invariably approached by people (whom I have never met) who tell me that it is largely because of reading that book as an undergraduate that they decided to become social psychologists.

There is a sense in which the major publishers were right. *The Social Animal* is not among the best-selling books in this country, largely because it is professors who order books. And most professors believe that a textbook should include the requisite 15 chapters, that it should contain a great many references, and that it should be written in a more formal style.

Moving From the Laboratory to Experiments in the Real World

From the very beginning, in the back of my mind I wanted to do the kind of research that would have a direct and positive influence on the lives of the participants in these experiments. I wanted to do some good in the world. But that desire was very much on the back burner. I was so thoroughly enjoying my work in the laboratory, testing theory, and pushing the boundaries of our basic knowledge that, somehow, I never had gotten around to doing good. Then, in the autumn of 1971, I happened to be in the right place at the right time—once again. I was teaching at the University of Texas, happily doing laboratory experiments on interpersonal attraction, when the schools of Austin were ordered to desegregate, and all hell broke loose. Within a few weeks, the schools were in turmoil. African American, White, and Mexican American youngsters were in open conflict; fistfights broke out between the various racial groups in the corridors and schoolyards throughout the city.

As it turned out, the assistant superintendent of schools was a former graduate student at the University of Texas who had become a friend of mine, and he invited me to enter the system with the mandate to do anything within reason to create a more harmonious environment. He suggested that we begin in elementary school, where the situation was tense but less volatile than in the high schools.

My students and I entered a newly desegregated elementary school, and spent several days systematically observing the classroom process to see if we could get any clues as to what was going on and how we might best intervene. We tried to do this with fresh eyes—as if we were anthropologists entering an exotic culture for the first time. This mindset was invaluable. The one thing that leapt out at us was, of course, something that anyone who has ever attended traditional public schools simply takes for granted: The typical classroom is a highly competitive place.

To further exacerbate the problem, the minority kids were underprepared for this competition. The schools they had been attending were substandard. When we tested them we found that, on average, their reading skills were approximately one full grade level behind the White kids' in their classroom. Thus, they were engaged in a highly competitive activity in which they were virtually guaranteed to lose. From what we could gather from interviews we conducted with the students, some of the existing stereotypes were confirmed and magnified: The White kids tended to conclude that the minority kids were stupid and lazy; the minority kids were of the opinion that the White kids were arrogant show-offs.

The events that took place in Austin were not an aberration but were a rather extreme exemplification of the fact that, across the nation, school desegregation was not progressing smoothly and was not having the salutary effects on behavior and attitudes that had been anticipated. In his review of the research literature, Walter Stephan (1978) found that, following school desegregation, the self-esteem of minority children underwent a further decrease, and there was virtually no clear evidence indicating even the slightest decrease in prejudice or stereotyping. In short, desegregation was not having the anticipated positive effects, but we didn't know why.

After observing classrooms and interviewing children, my students and I had one pretty good clue as to what might be going wrong. We surmised that it might be the highly competitive nature of the classroom that was preventing desegregation from working in the way it was intended to work. Accordingly, our intervention consisted of restructuring the dynamics of the classroom; we changed the atmosphere from a competitive one to a cooperative one. This involved inventing, developing, and implementing a technique that created small interdependent groups, designed to place the students of various racial and ethnic groups in a situation in which they needed to cooperate with one another to attain their personal goals. We called it the *jigsaw classroom*, because it resembled the assembling of a jigsaw puzzle (Aronson, 1978, 1992; Aronson, Blaney, Sikes, Stephan, & Snapp, 1975; Aronson & Bridgeman, 1979; Aronson & Gonzalez, 1988; Aronson & Patnoe, 1997).

We invented this technique within a few days of our first entry into the classroom. I am frequently asked how we were able to diagnose the problem and invent a solution as quickly as we did. Occasionally, the question is asked a bit more aggressively: "What made *you guys* so smart? How come the teachers weren't able to see that competition was the problem and cooperation the solution?" We weren't that smart; it's just that we were outsiders. In 1971, the competitive structure of the typical classroom was more or less taken for granted. At that time, most teachers were immersed in that structure and seemed to implicitly accept it as the way things had to be. I think that our coming from outside the system (and setting ourselves to observe the classroom as if we were anthropologists observing an exotic culture) gave us an enormous advantage. With that mind-set, the destructive aspects of competition fairly leapt out at us.

Within a week of instituting jigsaw, the impact was palpable. The entire classroom atmosphere changed as kids began to gain respect and liking for one another across racial lines. To witness this taking place was the single most exciting experience I had ever had as a researcher. The formal results of our experiment with the jigsaw classroom confirmed what we had seen with the naked eye. Compared with students in traditional classrooms, students in jigsaw groups showed a decrease in their general prejudice and stereotyping, as well as an increase in their liking for their groupmates, both within and across ethnic boundaries. In addition, they performed better on objective exams, showed a significantly greater increase in self-esteem, and liked school better (absenteeism was significantly lower in jigsaw classrooms than in traditional classrooms in the same school). Moreover, students in schools where the jigsaw technique was practiced showed substantial evidence of true integration—that is, in these schoolyards there was far more intermingling among the various races and ethnic groups than in the schoolyards of schools using more traditional classroom techniques. Finally, students in the jigsaw classrooms developed a greater ability to empathize with others and to see the world through the perspective of others than students in traditional classrooms did (Aronson & Bridgeman, 1979; Bridgeman, 1981).

This was truly an exciting event. My students and I had found a way to make desegregation work the way it was intended to work! I was so excited by the success of the jigsaw technique that I virtually stopped doing laboratory experiments for the next few years and devoted an enormous amount of time to trying to give my invention away. This was not considered a "smart" thing to do by the academic establishment, as you will see! Nevertheless, I decided to publish our initial findings, not in an esoteric psychology journal (that is read only by academic psychologists and their hapless graduate students) but in the popular magazine *Psychology Today* (Aronson et. al., 1975). I then made some 200 photocopies of the article and sent it to principals and school superintendents all over the country. In an accompanying letter, I offered to train their teachers to use jigsaw (in a 5-hour workshop) without charge.

Although I was invited into a handful of schools, to my surprise and great disappointment, during those first few years most school administrators were not at all interested in what I had to offer. They expressed a desire to avoid "rocking the boat." That is, as long as their schools were not in crisis, they seemed reluctant to introduce so radical a technique that might lead some White parents to complain.

For me, personally, those years were frustrating and disheartening. I was confident that we had a technique that would make desegregation work, and I had collected convincing experimental data to prove it. I was eager to give it away. Yet, very few administrators wanted it.

I now realize that my expectations were far too high. What I learned was that bureaucrats are reluctant to try anything new unless there is a crisis. Moreover, ideas sometimes need time to marinate, and sometimes the ideas need a little help through formal recognition. Such recognition came in 1979, when, in commemoration of the 25th anniversary of *Brown v. Board of Education,* the U.S. Civil Rights Commission named Austin as a model city in which school desegregation worked in the manner intended. Much of the credit went to jigsaw. Interest in jigsaw immediately picked up, and I subsequently received a great many invitations to enter school systems and train teachers to use the technique. The striking results described above have now been successfully replicated in dozens of classrooms in all regions of the country and abroad.

But the fact that I seemed to be turning my back on the laboratory did not go unnoticed by the social psychology establishment. In 1976, I was invited to give a keynote address at the annual meeting of social psychology's elite scientific organization, the Society of Experimental Social Psychologists. The suggested title of the address was "What Ever Became of Elliot Aronson?" I accepted the invitation and took their question seriously. I tried to answer it by describing the jigsaw classroom and why I was so passionate about it. Although it was not my intention, I have since learned that my talk encouraged several members of the audience to step out of their laboratory from time to time.

Hanging Out in the Real World—For a While

The jigsaw research enabled me to see how exciting it could be to use what I knew as a social psychologist to have a direct, positive impact on thousands of lives. Accordingly, when I felt ready to get back into doing research, instead of returning to the laboratory, I began looking around for another crisis. During this era, a major crisis was the shortage of energy. In addition to people enduring long lines at gasoline pumps, poor and elderly people on fixed incomes were being forced to choose between heating and eating.

At that time the major utilities had a home audit program in which customers could request an engineer to examine their homes and suggest ways to make them more energy efficient. Moreover, the utilities were offering zero-interest loans to cover the cost. It was a great service and a great bargain. Unfortunately, although a great many homeowners requested an audit, only a small percentage followed the suggestions of the auditors.

At the request of the utility companies, a few of my students and I accompanied auditors, observed their behavior, and made some simple suggestions. We urged them to get the homeowner more involved in the audit itself (commitment) by accompanying the auditor as he examined the house. In addition, we coached the auditors to use more vivid language in describing how the homeowner was currently wasting money. For example, the presence of a few cracks under the doors doesn't sound important to a homeowner. But if you informed the homeowner that if one added up all the cracks, they would form a hole the size of a basketball, that would get his or her attention. Our intervention tripled the success rates of the auditors we trained (compared with a control group). Our intervention not only had a salutary effect on the environment, but it also resulted in significant financial savings for the individual homeowner (Aronson & Gonzales, 1990; Gonzales, Aronson, & Costanzo, 1988; Yates & Aronson, 1983).

Somewhat later, my interest in real-world crises got me to turn toward the AIDS epidemic. AIDS is almost always caused by voluntary social behavior—unprotected sexual intercourse. Accordingly, it seemed logical for social psychologists to enter that realm. The only thing we had to do was persuade sexually active people to use condoms. (The word *only* in this context is one of the biggest words in the English language!) Ironically, this research, although aimed at saving the lives of sexually active people in the real world, took me back into the laboratory. In addition, this applied research resulted not only in a successful intervention strategy, but it also brought me full circle in my own career—back to theory building. That is to say, in pursuit of applying social psychology to an important real-world problem, I unintentionally ended up contributing further to our understanding of the theory of cognitive dissonance.

Here's how I got into the condom business. It was becoming increasingly clear to me that traditional advertising campaigns would not make much of a dent in the sexual behavior of young people. Our government had spent tens of millions of dollars on such campaigns to very little avail. Our surveys showed that, although sexually active college students are aware of AIDS as a serious problem and are aware that using condoms is an excellent protection against AIDS and other sexually transmitted diseases, only a surprisingly small percentage used condoms regularly. Most nonusers were in a state of denial. In effect, they were saying, "AIDS is a serious and deadly problem, all right, but not for me!"

How might we overcome the denial mechanism? My early research on dissonance theory had revealed that, in a situation like this, self-persuasion is far more effective than direct persuasion attempts. Specifically, instead of trying to convince sexually active young people of the virtues of safe sex through direct rational argument, I considered making an end run around the denial mechanism by applying the counterattitudinal advocacy paradigm, that is, by getting people to present an argument favoring condom use. However, it soon became obvious that counterattitudinal advocacy is not possible in this situation because sexually active young people already believe that AIDS is a problem, and they already believe that condom use is a good thing—for everyone else but not for them. Quite a dilemma: Not only are traditional persuasion tactics ineffective, but there is no counterattitude for them to advocate!

I puzzled over this issue for some time, until I hit on a solution. It took the form of a scenario: Suppose you are a sexually active college student and, like most, (a) you do not use condoms regularly, and (b) you have managed to blind yourself to the dangers inherent in having unprotected sex. Suppose, on going home for Christmas vacation, you learn that Charley, your 16-year-old kid brother, has just discovered sex and is boasting to you about his many and varied sexual encounters. What do you say to him? Chances are, as a caring, responsible older sibling, you will dampen his enthusiasm a bit by warning him about the dangers of AIDS and other sexually transmitted diseases, and you will urge him to, at least, take proper precautions by using condoms every time he makes love.

Suppose that I am a friend of the family who was invited to dinner and who happens to overhear this exchange between you and your kid brother. What if I were to pull you aside and say, "That was very good advice you gave Charley. I'm very proud of you for being so responsible; by the way, how frequently do *you* use condoms?"

In other words, I am confronting you with your own hypocrisy; I am making you mindful of the fact that you are not practicing what you preach. Most individuals have a need to see themselves as people of integrity. People of integrity practice what they preach. Your self-concept as a person of integrity is threatened by your own behavior—behavior that suggests you might lack integrity, that you might be behaving hypocritically. How might you reestablish your self-concept as a person of high integrity? There is only one surefire way: by beginning forthwith to put into practice what you have just finished preaching. In short, to start using condoms consistently.

In a series of experiments, my students and I constructed a procedure very much like the above scenario (Aronson, Fried, & Stone, 1991; Fried & Aronson, 1995; Stone, Aronson, Crain, Winslow, & Fried, 1994). The results of these experiments are powerful. Immediately after the experiment, those college students who were put in the "hypocrisy" condition, when given the opportunity to buy condoms at a reduced price, purchased substantially more condoms than students in the control conditions. The long-term effects of the hypocrisy intervention are even more impressive: Some 3 months later, when interviewed on the telephone about their sexual behavior, 92% reported that they were now using condoms regularly. This percentage is almost twice as high as that of participants in the control conditions.

In examining the early induced compliance experiments (in which participants are induced to tell a lie for either a small incentive or a large one), like Festinger and Carlsmith's (1959) classic $1–$20 experiment discussed earlier, Cooper and Fazio (1984) made an interesting discovery: In these experiments, not only was inconsistency present, but aversive consequences were also always present; that is, lying to another person is usually aversive because it can do the recipient harm. Cooper and Fazio then made an interesting but rather huge leap: that dissonance is not due merely to inconsistent cognitions at all—rather, it is aroused only when an individual feels personally responsible for bringing about an aversive or unwanted event. Or, to put it in my terms, dissonance is caused solely by harming another person, which threatens one's self-concept as a morally good human being.

I never bought into this analysis, but I had been at a loss as to how to perform the crucial experiment: to produce inconsistency in the Festinger/Carlsmith type of experiment without also producing aversive consequences for the recipient of one's message. After all, if you are misleading another person by telling him or her something you believe is false, then you are always bringing about aversive consequences, aren't you? But, without quite realizing it at the moment of conception, with the hypocrisy paradigm I seem to have stumbled onto the solution. In this procedure, the participants are preaching what they are not practicing (and are therefore experiencing dissonance), but where are the aversive consequences for the audience in the condom experiment? There are none. Indeed, to the extent that the "hypocrites" succeed in being persuasive, far from producing aversive consequences for the recipients, they may well be saving their lives. And still, it is clear from the data that our participants were experiencing dissonance. For a fuller discussion of this theoretical controversy see Thibodeau and Aronson (1992).

Jigsaw Revisited—Going Public in a Big Way

On April 20, 1999, at Columbine High School two students, consumed by rage and armed with an arsenal of guns and explosives, went on a rampage, killing a teacher and 12 of their fellow students and then turning their guns on themselves. It was the worst school massacre in U.S. history. It was one of nine that happened in a 2-year period, and it was not the last.

I was appalled at the naïve and feeble solutions proposed by our policymakers in the aftermath of that horrifying event: adding more security guards and metal detectors in our schools, forcing students to show respect for their teachers by addressing them as "sir" and "ma'am," and posting the Ten Commandments on school bulletin boards. But, by far, the most counterproductive measure of all involved a concerted effort by a great many school bureaucrats to profile potential rampage killers. My own grandson came home from school one day and reported that the principal of his school called an assembly of the entire student body and asked them to be on the lookout for loners, odd-balls, and other strange students and report them.

This is almost certainly a giant step in the wrong direction. My own analysis of the situation leads to the conclusion that, as horrendous as the killings were, they are merely the lethal, pathological tip of a huge iceberg—the poisonous social atmosphere that exists in virtually all high schools in this country. Almost all the recent rampage killings were the direct result of unpopular kids being pushed over the edge into patho-logical behavior by being taunted, bullied, and humiliated by their fel-low students.

Needless to say, there is no excuse or justification for what the killers did. But if we are to prevent such killings in the future, it is essential to get to the root cause of the problem, and to my mind, the root cause is the exclusionary social atmosphere of high schools in America. Most high schools consist of a hierarchy of cliques with the kids near the bottom of the social hierarchy being ostracized and ridiculed. A sizeable number of teenagers experience this kind of abuse.

Blessedly, very few kids lash out lethally against their classmates. When they do, their action understandably gets the headlines. But, for hundreds of thousands of kids who don't lash out, school can be a living hell. Most of them suffer in silence—but they suffer. Some seriously contemplate suicide. Asking the popular kids to point out the "losers and loners" is akin to giving them license to taunt them even more viciously because now the school authorities are labeling them as po-tential rampage killers.

With policymakers and school authorities going in the wrong direc-tion, I felt it was imperative for social psychologists to make their views known to the general public. So once again, I chose to leave the friendly confines of the laboratory. Our research on the jigsaw classroom had demonstrated that we can build empathy and compassion across the greatest clique divide imaginable—racial and ethnic prejudice. If we were successful at bridging that divide, surely we could drastically reduce the taunting that makes school so unpleasant for so many kids. And, by the way, it might put an end to rampage killings as well. So, in an attempt to bring social psychological wisdom into this situation, I wrote a jargon-free trade book aimed at teachers, school administrators, and parents (Aronson, 2000). To get my ideas as widely distributed as possible, I went public in a big way. I subjected myself to interviews with the *New York Times*, *National Public Radio*, *CNN*, *MSNBC*, and *Dateline NBC* as well as dozens of small local radio and television stations. I gave speeches around the country to Parent–Teacher Association groups, where I gave away hundreds of copies of my book. I set up my own Web site (http://www.jigsaw.org/), which enabled any teacher to download all the material they would need to use jigsaw in their classrooms —without charge. In short, I did the unacademic thing: I became a shameless huckster. Why? Because I strongly believe that when we are certain of what we know, it is our duty, as social psychologists, to get off our ass and go public—as loudly and as forcefully as we can.

That brings me to the present moment. What will I be up to next year or in the next decade? I have no idea—thank goodness!

References

Aronson, E. (1960). *The cognitive and behavioral consequences of the confirmation and disconfirmation of expectancies.* Grant proposal submitted to the National Science Foundation, Harvard University, Cambridge, MA.

Aronson, E. (1961). The effect of effort on the attractiveness of rewarded and unrewarded stimuli. *Journal of Abnormal and Social Psychology, 63,* 375–380.

Aronson, E. (1963). Effort, attractiveness, and the anticipation of reward. *Journal of Abnormal and Social Psychology, 67,* 522–525.

Aronson, E. (1966a, August). Problem: To find evidence of discomfort as a function of "dissonant" success. In L. Festinger (Chair), *Methodological problems of social psychology.* Proceedings of the XVIII International Congress of Psychology, 34th Symposium, Moscow.

Aronson, E. (1966b). The psychology of insufficient justification: An analysis of some conflicting data. In S. Feldman (Ed.), *Cognitive consistency* (pp. 109–133). New York: Academic Press.

Aronson, E. (1966c). Threat and obedience. *Trans-action,* March–April.

Aronson, E. (1968). Dissonance theory: Progress and problems. In R. P. Abelson, E. Aronson, W. J. McGuire, T. M. Newcomb, M. J. Rosenberg, & P. H. Tannenbaum (Eds.), *Theories of cognitive consistency: A sourcebook* (pp. 237–289). Skokie, IL: Rand-McNally.

Aronson, E. (1972). *The social animal.* New York: Worth/Freeman.

Aronson, E. (1978). *The jigsaw classroom*. Beverly Hills, CA: Sage.

Aronson, E. (1992). The return of the repressed: Dissonance theory makes a comeback. *Psychological Inquiry, 3,* 303–311.

Aronson, E. (1999). Dissonance, hypocrisy, and the self-concept. In E. Harmon-Jones & J. Mills (Eds.), *Cognitive dissonance: Progress on a pivotal theory in social psychology* (pp. 103–126). Washington, DC: American Psychological Association.

Aronson, E. (2000). *Nobody left to hate: Teaching compassion after Columbine*. New York: Worth/Freeman.

Aronson, E., Blaney, N., Sikes, J., Stephan, C., & Snapp, M. (1975). Busing and racial tension: The jigsaw route to learning and liking. *Psychology Today, 8,* 43–50.

Aronson, E., & Bridgeman, D. (1979). Jigsaw groups and the desegregated classroom: In pursuit of common goals. *Personality and Social Psychology Bulletin, 5,* 438–446.

Aronson, E., & Carlsmith, J. M. (1962). Performance expectancy as a determinant of actual performance. *Journal of Abnormal and Social Psychology, 65,* 178–182.

Aronson, E., & Carlsmith, J. M. (1963a). Effect of severity of threat on the valuation of forbidden behavior. *Journal of Abnormal and Social Psychology, 66,* 584–588.

Aronson, E., & Carlsmith, J. M. (1963b). Some hedonic consequences of the confirmation and disconfirmation of expectancies. *Journal of Abnormal and Social Psychology, 66,* 151–156.

Aronson, E., & Carlsmith, J. M., & Darley, J. M. (1963). The effects of expectancy on volunteering for an unpleasant experience. *Journal of Abnormal and Social Psychology, 66,* 220–224.

Aronson, E., Chase, T., Helmreich, R., & Ruhnke, R. (1974). A two-factor theory of dissonance reduction: The effect of feeling stupid or feeling "awful" on opinion change. *International Journal of Communication Research, 3,* 340–352.

Aronson, E., Ellsworth, P., Carlsmith, J. M., & Gonzales, M. H. (1990). *Methods of research in social psychology*. New York: McGraw-Hill.

Aronson, E., & Festinger, L. (1957). Some attempts to measure tolerance for dissonance [Wright Development Center, Technical Report 58–492, ASTIA Document No. 207–337].

Aronson, E., Fried, C., & Stone, J. (1991). Overcoming denial and increasing the intention to use condoms through the induction of hypocrisy. *American Journal of Public Health, 81,* 1636–1638.

Aronson, E., & Gonzalez, A. (1988). Desegregation, jigsaw, and the Mexican-American experience. In P. A. Katz & D. Taylor (Eds.), *Towards the elimination of racism: Profiles in controversy* (pp. 326–351). New York: Plenum Press.

Aronson, E., & Gonzales, M. (1990). The social psychology of energy conservation. In J. Edwards (Ed.), *Social influence processes and prevention* (pp. 247–278). New York: Plenum Press.

Aronson, E., Helmreich, R., & LeFan, J. (1970). To err is humanizing—Sometimes: Effects of self-esteem, competence, and a pratfall on interpersonal attraction. *Journal of Personality and Social Psychology, 16,* 259–264.

Aronson, E., & Linder, D. (1965). Gain and loss of esteem as determinants of interpersonal attractiveness. *Journal of Experimental Social Psychology, 1,* 156–171.

Aronson, E., & Mills, J. (1959). The effect of severity of initiation on liking for a group. *Journal of Abnormal and Social Psychology, 12,* 16–27.

Aronson, E., & Patnoe, S. (1997). *Cooperation in the classroom: The jigsaw method.* New York: Longman.

Aronson, E., & Sigall, H. (1967). Opinion change and the gain–loss model of interpersonal attraction. *Journal of Experimental Social Psychology, 3,* 178–188.

Aronson, E., Turner, J., & Carlsmith, J. M. (1963). Communicator credibility and communication discrepancy as determinants of opinion change. *Journal of Abnormal Social Psychology, 67,* 31–36.

Aronson, E., Willerman, B., & Floyd, J. (1966). The effect of a pratfall on increasing interpersonal attractiveness. *Psychonomic Science, 4,* 227–228.

Asch, S. E. (1951). Effects of group pressure upon the modification and distortion of judgments. In H. Guetzkow (Ed.), *Groups, leadership and men* (pp. 177–190). Pittsburgh, PA: Carnegie Press.

Berscheid, E., Brothen, T., & Graziano, W. (1976). Gain–loss theory and the "law of infidelity": Mr. Doting versus the admiring stranger. *Journal of Personality and Social Psychology 33,* 709–718.

Bridgeman, D. (1981). Enhanced role-taking through cooperative interdependence: A field study. *Child Development, 52,* 1231–1238.

Byrne, D. (1961). Interpersonal attraction and attitude similarity. *Journal of Abnormal and Social Psychology, 62,* 713–715.

Chapanis, N. P., & Chapanis, A. (1964). Cognitive dissonance. *Psychological Bulletin, 61,* 1–22.

Cooper, J., & Fazio, R. H. (1984). A new look at dissonance theory. In L. Berkowitz (Ed.), *Advances in experimental social psychology* (Vol. 17, pp. 229–266). Orlando, FL: Academic Press.

Festinger, L. (1957). *A theory of cognitive dissonance.* Evanston, IL: Row, Peterson.

Festinger, L., & Aronson, E. (1960). Arousal and reduction of dissonance in social contexts. In D. Cartwright & E. Zander (Eds.), *Group dynamics* (3rd ed., pp. 125–136). New York: Harper & Row.

Festinger, L., & Carlsmith, J. M. (1959). Cognitive consequences of forced compliance. *Journal of Abnormal and Social Psychology, 58,* 203–211.

Fried, C., & Aronson, E. (1995). Hypocrisy, misattribution, and dissonance reduction: A demonstration of dissonance in the absence of aversive consequences. *Personality and Social Psychology Bulletin, 21,* 925–933.

Gonzales, M., Aronson, E., & Costanzo, A. (1988). Increasing the effectiveness of energy auditors: A field experiment. *Journal of Applied Social Psychology, 18,* 1049–1066.

Homans, G. C. (1961). *Social behavior: Its elementary forms.* New York: Harcourt Brace & World.

Hovland, C. I., & Weiss, W. (1951). The influence of source credibility on communication effectiveness. *Public Opinion Quarterly, 15,* 635–650.

Lewin, K., Lippitt, R., & White, R. K. (1939). Patterns of aggressive behavior in experimentally created "social climates." *Journal of Social Psychology, 10,* 271–299.

Lott, B. E. (1963a). Rejoinder. *Journal of Abnormal and Social Psychology, 67,* 525–526.

Lott, B. E. (1963b). Secondary reinforcement and effort: Comment on Aronson's "The Effect of Effort on the Attractiveness of Rewarded and Unrewarded Stimuli." *Journal of Abnormal and Social Psychology, 67,* 520–522.

Mettee, D. R. (1971). Changes in liking as a function of the magnitude and affect of sequential evaluations. *Journal of Experimental Social Psychology, 7,* 157–172.

Mettee, D. R., Taylor, S. E., & Friedman, H. (1973). Affect conversion and the gain-loss liking effect. *Sociometry, 36,* 494–513.

Neruda, P. (1992). La poesia (D. Whyte, Trans.). In D. Whyte (Ed.), *Fire in the earth.* Langley, WA: Many Rivers Press.

Stephan, W. G. (1978). School desegregation: An evaluation of predictions made in *Brown v. Board of Education. Psychological Bulletin, 85,* 217–238.

Stone, J., Aronson, E., Crain, A. L., Winslow, M. P., & Fried, C. B. (1994). Inducing hypocrisy as a means of encouraging young adults to use condoms. *Personality and Social Psychology Bulletin, 20,* 116–128.

Thibodeau, R., & Aronson, E. (1992). Taking a closer look: Reasserting the role of the self-concept in dissonance theory. *Personality and Social Psychology Bulletin, 18,* 591–602.

Yates, S., & Aronson, E. (1983). A social psychological perspective on energy conservation in residential buildings. *American Psychologist, 38,* 435–444.

Zimbardo, P., Weisenberg, M., Firestone, I., & Levy, B. (1965). Communicator effectiveness in producing public conformity and private attitude change. *Journal of Personality, 33,* 233–255.

Ellen Berscheid was a principal figure in what she terms "the Proxmire affair," a political debacle instigated by the powers that be in Washington, DC. Berscheid is a recipient of Sen. William Proxmire's (D-WI) Golden Fleece award for egregious misuse of taxpayer funds, as he termed her National Science Foundation (NSF) proposal to study, among other things, romantic love. In the days when the American divorce rate hovered around 50%, a fact which political figures did not hesitate to publicly lament, Proxmire thought the topic frivolous and that the NSF should "get out of the love business" and leave the matter to poets and composers. In the course of the uproar that followed Proxmire's attack, Berscheid learned several difficult lessons, including the importance of keeping one's mouth shut from time to time and the true meaning of the word *journalist*. Her trials and tribulations resulted in numerous important studies on close interpersonal relationships and romantic love.

Ellen Berscheid

On Stepping on Land Mines 2

"**H**e's naked!" cried the little boy in the fairy tale "The Emperor's New Clothes" when he saw the emperor proudly parading his invisible finery. For his observation, the boy no doubt got a cuff on the ear from his mother and the admonition that "Nice boys don't say things like that about the emperor." He had simply spoken the truth as he saw it, and what he saw was a naked old man strutting about. Like many nonconformists who appear to "defy" the crowd, the boy acted out of ignorance. He didn't know what everyone else in the kingdom knew—that the emperor's sartorial splendor was visible to everyone but themselves. Had he been aware of the establishment norm, he might have chosen to keep his mouth shut and cheerfully forgone the badge of courage generations of children subsequently bestowed on him.

Had I known that Sen. William Proxmire (D-WI) would select my National Science Foundation (NSF) research grant to receive his first "Golden Fleece" award in 1976 and that the ensuing controversy would consume my personal and professional life for the next few years, I, too, might have chosen to study something other than interpersonal attraction. I most certainly would not have mentioned in the abstract of my research proposal that I hoped to study one of the strong forms of attraction, romantic love, in the last year of the project. As it happened, however, I did not know that romantic love was a politically sensitive topic. Perhaps I should have. A few decades earlier, Harry Harlow (1958) had been pilloried by a congressional investigating committee and ridiculed by the press for studying "monkey love." At the time I wrote my proposal, however, it seemed only common sense that more should be known about romantic love, for it had become the sine qua non of marriage in the United States (e.g., Kephart, 1967). Moreover, politicians were expressing their concern about the then-escalating divorce rate with the same frequency with which they praised motherhood and apple pie. It would have been hard to guess that those concerned with what they routinely called the "disintegration of the family" would not welcome greater understanding of the basis on which marriages were being contracted and dissolved.

There were other reasons why I did not foresee that I had stepped on a land mine about to explode. Positive and negative sentiment toward others is the underlying theme of all human relationships; thus, matters of interpersonal attraction lie at the heart of all of the sciences endeavoring to understand the processes and products of human association, which is to say, matters of attraction lie at the core of the social and behavioral sciences and many of the biological sciences as well. Moreover, identification of the antecedents and consequences of attraction long had been a staple of social psychological inquiry. As early as 1969, sufficient attraction theory and research had accumulated that my colleague Elaine Walster [Hatfield] and I were able to publish a thin book, *Interpersonal Attraction*, that subsequently was translated into several languages and used by scholars throughout the world. The bulk of my NSF project, in fact, was simply attraction "business as usual"; its only departure from the mainstream of conventional attraction research was my hope of making a preliminary foray into the mysterious thicket of romantic love.

Not only was I not aware that I was proposing anything singular, I was ignorant of the facts that Proxmire chaired the Senate Appropriations Committee responsible for NSF funding and that he had been warring with the foundation for some time. Finding the NSF unresponsive to his concerns, he had begun to attack individual NSF principal investigators. These attacks, too, had escaped my notice, although several distinguished contributors to psychology and other disciplines had received the senator's public opprobrium.

Thus, I was surprised—but not unduly concerned—when one afternoon in February 1976 (shortly before Valentine's Day and just as many Americans were wincing at their federal tax bills), I received a call from a reporter from the *Los Angeles Times* who requested my comment on a press release issued by Proxmire attacking as a waste of taxpayer money a number of research projects funded by the NSF; these included my own project and, if I recall correctly, one on the Alaskan brown bear and one on an endangered South American bird. It soon became evident that Proxmire had constructed a new and effective publicity vehicle for his attacks on the NSF: Golden Fleece awards for the most egregious misuses of taxpayer funds. Fortunately for the bear and the bird, the only portion of the release that captured the attention of the press was my research project—inaccurately described by Proxmire as a "study of romantic love"—and the senator's claim that of all the things people did not want investigated, romantic love was at the top of the list. He declared that the NSF should get out of the "love business" and leave the matter to Elizabeth Barrett Browning and Irving Berlin.

In a brief but front-page article, accompanied by a photo of me and of Proxmire, the *Los Angeles Times* reporter accurately relayed what he termed my "soft-spoken" rejoinder. That was the last time for many years that I could be described as soft-spoken. A media blitz, accompanied by thundering salvos from other quarters, immediately began with terrifying ferocity, and it lasted much longer than the customary "15 minutes." It is no exaggeration to say that virtually every newspaper and radio station in this and other countries (the only exception being mainland China, not yet open to the West) ran articles on the controversy, usually with my photo and Proxmire's and usually on the front page. (One befuddled psychologist, apparently glancing at the photos and the word *love* in the headline, sent me a congratulatory note on my engagement to Proxmire.) Almost all syndicated print columnists weighed in on the issue, as did the likes of Johnny Carson, Phil Donohue, and numerous other television personalities and celebrities, including Warren Beatty, who requested that I appear on television with him. My telephone, both at home and at the office, rang continuously, night and day. The bushel baskets of mail I received contained requests for interviews and for information from all over the world—often from people in countries I had never heard of and also from those still behind the communist Iron Curtain, including Albania, a country I recognized only from James Bond movies. A friend on a mission to Moscow was being given a tour of the GUM department store, which continuously broadcasted official news over its loudspeakers, when he heard my name and Proxmire's boom throughout the store; not understanding Russian, he could not imagine what I'd done that the government of the USSR considered newsworthy.

The heavy bombardment continued for a year or two, during which time the casualties in my personal life directly traceable to it included the death of my beloved dog, the destruction of my car, and the disintegration of my marriage. These were painful events, but it was fear for my life that took the greatest toll on my mental and physical well-being. The mail and telephone brought death threats from people who obviously not only had the will but the means to carry out their wishes. I recall that one Hannibal Lector wannabe described in prose and drawing how he would take a knife and cut out my ovaries. A woman writing in perfect Palmer method on expensive vellum stationery described how she would like to put her gun to my head and pull the trigger. I was advised by the authorities to save my mail and phone messages so that if I was murdered, they could sift through them for clues to the culprit. I personally thought more attention ought to be given to preventing the act than finding the perpetrator after the fact, but the only help I received on that score was from my German shepherd and, after he died, from the installation of a state-of-the-art security system in my home.

What remains after all these years is only a jumbled kaleidoscope of images, some still vivid but most blessedly faded or, I suspect, forgotten altogether. I vowed long ago never to revisit those years or to second-guess my behavior or that of others. The boxes of mail and other materials associated with the event were thrown out just a few years ago when our laboratory needed more storage space. I no longer even have the original press release. Thus, it is with some reluctance that I descend into the catacombs of memory and pry open the cobwebbed door I've mentally labeled "the Proxmire affair." I do so only because the editor of this book is a good friend and no stranger to controversy himself and because it might be useful to someone similarly afflicted in the future to have a listing of a few of the things I learned.

Sometimes it is best to turn the other cheek and keep your mouth shut.

There were many reasons I replied to that first newspaper reporter. First, I was taken unaware, interrupted in the middle of a research meeting; I simply wanted to get off the phone as quickly as possible and so replied in a routine, matter-of-fact way to the reporter's questions. There was an alternative, but it never occurred to me to use it. I did not have the press release (Proxmire did not forewarn his victims, and the NSF had not told me that the abstract of my proposal had been requested or, indeed, that Proxmire had been attacking NSF principal investigators). I could have told the reporter that I would reply after I had read and studied what Proxmire had to say; then, I either could have remained incommunicado until the press got interested in someone or something else, or I could have issued a responding press release through the university's news service (if I could have reached the news service, which did not answer its telephones for days at a time and, as my bad luck would have it, this was one of those times).

It would not have occurred to me not to respond to a reporter, however, because I never considered the press an enemy. My husband was a working newspaperman, my mother had been a newspaper-woman, and many friends were reporters and editors. Over the years, I had thoroughly absorbed their perpetual First Amendment and "the truth shall make you free" propaganda. Moreover, George Miller (1969) had given an influential presidential address to the American Psychological Association in which he enjoined psychologists to "give psychology away"; his message had made its mark on me as well as many others. In addition, I had always believed that my PhD carried the obligation to speak the truth as I saw it, regardless of consequence, and that a professorship in a public university carried the responsibility to disseminate what information I had on request. Although I still believe these things, I learned also that—

Not everyone carrying a pencil stub and a piece of paper is a journalist.

From my original orientation toward the media as "friendlies," I quickly moved to Oscar Wilde's putative view that they are a pack of "scurrilous scoundrels," willing to tell any lie (including representing themselves as a student or research colleague in need of my aid) to get a story and write any drivel or fiction to make that story interesting. Journalists are not licensed, nor do they have a professional code of ethics; hence, the perennial debate about whether journalism is a profession or a trade (I vote for trade). Thousands of freelance writers do not represent themselves as such but, rather, as working for the publication to which they hope to sell their story. Some freelancers are responsible and talented, but many are not. I learned that good science writers are rare and that most editors are acutely aware of the difficulties involved in covering science news. I found that the few science writers who had even a modicum of background for their task mostly worked for three of the country's best newspapers: the *Los Angeles Times*, the *New York Times*, and the *Washington Post*. There is a reason these newspapers have the reputations they do; not only do they have the most talented reporters, their reporters are carefully supervised by editors who routinely check their reporters' accuracy. In the end, I came to realize that, although I had a responsibility to disseminate information to the public—

No one has a responsibility to cooperate in the dissemination of falsehoods.

Most reporters get their story ideas from reading other newspapers, magazines, and watching television. As a consequence, giving an interview to one outlet almost always results in a year's trail of articles in other outlets, often warmed over and embellished in various ways from the original and written without recontacting the source. Moreover, most reporters start with an "angle," which is worth one's while to discover as quickly as possible. Most know what they want to write before they talk to anyone; they want only a few quotes to give their article an air of legitimacy and currency. They are banking on their interviewee saying something congruent with their preformed opinions and theme; if that turns out to be a single sentence in an hour-long interview, that sentence will be quoted and the opposing remainder discarded. This practice is true even of the best. For example, one morning in the heat of the controversy I received a call from the late and highly respected James Reston. I was eager to tell him "my side," but I couldn't get a word in edgewise. Cutting me off almost immediately, he said, "Let me tell you what I'm going to write." The speed with which he reeled off his opinion suggested he had already written his column, but he did finally ask, "What do you think?" Because it was a favorable column in a sea of calumny, I replied "It's fine but. . . ." I heard the dial tone before I could finish the sentence.

Part of the strain on my marriage was that my newspaperman husband got a glimpse few journalists ever get of the seamy tactics and havoc his colleagues often wreak on the lives of the subjects of their work (few journalists are newsmakers and ever personally experience what it is like to be on the other side of the fence), and he often tried to defend the indefensible. Most journalists in the United States operate with impunity. At that time, for example, the conventional legal wisdom was that I could sue neither Proxmire nor any member of the media for slander or libel because by accepting federal research monies, I had become a public figure. In contrast to the legal standards for proving slander and libel for ordinary citizens, the standards for public figures are extraordinarily (some would say impossibly) high. However, one of the researchers Proxmire subsequently attacked sued him anyway. The case went all the way to the Supreme Court, which decided that acceptance of federal research funds did not make one a public figure. On hearing the happy news, I took a box of materials to a well-known First Amendment lawyer with the intention of suing *Time* magazine, among others. Unfortunately (or fortunately, as the case may be), it was the attorney's opinion that throughout the controversy I had defended myself well and thus would have trouble proving harm; the dog, the car, the marriage, and my health didn't count.

The Supreme Court's decision was a victory for all researchers, however, and in my own case it probably forestalled a particularly vicious revival of the controversy. One afternoon some time after the Court's decision, I received a call from an NSF administrator who cheerfully reported that he and Proxmire had just taped separate segments for a new television program in which the audience "voted" for sides in controversial issues and that I might want to tune in. I was dismayed because the show already had been lambasted by reviewers for being a particularly sleazy example of yellow journalism, and the NSF had so far not proved to be an effective supporter of its principal investigators, its projects, or itself. I cautioned the administrator that although he may have done as fine a job as he believed he had, I had learned that editing and context placement could make anyone look like a drooling fool. His enthusiasm for his impending television appearance was undimmed, however, until I added that my lawyers would tape the program and that I would sue all concerned if damaging remarks had been made about me or my research. My warning statement was greeted by a chilly silence, and when the program was shown a few days later, the "love" segment did not appear. Shortly afterward, the network cancelled the program.

Much of the harm I experienced was not the direct result of the searing criticism of me and my research but, rather, a byproduct of the publicity and the absence of staff to help me cope with it. Politicians such as Proxmire and most other public figures are buffered and protected from the consequences of their fame and notoriety by a cadre of professional publicists and security experts that ordinary citizens, such as professors, do not have. For example, I could put a security system in my home, but I worked on public property which, unlike the U.S. Senate, has no security procedures and is open to any crackpot or homicidal maniac. This was a source of much anxiety, because I learned that—

Anyone in the news is likely to hear from those who are mentally ill and also from many lonely people, a large portion of whom are in prison.

As troubling and as potentially dangerous as the death threats I received were the attentions Proxmire's attack brought from those who aspired to be my friend, lover, or spouse. Men from all over the world sent their personal stories, horoscopes, and numerological analyses purporting to reveal our joint destiny, their divorce papers, financial statements testifying to their solvency (and, in some cases, their considerable wealth), photos of their houses and other properties and, of course, photos of themselves. (One memorable photo of a Middle Eastern "sheik" in white robes and headpiece standing in front of what looked like a sand dune was accompanied by a letter written by his British secretary explaining that arrangements were being made for me to join his employer at his Paris residence.) Men in prison expressed their intention of visiting me as soon as they were released, and many nonincarcerated men called continually.

Most people, however, were simply calling and writing for advice —for themselves, for their friends, and for their relatives, often for their children. The painful irony, of course, was that neither I nor anyone else knew much of anything about romantic love. In 1974, Walster [Hatfield] and I had published an article titled "A Little Bit About Love" (the "little bit" was an accurate characterization of the content), and Rubin (1970) had published his liking and love scales, but apart from those efforts, Abraham Maslow (1954) was right: Psychology had surprisingly little to say about love, romantic or otherwise. Nevertheless, Proxmire had represented my project as a study of love, and people all over the world wanted to know what I had "found." Moreover, given the worldwide publicity, I had become the only psychologist many people had ever heard of and, as a consequence, I received hundreds of requests from laypersons and scholars for information on every kind of close relationship problem as well as other psychological phenomena. A great number of these requests came from people in countries that did not have access to journals and up-to-date libraries. Some of their pleas for understanding were heartrending, and for several years I acted as a kind of clearinghouse for such books and journal articles as I thought might be of help. The postage and copying costs, as well as the cost of my time, were horrific. (My department chair insisted that I ask NSF to add a continuation year to my grant to help defray the expense, which it did.) From this worldwide flood of requests for information, I learned that—

At the top of the list of what people all over the world wanted to know about was romantic love and all other aspects of their close personal relationships.

If I ever had any doubt there was a need to learn more about close relationships in general and romantic love in particular, it was forever erased by the mail I received at that time. Intellectually, many attraction researchers, including myself, had come to believe that we needed to move beyond investigations of attraction in first encounters between strangers in the context of a psychology experiment; that is, we recognized that we needed to investigate attraction and other relationship phenomena in vivo and in situ. The mention of romantic love in my mundane attraction proposal was only a baby step in that direction, for I could not really fathom how we could accomplish the objective. Frustrated, and feeling I was contributing little of enduring value to the knowledge enterprise, I had planned to retire soon. In fact, 2 months prior to the attack, in December 1975, I had purchased a retirement house in the country and was looking forward to spring and planting roses to cover my little Arcadian stone cottage. Thus, another irony of the Proxmire affair was that if the senator had simply kept his mouth shut, he would have rid the world of "the love researcher" (as I was called).

Because my intention to resign was known only to my family and to my department chair, I sadly realized that I would have to delay my plans or risk being branded a spineless coward and setting a bad example for my students and for anyone else who ever hoped to study love. Quitting at that time also, I knew, would dismay my supporters, including a group of Nobel Prize-winning scientists at the University of Chicago who were outspoken in their condemnation of Proxmire and his attacks. Unlike some in the academy, these scientists went to the barricades almost immediately, because they were smart enough to know that throwing the vulnerable baby overboard to appease the appetite of the sharks was far more likely to whet it for bigger game. Psychology, then as now, was viewed as a "soft" science, and social psychology was viewed as lying on the softest fringe of that soft discipline. Anything having to do with close relationships was regarded as even further out in the stratosphere of mushiness (Berscheid, 1986). As former American Psychological Association President Martin Seligman described (1998), in previous years the elite departments of psychology had made a deliberate decision to exclude such "applied" phenomena from their purview. Thus, many psychology departments at the time, including my own, would have been delighted to exile social psychology from their midst. Proxmire's attack simply confirmed their suspicion that social psychology represented an embarrassing obstacle to the achievement of scientific respectability and stature for the discipline (see Berscheid, 1992).

Because Proxmire slammed the door on my retirement plans, it was clear to me that I would have to stagger on until such time as I could slip away quietly because, welcome as it might have been at the time, there was little danger of my being fired. I had tenure. Although I had never really known the purpose of tenure, I learned that—

Tenure is an essential ingredient in every researcher's survival kit.

General Patton was right: The first duty of every soldier is to survive. A dead researcher is an ineffective soldier in the war on ignorance. As a result of Proxmire's attack on me, some researchers did die. They lost their jobs. For example, one researcher (of sex—close enough to love to be suspect) was fired almost overnight as a result of the intervention of the Illinois legislature. I myself noticed a series of gray-haired men in suits and ties dropping in on my lectures. They were noticeable not only because of their appearance but because they listened to my lectures with an intensity rarely seen in the typical undergraduate. Only years later did I learn that the strangers were members of my university's board of regents. I was fortunate in having the support of my chair (the redoubtable Jack Darley, previously executive officer of the American Psychological Association), my dean, and also my university president (C. Peter Magrath, currently president of the National Association of State Universities and Land Grant Colleges), who asked one of his aides to check in on me from time to time to see how I was "holding up," a kindness I've never forgotten. Whether this trio would have been able to protect me had I not had tenure is doubtful. Living mostly in the world of sweet reason, few professors can imagine the bone-crushing pressure that can be put on university officials to fire those who arouse the ire of the politically and financially powerful.

Everything I learned in the Proxmire affair about the media, about politicians, and about the value of tenure was put to use when my university's board of regents decided just a few years ago that they were going to make history by being in the "vanguard" (as they put it) of a national movement to eliminate tenure. Had it not been for Proxmire's attack, I am sure I would have reacted as many of my colleagues did to the tenure threat. Most blithely assumed that they themselves were so valuable, and their work so worthy and noncontroversial, that no one would ever think of firing them, and because Professor Snerdley down the hall would be no great loss, defending tenure was not worthy of their own valuable time and effort. Although too many professors were content to give only an absent-minded cheer from the bleachers, I was surprised by how many researchers, in a wide variety of disciplines and often in the forefront of their fields, had been burned in the crucible of controversy, were acutely aware that they owed their jobs and the continuation of their research to the protection of tenure, and immediately abandoned their ongoing work to try to beat back the philistines.

It was during the tenure battle that my view of the media flip-flopped again. Tenure, which protects freedom of thought and inquiry, is akin to the press's First Amendment and, thus, it was easy for many (but not all) journalists to understand and appreciate what we, the faculty, were fighting for. As a disorganized collection of naïve Davids up against the well-oiled and politically connected Goliathan machine of the board and their supporting politicians and businessmen, we were dependent on the good will and fairness of the press and other media to help us reach the public and educate them about how tenure serves society. At crucial times, some members of the Fourth Estate even dropped their cloak of impartiality and gave much needed personal support. One day, for example, long into the exhausting battle when I was ready to throw in the towel and unwilling to give yet another interview or devote one more nanosecond to what I had concluded was a lost cause, I said as much to the seemingly unsupportive journalist on the other end of the line. I was surprised to hear the passionate reply, "You can't give up now! You're so close! You're winning—just hold on a little longer!" We did and, shortly after, the board backed off. With the certainty of death and taxes, however, researchers can expect to see the barbarians at their gates again. (I might mention parenthetically that supportive actions from some institutions, such as University of California at Berkeley and University of California at Los Angeles, were extremely helpful, but the silence from many others was puzzling. Tenure threats need to be taken seriously wherever they occur.)

Finally, the Proxmire affair reaffirmed the truth of the old saws that—

What doesn't kill you will make you stronger, and it's an ill wind that doesn't blow some good.

The stone cottage is still sitting empty, the garden full of weeds, not roses. At the nadir of my professional life, when I most acutely felt the need for psychology to study close relationship phenomena but sadly believed that I had been instrumental in dooming the achievement of that objective, Harold H. Kelley saddled up his white horse and rode to the rescue. Knowing that one cannot get from point A to point B in science without a conceptual map, Kelley proposed to the NSF that it fund a consortium of psychologists to develop a blueprint for the systematic study of close relationships. It did, and the result was *Close Relationships* (Kelley et al., 1983/2002). Today, a coherent science of relationships is becoming a reality (Berscheid, 1999). Because relationships are both the foundation and theme of human life, most human behavior takes place in the context of people's relationships with others. Thus, psychologists are realizing that a science of human behavior and development that neglects the influence of the individual's interpersonal relationships not only is destined to be incomplete but will also be inaccurate and misleading (Kelley et al., 1983; Reis, Collins, & Berscheid, 2000). As for romantic love, theory and research on love now fill whole books (e.g., Hendrick & Hendrick, 1992; Sternberg & Barnes, 1988) and will fill many more by the time psychologists are finished with it. The public and political zeitgeist has changed, and the way for relationship research is clear. Perhaps the greatest irony of all in the Proxmire affair is that we have the senator to thank for exposing, not a waste of taxpayer monies, but the phenomenal interest people have in understanding their relationships with others and for turning the tide of public opinion toward supporting the development of knowledge about close relationships.

References

Berscheid, E. (1986). Mea culpas and lamentations: Sir Francis, Sir Isaac, and "The slow progress of soft psychology." In S. Duck & R. Gilmour (Eds.), *The emerging field of personal relationships* (pp. 267–286). Hillsdale, NJ: Erlbaum.

Berscheid, E. (1992). A glance back at a quarter century of social psychology. *Journal of Personality and Social Psychology, 63,* 525–533.

Berscheid, E. (1999). The greening of relationship science. *American Psychologist, 54,* 260–266.

Berscheid, E., & Walster [Hatfield], E. (1969). *Interpersonal attraction.* Reading, MS: Addison-Wesley.

Berscheid, E., & Walster [Hatfield], E. (1974). A little bit about love. In T. L. Huston (Ed.), *Foundations of interpersonal attraction* (pp. 355–381). New York: Academic Press.

Harlow, H. H. (1958). The nature of love. *American Psychologist, 13,* 673–685.

Hendrick, S. S., & Hendrick, C. (1992). *Romantic love.* Newbury Park, CA: Sage.

Kelley, H. H. (1983). Epilogue: An essential science. In H. H. Kelley, E. Berscheid, A. Christensen, J. H. Harvey, T. L. Huston, G. Levinger, et al., *Close relationships* (pp. 486–503). San Francisco: Freeman.

Kelley, H. H., Berscheid, E., Christensen, A., Harvey, J. H., Huston, T. L., Levinger, G., et al. (2002). *Close relationships.* New York: Percheron. (Original work published 1983)

Kephart, W. M. (1967). Some correlates of romantic love. *Journal of Marriage and the Family, 29,* 470–474.

Maslow, A. H. (1954). *Motivation and personality.* New York: Harper & Row.

Miller, G. A. (1969). Psychology as a means of promoting human welfare. *American Psychologist, 24,* 1063–1075.

Reis, H. T., Collins, W. A., & Berscheid, E. (2000). The relationship context of human behavior and development. *Psychological Bulletin, 126,* 844–872.

Rubin, Z. (1970). Measurement of romantic love. *Journal of Personality and Social Psychology, 16,* 265–273.

Seligman, M. E. P. (1998, August). Work, love and play (President's column). *American Psychological Association Monitor,* p. 2.

Sternberg, R. J., & Barnes, M. L. (Eds.). (1988). *The psychology of love.* New Haven, CT: Yale University Press.

The general public might not know his name, but it certainly knows Kelly Brownell's work. The man who coined the term "yo-yo dieting" most certainly defied the crowd when he suggested in a 1994 *New York Times* editorial that the United States combat its current epidemic of obesity by instituting, among other things, a so-called fat tax on foods of poor nutrient quality. Brownell, who has been called a "dingbat health freak" and a member of the "high-fat gestapo," has made significant contributions in the fields of obesity and public policy and might one day solve the obesity ills of the world, that is, unless one Brownell critic follows up on his promise to "throw every brussel sprout, head of lettuce, celery stick, and container of no-fat yogurt" he can find into the New Haven harbor, and Brownell in after it.

Kelly D. Brownell

Diet, Obesity, Public Policy, and Defiance

3

Few tasks rival the importance of promoting innovation. Explaining innovation is difficult, however, because it forces scholars beyond recitation of their work to understanding its genesis. I hope to accomplish more in this chapter than recite my story. To the extent that I have defied the crowd, I would like to discuss how and why this has occurred, its effects on my professional life, and whether there are lessons to be learned. I use three examples from my research. The first involves a methodological inquiry; the second a theory of behavior, metabolism, and health originating from my clinical experience; and the third a view of diet and health that has led to a social mission based in public policy.

The Integrity of the Double Blind

My earliest work involved clinical trials on dietary change and weight loss, done in the mid- to late 1970s, when the theory and principles of behavior therapy were being refined and tested. My dissertation, done with G. Terence Wilson at Rutgers University, tested manipulation of the social environment in the treatment of a most defiant disorder—obesity (Brownell, Heckerman, Westlake, Hayes, & Monti, 1978). The results were promising and led to a second study, done in my first faculty position, at the University of Pennsylvania School of Medicine.

This study was designed to test whether a weight loss medication (fenfluramine), a social support intervention, or their combination would prevent relapse following treatment for obesity (Brownell & Stunkard, 1981). Drugs and placebos were administered using double-blind methodology (both patients and physicians were "blind" to medication or placebo assignment). Blinding of patients and physicians was central to the conduct of the trial, so it was logical to test the integrity of the design, that is, whether blinding actually occurred. Hence, we assessed whether patients and physicians believed each individual was using drug or placebo. This was not common practice in the field.

The results did not reflect well on the double blind. Seventy percent of patients and physicians correctly guessed medication assignments, and correct guesses were associated with positive clinical outcome. Correct identification can occur when patients infer assignment from side effects, clinical improvement, or other factors. Whatever the reason, the double blind did not accomplish its aim.

The double blind is the foundation of thousands of pharmacology trials and is still the standard for evaluating new drugs. It became apparent to us in the early 1980s that patients and physicians may not be "blind" and that this may affect the outcome of trials. We wrote the results in an article that we were certain would prompt the field to reexamine this method, and we expected a receptive audience.

We were wrong. A number of top medical journals rejected the article, with the typical review saying the topic was unimportant. I refused to accept this as a final conclusion, so we were persistent and eventually published it (Brownell & Stunkard, 1982). This felt like defying the crowd for the first time, because a valid and important scientific observation had been rejected, perhaps because it challenged orthodoxy. I reacted with resolve to fight harder to publish new studies and to not shy from criticism. This willingness to stand firm seems to be one necessary ingredient in defying the crowd.

The immediate response to this article was additional questioning of the double blind (e.g., Barsa, 1983), but still not routine assessment of its integrity, despite confirming evidence that the blind can be breached (Howard, Whittemore, Hoover, & Panos, 1982). Other scholars later challenged the double blind, questioning it on much the same grounds as we did originally (Caspi, Millen, & Sechrest, 2000; Day & Altman, 2000; Devereaux et al., 2001; Double, 1990; Even, Siobud-Dorocant, & Dardennes, 2000; Meinert, 1998; Oxtoby, Jones, & Robinson, 1989).

Most encouraging is that there is now more testing of whether physicians and patients are blinded to drug assignment and recognition that conclusions about a drug's efficacy can be influenced by breaking of the blind. This has occurred across many fields, including neurology (Noseworthy et al., 1994), medicine (Byington, Curb, & Mattson, 1985), pharmacology (Kirsch & Rosadino, 1993), psychology (Margraf et al., 1991), and psychiatry (Basoglu, Marks, Livanou, & Swinson, 1997). Nevertheless, the integrity of this design has undergone too little assessment.

This work on the double blind occurred early in my career and was not central to my research, so the ramifications of challenging the field were minimal. Such was not the case with the second area, weight cycling.

Weight Cycling (aka "Yo-Yo Dieting")

The treatment of obesity is a frustrating enterprise, with estimates of relapse rates ranging from 75% to 95% (Brownell & Rodin,1994a; Wilson & Brownell, 2002). Some have questioned the morality of recommending weight loss, given the high failure rates (Foster, 2002).

The scientific debate on dieting notwithstanding, there is the human torment of people desperate to lose weight. My clinical work with one such person, a woman who had struggled with weight for many years, led to a theory, research to test the theory, and a controversy still not settled.

In 1984–1985, Thomas Wadden, Albert Stunkard, and I set out to test very-low-calorie diets in our clinic at the University of Pennsylvania (Wadden, Stunkard, & Brownell, 1983; Wadden, Stunkard, Brownell, & Dey, 1985). Very-low-calorie diets are very strict diets, providing 800 calories or less per day (Wadden & Berkowitz, 2002). I was a therapist for individuals on this diet and came to know them very well because we hoped to learn as much as possible from patient experiences with the diet. I was struck with the variability in weight loss among these individuals, all of whom were prescribed the same diet. Variability is common in such trials, but it had been attributed to differing adherence to the diet. (Patients losing less weight than expected were assumed to be "cheating.")

One patient, Cathy, lost little weight but was firm in her claims of adherence to the prescribed diet. After much discussion, I was convinced she was adhering. I speculated whether one's body could resist weight loss, even when calorie intake is quite low, and what factors might be responsible.

Cathy and I discussed her weight and eating history, family environment, and many other issues. My strongest impression was of her extensive history of dieting, remarkable even in the face of the multiple diets of the typical patient. I remember the urgency with which a thought, soon a theory, came to me—that repeated dieting (weight cycling) might cause resistance to subsequent weight loss.

My weight-cycling theory stated that the body, for teleological reasons, defended itself against the threat of energy deprivation (dieting) by making metabolic adjustments to minimize weight loss and maximize regain with successive periods of restriction. A "smart" body would protect itself against unpredictable cycles of scarcity by becoming more efficient with calories, thus creating slower weight loss during deprivation and more rapid regain during abundance. This ability would increase the likelihood of survival; maximize reproductive capacity; and, through natural selection, become prominent in the species (Brownell & Rodin, 1994b).

This theory seemed ideally suited for testing in animals, but I had only done human research. I was fortunate to know two leading researchers on the physiology of body weight regulation, Eliot Stellar at Penn and M. R. C. Greenwood, then at Vassar. Flooded with excitement of testing the theory, I rushed to meet with Eliot Stellar, who was encouraging and helped assemble the resources, space, animals, and a talented postdoctoral fellow, Eileen Shrager.

Our first animal study, with Sprague–Dawley rats, examined animals subjected to repeated bouts of weight loss and regain (Brownell, Greenwood, Stellar, & Shrager, 1986). The results supported the theory; weight loss on a second bout of energy restriction was slower than on a first, and regain was more rapid the second time. In one of our research meetings, I proposed *yo-yo dieting* as a colloquial term to describe the phenomenon we were studying. The results, published in a physiology journal, generated attention in the field but also drew in the national press. A generation of newspaper and magazine articles on yo-yo dieting was born.

The most gratifying aspect of this study was the interest taken by fellow scientists, including Judith Rodin at Yale, G. Terence Wilson at Rutgers, Judith Stern at the University of California at Davis, Albert Stunkard at Penn, and George Blackburn at Harvard Medical School. We, and the individuals involved originally, came together to form something quite unique, the Weight Cycling Project.

The Weight Cycling Project was a collaboration among many scientists, some studying animals and others humans. The multidisciplinary group represented many fields, including nutrition, biochemistry, physiology, surgery, psychiatry, psychology, and exercise physiology. Our interactions were magical. A group of bright, creative people, secure in their own areas but eager to learn from others, created a great sense of excitement and energy.

We received funding from the MacArthur Foundation, which supported creative, collaborative, scientific projects. Our main focus was on understanding whether dieting made later dieting more difficult, whether regain would be more rapid with successive cycles of loss and regain, the physiology underlying these effects, and the health consequences of the cycles, using both human and animal models. Some excellent people early in their careers joined the group, including Suzanne Steen and Leslie Stein, and several outstanding senior researchers, Steven Blair and Jack Wilmore, became involved.

Being able to interact with these people early in my career and to feel responsible for bringing them together gave me great satisfaction and placed me at the center of a group of first-rate scientists. Ideas were shared freely, and each person was enriched intellectually and personally from the others. The ordinary competition, disputes over status and credit, and other common problems were absent.

Some early signs of disapproval in the field became apparent. Several of us met once with Jules Hirsch of the Rockefeller University, a revered figure in the obesity field. He dismissed the work as trivial and claimed the theory was wrong. I was shaken by the harsh response of an esteemed figure but reacted with increased resolve to do the science necessary to prove Hirsch correct or not. I was convinced that the issue we were studying (the effects of repeated diets) was terribly important, that the theory still needed testing, and that Hirsch was being negative for his own reasons. My deep conviction in our science and in the creativity of our group made me certain that, although Hirsch had useful input, we were right. Tolerating criticism and not succumbing to self-doubt were key.

Our work took many exciting turns, and consistent with the multidisciplinary nature of the group, we published our results in an array of journals. A study led by Terry Wilson in collaboration with George Blackburn's group at Harvard University tested whether humans lost weight differently a second time on a very-low-calorie diet compared with the first, and it was published in the *American Journal of Clinical Nutrition* (Blackburn et al., 1989). Suzanne Steen coordinated several projects with collegiate and high schools wrestlers, a group known for dramatic cycles of weight loss and regain, and published articles in the *Journal of the American Medical Association* and in *Medicine and Science in Sports and Exercise* (Steen & Brownell, 1990; Steen, Oppliger, & Brownell, 1988). This work with athletes led to reviews and a book (Brownell, Rodin, & Wilmore, 1992; Brownell, Steen, & Wilmore, 1987). Another animal study, examining how exercise affected the response to weight cycling, was published in the *American Journal of Physiology* (Gerardo-Gettens et al., 1991).

The study with the greatest ultimate significance was born from my interest in the health consequences of weight cycling, and again, became possible after much interaction with new scientists and the collaboration of a team. Research had shown that coronary heart disease risk factors (e.g., blood pressure, lipids) changed with variations in body weight, but no one knew whether repeated cycles of loss and gain would be deleterious.

I contacted Joseph Stokes, a physician and epidemiologist at Boston University who was an investigator involved with the Framingham Heart Study, one of the longest running and largest cardiovascular epidemiology studies. A cohort of more than 5,000 adults in Framingham, Massachusetts, had been followed for many years, with detailed medical exams taking place every other year. The large sample, prospective nature of the data, and range of assessments on the participants provided an ideal opportunity to examine weight variability over time, account for variables related to both weight change and health (e.g., exercise, smoking, age), and test "hard" endpoints (cardiovascular morbidity and mortality).

Persistence was needed just to obtain permission to conduct the study. Many scientists petition for access to the Framingham data, with requests sometimes denied or delayed for long periods. I was determined to do the study and therefore spent several years interacting with Framingham investigators and another year planning the study. It was worth the effort.

The results of the study were striking. Increased weight variability was associated with risk of cardiovascular disease and of all-cause mortality, with relative risks approximating those for established risk factors such as hypertension. The article was published in the *New England Journal of Medicine* (Lissner et al., 1991) and was followed by an explosion of coverage in the press and by interest in the health field. Steve Blair and our group subsequently obtained similar results in a study using data from the Multiple Risk Factor Intervention Trial (Blair, Shaten, Brownell, Collins, & Lissner, 1993).

At this point funding from the MacArthur Foundation was ending, so our group faced the choice of scaling back the work or applying for more traditional federal funding. We were unanimous in our desire to keep the group together, as a commitment to both the science and our collaborations. We embarked on the lengthy process of preparing a program project grant proposal for consideration by the National Institutes of Health. This is where we met the greatest resistance.

We were confident that the innovative nature of the work, our unique collaborative ties, and the creativity of our studies would be welcomed. However, our site visitors stayed within their areas of expertise and seemed uninterested in the overall innovation of the project. In their defense, this was not a time when collaboration was common, especially spanning so many disciplines and involving both animal and human work. The animal experts on the group picked at the animal studies, the human experts did the same with the human studies, and the mood of the group, instead of working with us to build on a unique foundation, was somewhat antagonistic. Our grant proposal was not approved.

Several interpretations are possible. Weak science, a field not ready for our unique collaborations, or animosity engendered by the attention the work received in the field and the media were all possible explanations. We did sense that challenging orthodoxy and embracing a theory that some prominent people felt was wrong led to problems.

Without federal funding, we were able to keep the team together for a short while, so work continued on several studies. A number of the investigators accepted new professional positions; I moved from Penn to Yale, Greenwood became chancellor of the University of California at Santa Cruz, Rodin became president at Penn, and professional interests changed. As a result, the collective work we did on weight cycling ended in the early 1990s.

Work on weight cycling has continued, with many research groups around the world tackling the topic using both human and animal models. Examples are studies of the effects of weight cycling on lipid metabolism (Olson et al., 2000), blood pressure (Miller, Dimond, & Stern, 2000), and fatty acid metabolism (Sea, Fong, Huang, & Chen, 2000); the association of weight cycling with health risk in humans (Field et al., 1999; Guagnano et al., 2000; Petersmarck et al., 1999); the psychological correlates of weight cycling (Carmody, Brunner, & St. Jeor, 1999; Friedman, Schwartz, & Brownell, 1998); and even the effects of food restriction and realimentation during pregnancy in farm animals (Freetly, Ferrell, & Jenkins, 2000).

The original metabolic hypothesis, that rates of weight loss and regain would change with successive diets, has been supported in some studies but not others, and so at this point, cannot be fully supported. The work on weight cycling and health has been consistent in showing negative health consequences of body weight variability.

What did I learn? The greatest rewards of the weight cycling work were the personal and professional connections I developed with scientists outside my area of expertise. The learning and stimulation were tremendous. We created a climate that generated many new ideas and new methods to test them. This was different from the way most people did science, and in some ways, may have hindered me from accomplishing some of the usual measures of success (e.g., writing traditional grants). Looking back, however, I would not trade the experience for anything.

Although this work on weight cycling generated controversy and debate, it was nothing compared to the work I took on next dealing with public policy and diet.

The "Toxic Environment" and a Call for Public Policy

I have had a long and vital interest in public health (Brownell, Cohen, Stunkard, Felix, & Cooley, 1984). Its models and methods are quite different from traditional psychological and medical models, focusing on risks to populations rather than individuals, on control rather than cure, and on prevention more than treatment. This template led me in the early 1990s to ask why the rates of obesity and related diseases (e.g., diabetes) were increasing to such an alarming degree in the United States and in places previously thought to be immune (e.g., China). Work was being done to document the problem but not to explain it.

Long before Freud, obesity was considered to be a personal failing, a view generally still held today (Puhl & Brownell, 2001). Biology and genetics emerged as explanatory factors among professionals (but not the general public) in the mid-1980s, and today this view dominates the field. Early heritability estimates for body weight as high as .75 (now lowered to .25–.40) led to a frenetic search for obesity genes. Today at professional meetings and in journals, the number of presentations and articles on molecular biology, physiology, and pharmacology dwarfs that of articles on the psychosocial causes of the obesity epidemic. There is almost nothing on prevention.

Our field has confused knowledge with wisdom. Receptor sites, gene maps, and uncoupling proteins sound awfully impressive, but they cannot explain why we are the most overweight nation on earth and why prevalence spirals out of control here and elsewhere. Changes in the gene pool cannot explain such rapid increases, why ethnic groups migrating to the United States get fatter, and why immigrants in the United States weigh more than their biological relatives who remain in native countries. The environment is the causative agent, yet our field has been blinded to this reality (Brownell, 2002a).

We are exposed to a "toxic environment" of poor foods and physical inactivity, a crisis that has produced a predictable and inevitable epidemic of obesity. The toxic environment exerts an effect on the majority of the population, with children being the most tragic victims.

By a *toxic environment*, I refer to the almost ubiquitous presence of high-fat and high-calorie foods, food that is promoted heavily and sometimes deceptively by a powerful industry, and provided at low cost as an incentive to eat; I refer to the massive portions served, to food available in places previously inconceivable (e.g., drug stores, gas stations, shopping malls), to the ubiquitous inducements for children to eat a poor diet (e.g., poor foods in the schools), and to a culture that discourages physical activity in a variety of ways.

Concerning ourselves less with why individuals become obese (which directs the focus to biology and genetics) and more with why the nation is overweight underscores the importance of environmental causes. Genes help specify which individuals will succumb to a toxic environment, but prevalence and the public health impact are determined by the environment itself. Without a toxic environment, as in very poor countries, obesity will almost disappear.

This stance has been controversial among professionals because the field is dominated by a biological perspective. However, what has generated the greatest debate are the public policy proposals I have made on the basis of this environmental argument.

THE CONTROVERSY

Rarely are treatments for obesity based on causes or even theoretical models of cause, they are rarely effective, and their cost would be prohibitive if used on a large scale. In addition, treatment implies that biological or personal problems must be corrected. If the environment causes obesity, the environment must change or the problem will worsen. Treatment will never reduce prevalence. Prevention must be the priority.

I have written about these ideas for a decade or more, but the first time they crystallized into specific policy proposals was in an op-ed piece I wrote for the *New York Times* in late 1994 (Brownell, 1994). The proposals have subsequently been refined and expanded (Brownell, 2002a, 2002b; Horgen & Brownell, 1998; Horgen, Choate, & Brownell, 2001). My current policy proposals are as follows (Brownell, 2002b):

1. Use public funds to create more opportunities and incentives for physical activity.
2. Regulate food advertising aimed at children by mandating equal time for messages on nutrition and physical activity.
3. Modify school lunch programs to become part of the educational mission of the schools and to improve their quality.
4. Prohibit fast foods and soft drinks for sale in schools.
5. Subsidize the sale of healthy foods at the national level.
6. And, if needed to support the other proposals, tax foods of poor nutrient quality.

THE FIRESTORM

A firestorm of controversy, still active today, erupted the day the editorial in the *New York Times* was published. The notion of taxing foods has drawn the greatest ire. The controversy went well beyond polite scientific debate. Radio talk shows, newspaper editorials, Web sites, and television debates with people from political think tanks were but a few of the arenas in which I was either applauded or, more often, condemned. Examples are the e-mails I received from the general public:

> The amazing thing to me is not that there are people like you,
> who insidiously gain positions of voice and relative power even
> in a country which was designed to prevent your influence, but
> that our government has grown to the point where you Nazis can

actually voice your absurd opinions with conviction on public television. (Personal communication, September 3, 1999)

Your statement about Ronald McDonald and Joe Camel is patently stupid! . . . You have no business telling me what or how to eat. I do not accept your arrogant self-appointed guardianship of my life so butt out and shut up!" (Personal communication, April 24, 1998)

What gives you or the government the right to decide what others should or shouldn't eat? Ever hear of the U.S. Constitution? (Personal communication, April 14, 1998)

I suggest you get a job digging ditches because it appears that you are totally unqualified to be associated with a university. (Personal communication, December 20, 1994)

Let's get something straight right now. This is a free country, and don't you ever forget it! If your proposals ever see the light of day, I will do whatever it takes to resist such communistic oppression, by whatever means necessary. For starters, I will personally throw every brussel sprout, head of lettuce, celery stick, and container of no-fat yogurt I can find into New Haven harbor, and throw you in there after it! (Personal communication, December 21, 1994)

Conservative media figures have been extremely critical. Rush Limbaugh, for example, called me part of the "high-fat gestapo" and was very harsh about my proposals on at least three shows. Editorials from some newspapers were also quite critical:

Everyone was wondering which legal product would be targeted next once the health fascists and their trial lawyer piranhas finished with the carcass of the tobacco industry. Now we know. ("Dr. Pepper, Please Call Your Office," 1998, p. 26)

First, public health groups will determine that hamburgers cause cancer and heart disease. The trial lawyers will begin class actions on behalf of adults who blame their illness on . . . special sauce. ("Who's Next?", 1998, p. A22)

Do you think the lifestyle police will stop goosestepping . . . ?

Brownell . . . isn't satisfied with trying to persuade you to eat less junk food. He wants Big Brother to *make* you eat less junk food.

Ben and Jerry will be transformed from kindly Vermont hippies to foul peddlers of heart disease. Preposterous, you say! Laughable! Absurd! Philip Morris used to think so too. ("The Bullies' Next Target," 1998, p. A25)

The less revered *Weekly World News* had a headline entitled, "Dingbat Health Freaks Call for a Fat Tax . . ." (Anger, 1997, p. 17).

I guess this qualifies as defying the crowd. There were also many positive reactions. Among them was an article in the *New Republic* that stated, "Is it really such a crazy idea? . . . It's too bad Brownell isn't more popular" (Rosin, 1998, p. 18). In early 1998, *U.S. News and World Report* released a cover story entitled, "16 Silver Bullets; Smart Ideas to Fix the World." It discussed my environmental argument and several of the proposals, and said, "This would be unabashed social engineering, but so is virtually everything the government does about public health dangers, such as air pollution or drunk driving, that pose smaller threats to most people's life expectancy" (Ahmad, 1998, pp. 62–63).

MY REACTION

This controversy has enriched me. With more debate and the accumulation of additional science, I have grown more resolute in my opinion that the environment must change and that public policy offers our best hope for progress. I dismiss some objections and embrace others, but I continue to write and speak on the subject in what I hope is a powerful, thoughtful manner.

I accept nearly every opportunity to debate the issue, be it with friendly audiences or foes. I have debated at scientific meetings whether genetics or environments are more responsible for obesity, spoken after the Surgeon General at the annual meeting of the Institute of Medicine, presented at a meeting of food industry officials and lobbyists, and faced off with opponents in hostile environments (a debate with a spokesperson from the conservative Cato Institute on CNN and a meeting of state attorneys general held by the Manhattan Institute).

It is easy to absorb positive comments, but the negative ones have been more interesting and in many ways more enlightening. In the barrage of negative comments coming in the press, in e-mails, and in letters, I have responded in two ways to two types of feedback. One, epitomized by Rush Limbaugh and other conservative commentators, has been philosophical and nearly without substance. To say, as they do, that ideas are stupid and that government involvement of any type is evil, is itself stupid. If these individuals would engage in a discussion of why they disagree, could be opened-minded even a little, and could propose more creative solutions to an international problem (an epidemic of obesity), a sensible conversation could occur with both sides benefitting.

The second type of feedback is more thoughtful and engaging. Often people disagree, sometimes quite strongly, but have a rationale for doing so and can challenge what I say in an informed and thoughtful way. Some of those challenges have been telling. People have argued that I cannot be certain that altering the price of food will have the intended effect. I agree we can only speculate from incomplete data. Others have argued that a tax on nonnutritious foods would be regressive in nature, that is, that poor people would be the most adversely affected. Still others have questioned my proposals on economic grounds. I welcome this input, because it helps me strengthen some arguments and abandon others.

In analyzing this experience and the others I mentioned earlier, I can summarize what has been important in my defying the crowd and reflect on the issue of creativity.

Reflections and Advice on Creativity and Defying the Crowd

In 1890, Oscar Wilde had this to say on the topic of advice: "People are very fond of giving away what they need most themselves" (1890/1994, p. 46). Therefore, I reflect rather than advise.

Creative scientific contributions have multiple origins (Sternberg, 1999). My own belief is that innovation is most likely when synergy occurs between characteristics of the scientist, the style in which she or he was mentored, and the work setting.

INDIVIDUAL DIFFERENCE FACTORS

To persevere in the face of criticism and attack, several personal and intellectual qualities seem to be helpful. Confidence in one's beliefs is important. Dogged persistence is often necessary to convince others that ideas are worthwhile. Willingness to have people disagree, feistiness in welcoming debate, and eagerness to hear opposing views is central to intellectual integrity, which in turn permits clear and honest thinking.

Separating criticism from substance is also essential. Criticism is unpleasant and often gets internalized, particularly by students and people early in their careers. It can be experienced as a damning, even fatal blow, whether or not the criticism is reasonable. If one attends to substance and is open to reasoned, thoughtful input but is not wounded by criticism, advances in thinking are more likely. People who disagree with me are often right. Learning from them makes me stronger and is a sign of wisdom, not weakness.

I also believe that working well with others is important. I know that some people prefer to work in isolation, but in my case, being collaborative, giving credit to others when it is due, enjoying it when people working with me prosper, and learning from colleagues and students are both necessary and gratifying.

MENTORING STYLES

I have observed many styles of mentoring. It is intuitive that mentors who are open-minded, welcome critiques of their work, and are enthusiastic about new ideas would be in a position to nurture creativity in developing scientists. Believing that students are partners rather than employees, encouraging them to develop and pursue new ideas, reinforcing creative thinking, offering an environment where bold thinking is safe, and providing resources seem essential for fostering innovation.

I was blessed with superb mentors at key stages in my career. My mentor in graduate school, G. Terence Wilson at Rutgers, is brilliant but not conceited. He appreciated my ideas and encouraged me to carry out studies I proposed. It is no accident that many leading figures in the field had Wilson as a mentor. I could not have had a better model, supervisor, and friend. David Barlow, director of the internship program at Brown University, and Albert Stunkard, who hired me at Penn for my first job, were very helpful mentors as well. Barlow has a consummate professionalism and great scientific mind, and Stunkard is one of the freest and most creative thinkers I have known. Both possess a genuine enthusiasm for new ideas.

I would advise young people to seek mentors who are creative. In addition, one wants mentors who seek ideas from trainees, are enthusiastic, and support one's work in tangible ways.

SCIENTIFIC ENVIRONMENT

Psychologists work in a variety of settings, and in my belief, some settings lend themselves to creativity more than others. Most noteworthy is the distinction between academic (psychology department) and professional (medical school) settings.

Researchers in medical schools survive on grants. Creativity is possible, but often scientists are forced to chase money and to conduct research someone else designs and considers important. Young scientists are drawn to those with money and then get socialized into the grant mentality, whereby levels of funding are more important than the work itself.

I was recently at a presentation by a highly regarded figure in the obesity field, who was discussing the work done by his group in a medical school. He boasted of the amount of grant money he had, the number of square feet he controlled, the number of people he employed, and the laboratories he governed; finally he mentioned the nature of his research. The medical school setting so values grant money that it is often the first issue mentioned in promotion evaluations. There are lavishly funded and hence esteemed figures in medical schools who do little but conduct clinical trials for pharmaceutical companies. They are research subcontractors.

Psychology or other liberal arts and social science departments can be quite different. Grants are valued, of course, but the intellectual quality of the work is more likely to be the primary emphasis. Some top contributors to the field have little grant money.

Not to succumb to overstatement, I admit that the setting does not create the person. Many creative people are in medical school settings, many young people emerge from these settings to be fine scientists, and plenty of people in other settings are not creative. It is defensible to argue that creative scientists may be creative wherever they are, but it is also true that the setting creates expectations, rewards different activities, and provides an environment in which creativity is likely or not. I have found that a university psychology department is an excellent atmosphere in which creativity can thrive.

Final Comments

Defying the crowd requires creativity, confidence, willingness to debate, flexible thinking, willingness to learn from critics, persistence, and determination when attacked. Defiance creates breakthroughs. Breakthroughs are needed to ensure the vitality of our field and the well-being of the population. Better understanding of creativity and innovation is essential.

References

Ahmad, S. (1998, December 29). Time for a twinkie tax? How to slim down the world's fattest society. *U.S. News and World Report*, pp. 62–63.

Anger, E. (1997, August 19). Dingbat health freaks push for "fat tax" on all junk food. *Weekly World News*, p. 17.

Barsa, J. A. (1983). More on the fallibility of the double-blind. *American Journal of Psychiatry, 140*, 820–821.

Basoglu, M., Marks, I., Livanou, M., & Swinson, R. (1997). Double-blindness procedures, rater blindness, and ratings of outcome. Observations from a controlled trial. *Archives of General Psychiatry, 54*, 744–748.

Blackburn, G. L., Wilson, G. T., Kanders, B. S., Stein, L. J., Lavin, P. T., Adler, J., et al. (1989). Weight cycling: The experience of human dieters. *American Journal of Clinical Nutrition, 49*, 1105–1109.

Blair, S. N., Shaten, J., Brownell, K. D., Collins, G., & Lissner, L. (1993). Body weight change, all-cause mortality, and cause-specific mortality in the Multiple Risk Factor Intervention Trial. *Annals of Internal Medicine, 119,* 749–757.

Brownell, K. D. (1994, December 15). Get slim with higher taxes [Editorial]. *New York Times,* p. A29.

Brownell, K. D. (2002a). The environment and obesity. In C. G. Fairburn & K. D. Brownell (Eds.), *Eating disorders and obesity: A comprehensive handbook* (2nd ed., pp. 433–438). New York: Guilford Press.

Brownell, K. D. (2002b). Public policy and the prevention of obesity. In C. G. Fairburn & K. D. Brownell (Eds.), *Eating disorders and obesity: A comprehensive handbook* (2nd ed., pp. 619–623). New York: Guilford Press.

Brownell, K. D., Cohen, R. Y., Stunkard, A. J., Felix, M. R. J., & Cooley, N. B. (1984). Weight loss competitions at the work site: Impact on weight, morale, and cost-effectiveness. *American Journal of Public Health, 74,* 1283–1285.

Brownell, K. D., Greenwood, M. R. C., Stellar, E., & Shrager, E. E. (1986). The effects of repeated cycles of weight loss and regain in rats. *Physiology and Behavior, 38,* 459–464.

Brownell, K. D., Heckerman, C. L., Westlake, R. J., Hayes, S. C., & Monti, P. M. (1978). The effect of couples training and partner cooperativeness in the behavioral treatment of obesity. *Behaviour Research and Therapy, 16,* 323–333.

Brownell, K. D., & Rodin, J. (1994a). The dieting maelstrom: Is it possible and advisable to lose weight? *American Psychologist, 49,* 781–791.

Brownell, K. D., & Rodin, J. (1994b). Medical, metabolic, and psychological effects of weight cycling. *Archives of Internal Medicine, 154,* 1325–1330.

Brownell, K. D., Rodin, J., & Wilmore, J. H. (Eds.). (1992). *Eating, body weight and performance in athletes: Disorders of modern society.* Philadelphia: Lea & Febiger.

Brownell, K. D., Steen, S. N., & Wilmore, J. H. (1987). Weight regulation practices in athletes: Analysis of metabolic and health effects. *Medicine and Science in Sports and Exercise, 19,* 546–556.

Brownell, K. D., & Stunkard, A. J. (1981). Couples training, pharmacotherapy, and behavior therapy in the treatment of obesity. *Archives of General Psychiatry, 38,* 1224–1229.

Brownell, K. D., & Stunkard, A. J. (1982). The double-blind in danger: Untoward consequence of informed consent. *American Journal of Psychiatry, 139,* 1487–1489.

The bullies' next target: Junk food [Editorial]. (1998, November 12). *Boston Globe,* p. A25.

Byington, R. P., Curb, J. D., & Mattson, M. E. (1985). Assessment of double-blindness at the conclusion of the beta-Blocker Heart Attack Trial. *Journal of the American Medical Association, 253,* 1733–1736.

Carmody, T. P., Brunner, R. L., & St. Jeor, S. T. (1999). Hostility, dieting, and nutrition attitudes in overweight and weight-cycling men and women. *International Journal of Eating Disorders, 26,* 37–42.

Caspi, O., Millen, C., & Sechrest, L. (2000). Integrity and research: Introducing the concept of dual blindness: How blind are double-blind clinical trials in alternative medicine? *Journal of Alternative and Complementary Medicine, 6,* 493–498.

Day, S. J., & Altman, D. G. (2000). Statistics notes: Blinding in clinical trials and other studies. *British Medical Journal, 321,* 504.

Devereaux, P. J., Manns, B. J., Ghali, W. A., Quan, H., Lacchetti, C., Montori, V. M., et al. (2001). Physician interpretations and textbook definitions of blinding terminology in randomized controlled trials. *Journal of the American Medical Association,* 285, 2000–2003.

Double, D. B. (1990). Limitations of double-blind trials. *British Journal of Psychiatry, 157,* 300.

Dr. Pepper, please call your office [Editorial]. (1998, October). *New York Post,* p. 26.

Even, C., Siobud-Dorocant, E., & Dardennes, R. M. (2000). Critical approach to antidepressant trials. Blindness protection is necessary, feasible and measurable. *British Journal of Psychiatry, 177,* 47–51.

Field, A. E., Byers, T., Hunter, D. J., Laird, N. M., Manson, J. E., Williamson, D. F., et al. (1999). Weight cycling, weight gain, and risk of hypertension in women. *American Journal of Epidemiology, 150,* 573–579.

Foster, G. D. (2002). Non-dieting approaches. In C. G. Fairburn & K. D. Brownell (Eds.), *Eating disorders and obesity: A comprehensive handbook* (2nd ed., pp. 604–608). New York: Guilford Press.

Freetly, H. C., Ferrell, C. L., & Jenkins, T. G. (2000). Timing of realimentation of mature cows that were feed-restricted during pregnancy influences calf birth weights and growth rates. *Journal of Animal Science, 78,* 2790–2796.

Friedman, M. A., Schwartz, M. B., & Brownell, K. D. (1998). Differential relation of psychological functioning with the history and experience of weight cycling. *Journal of Consulting and Clinical Psychology, 66,* 646–650.

Gerardo-Gettens, T., Miller, G. D., Horwitz, B. A., McDonald, R. B., Brownell, K. D., Greenwood, M. R. C., et al. (1991). Exercise decreases fat selection in female rats during weight cycling. *American Journal of Physiology, 260,* R518–R524.

Guagnano, M. T., Ballone, E., Pace-Palitti, V., Vecchia, R. D., D'Orazio, N., Manigrasso, M. R., et al. (2000). Risk factors for hypertension in obese women. The role of weight cycling. *European Journal of Clinical Nutrition, 54,* 356–360.

Horgen, K. B., & Brownell, K. D. (1998). Policy change as a means for reducing the prevalence and impact of alcoholism, smoking, and obesity. In W. R. Miller & N. Heather (Eds.), *Treating addictive behaviors* (2nd ed., pp. 105–118). New York: Plenum Press.

Horgen, K. B., Choate, M., & Brownell, K. D. (2001). Food advertising: Targeting children in a toxic environment. In D. G. Singer & J. L. Singer (Eds.), *Handbook of children and the media* (pp. 447–462). Thousand Oaks, CA: Sage.

Howard, J., Whittemore, A. S., Hoover, J. J., & Panos, M. (1982). How blind was the patient blind in AMIS? *Clinical Pharmacology and Therapeutics, 32,* 543–553.

Kirsch, I., & Rosadino, M. J. (1993). Do double-blind studies with informed consent yield externally valid results? An empirical test. *Psychopharmacology, 110,* 437–442.

Lissner, L., Odell, P. M., D'Agostino, R. B., Stokes, J., Kreger, B. E., Belanger, A. J., et al. (1991). Variability in body weight and health outcomes in the Framingham population. *New England Journal of Medicine, 324,* 1839–1844.

Margraf, J., Ehlers, A., Roth, W. T., Clark, D. B., Sheikh, J., Agras, W. S., et al. (1991). How "blind" are double-blind studies? *Journal of Consulting and Clinical Psychology, 59,* 184–187.

Meinert, C. L. (1998). Masked monitoring in clinical trials—Blind stupidity? *New England Journal of Medicine, 338,* 1381–1382.

Miller, G. D., Dimond, A. G., & Stern, J. S. (2000). The effect of repeated episodes of dietary restriction and refeeding on systolic blood pressure and food intake in exercise-trained normotensive rats. *Obesity Research, 8,* 324–336.

Noseworthy, J. H., Ebers, G. C., Vandervoort, M. K., Farquhar, R. E., Yetisir, E., & Roberts R. (1994). The impact of blinding on the results of a randomized, placebo-controlled multiple sclerosis clinical trial. *Neurology, 44,* 16–20.

Olson, M. B., Kelsey, S. F., Bittner, V., Reis, S. E., Reichek, N., Handberg, E. M., et al. (2000). Weight cycling and high-density lipoprotein cholesterol in women: Evidence of an adverse effect: A report from the NHLBI-sponsored WISE study. Women's Ischemia Syndrome Evaluation Study Group. *Journal of the American College of Cardiology, 36,* 1565–1571.

Oxtoby, A., Jones, A., & Robinson, M. (1989). Is your "double-blind" design truly double-blind? *British Journal of Psychiatry, 155,* 700–701.

Petersmarck, K. A., Teitelbaum, H. S., Bond, J. T., Bianchi, L., Hoerr, S. M., & Sowers, M. F. (1999). The effect of weight cycling on blood lipids and blood pressure in the Multiple Risk Factor Intervention Trial Special Intervention Group. *International Journal of Obesity and Related Metabolic Disorders, 23,* 1246–1255.

Puhl, P., & Brownell, K. D. (2001). Bias, discrimination, and obesity. *Obesity Research, 9,* 788–805.

Rosin, H. (1998, May 18). The fat tax: Is it really such a crazy idea? *New Republic,* pp. 18–19.

Sea, M. M., Fong, W. P., Huang, Y., & Chen, Z. Y. (2000). Weight cycling-induced alteration in fatty acidmetabolism. *American Journal of Physiology—Regulatory Integrative and Comparative Physiology, 279,* R1145–R1155.

Steen, S. N., & Brownell, K. D. (1990). Patterns of weight loss and regain in wrestlers. Has the tradition changed? *Medicine and Science in Sports and Exercise, 22,* 762–768.

Steen, S. N., Oppliger, R. A., & Brownell, K. D. (1988). Metabolic effects of repeated weight loss and regain in adolescent wrestlers. *Journal of the American Medical Association, 260,* 47–50.

Sternberg, R. J. (1999). A propulsion model of types of creative contributions. *Review of General Psychology, 3,* 83–100.

Wadden, T. A., & Berkowitz, R. I. (2002). Very-low-calorie diets. In C. G. Fairburn & K. D. Brownell (Eds.), *Eating disorders and obesity: A comprehensive handbook* (2nd ed., pp. 534–538). New York: Guilford Press.

Wadden, T. A., Stunkard, A. J., & Brownell, K. D. (1983). Very-low-calorie diets: Their efficacy, safety, and future. *Annals of Internal Medicine, 99,* 675–684.

Wadden, T. A., Stunkard, A. J., Brownell, K. D., & Dey, S. C. (1985). A comparison of two very-low-calorie diets: Protein-sparing-modified fast and protein formula liquid diet. *American Journal of Clinical Nutrition, 41,* 533–539.

Who's next? [Editorial]. (1998, April 22). *Wall Street Journal,* p. A22.

Wilde, O. (1994). *The picture of Dorian Gray.* Hertfordshire, United Kingdom: Wordsworth. (Original work published 1890)

Wilson, G. T., & Brownell, K. D. (2002). Behavior therapy for obesity. In C. G. Fairburn & K. D. Brownell (Eds.), *Eating disorders and obesity: A comprehensive handbook* (2nd ed., pp. 524–528). New York: Guilford Press.

John Garcia took a long time finding his place in the field of psychology, but once he found it, he dove in headfirst. The one-time self-titled "perennial dropout" made his way into the National Academy of Sciences with his extensive work on conditioned taste aversion. His work has had widespread impact, including, for an unfortunate group of subjects, a documented aversion to what had formerly been some very tasty mutton.

John Garcia

Psychology Is Not an Enclave

4

T he stuff of my psychology has been all around me since I was born. My mother and father were aliens from a different world, the northwest corner of Spain, a misty mountainous region cut by fjords where rivers drain into the Bay of Biscay and the Atlantic Ocean. Ethnographers refer to the old country as "Celtic Spain." They met and married in northern California while working in the vineyards. Pop was unschooled, but he was intelligent, pragmatic, and candid. Mom left school after the fifth grade, but she was bright, sparkling, and self-educated in English and Spanish. I was a child when she taught me that her chocolate aversion was due to seasickness, foreshadowing my career. As farm workers, we were drawn to compadres from other Hispanic regions and gained empathy for other minorities, including our interned Japanese friends. Mom and Pop raised six strong healthy sons: Frank, John, Ted, Ben, Bob, and Dick. I was Mom's built-in baby-sitter. I learned that babies do not babble, that they talk in sentences before they have mastered words, and that the second decade of life is a confusion of changing social and sexual roles.

I was set in my way of learning by 1929, when I was 12; thereafter, I took from teachers and books only what agreed with my set way. Domestic animals taught me conditioning before I ever heard of Ivan Pavlov. Fishing, hunting, and staring at wildlife through field glasses taught me ethology before I knew Konrad Lorenz. I met Inez Robertson in a dance hall with a big swing band playing in turbulent times circa 1940. I was a mechanic and she was a smart spunky teenager when we decided to go the distance together. Working on company trucks, navy ships, and army planes gave me a knack for devising experimental laboratory equipment. When I was unemployed, I attended Santa Rosa Junior College sporadically. In the Army Air Corps, I was an omnivorous reader like Mom. Leo Tolstoy, Sigmund Freud, Charles Darwin, and

Robert Woodworth attracted me to psychology. In 1946 at age 29, veterans benefits gave me the wherewithal to enter the University of California in Berkeley as a full-time probationary third-year undergraduate majoring in psychology and minoring in zoology. I knew animals had brains, minds, and ways of coping with the natural world; thus, the cognitive behaviorism of Edward C. Tolman and David Krech was infinitely more congenial to my thinking than the eviscerated behaviorism of John B. Watson, B. F. Skinner, and Clark L. Hull. In 1951, goaded by a growing family and tired of PhD exams, wherein I failed to convince academics of true animal ways, I reverted to my old ways of learning on the job for pay.

Radiation Research

For the next 17 years I worked in a succession of multidisciplinary labs: the U.S. Naval Radiological Defense laboratory in San Francisco, the University of California at Los Angeles (UCLA) research facilities in the Long Beach Veterans Administration (VA) Hospital, and the Harvard Medical School facilities in Massachusetts General Hospital. At the Navy radiology laboratory on my first day, I was summoned before the acting director, a biochemist who harangued me with that specious hierarchy of sciences, graded according to their use of the mathematical idiom, with physics and chemistry on top, psychology on the bottom. He also opined that psychology was a weak and useless pawn in radiation research. I had weathered countless such interdisciplinary hassles at Berkeley, so as I stood up to leave I shot back, whether a biochemical fact be vital or trivial depends on perception and judgment, two processes in the purview of psychology, the queen of sciences.

Bob Koelling, a hospital corpsman at the time, became my radiation research partner. Our breakthrough came after we learned what many people already knew: that rats exposed to an extremely low flux of ionizing radiation for hours progressively decrease their food and water consumption during repeated exposures. Because the rats showed no signs of illness, no one was concerned.

The decrease looked like a learning curve to Koelling and me. We suspected the rats were discriminating the subtle difference between the water in plastic tubes used in the radiation room and the water in glass bottles in the animal room. We put plastic tubes in both rooms and flavored the water in the radiation room with saccharin; the result was a strong conditioned taste aversion (CTA) for saccharin in one trial. When a distinctive place was substituted for the distinctive taste, avoidance was very weak and transient. I wrote a review replete with graphs and sketches directed at learning experts who paid no attention what-soever (Garcia, Kimeldorf, & Hunt, 1961). Ultimately our search for the cause of CTA culminated at Massachusetts General Hospital, where we found that blood serum taken from irradiated donor rats and injected into recipients caused a CTA. The culprit is probably histamine released from the viscera (Garcia, Ervin, & Koelling, 1967).

Early on, others were unable to replicate our CTA effect in their radiation labs. We knew people thought radiation was an implacable force, not realizing that CTA was a learned response subject to distrac-tion. So Caroline Wakefield and I varied the degree of habituation to the bustle of x-ray procedures. Animals given much habituation ac-quired a CTA in one saccharin-x-ray trial. Less habituation yielded am-biguous data (Garcia, Buchwald, Feder, & Wakefield, 1962). That little study won me a trip to the International Energy Agency in Vienna, Austria. At the reception, I was totally unknown until two senior Soviet scientists spotted my name tag and hustled me to an American who understood their excited jabber. The amazed American informed me that the Russians were saying that they got their information on the effects of extremely low doses of radiation from me. Later at the opening session in the grand United Nations auditorium, where instantaneous translations of foreign languages reached our earphones, the Soviet key-note speaker singled me out, along with my friend C. S. Bachofer, a Catholic priest and scientist, congratulating us for our demonstrations of the effects of low-dose radiation. A young English scientist leaned over to me and whispered, "Damned awkward for you, old man, caught between the commissar and the priest."

At the Long Beach VA Hospital, we discovered that a brief flash of x-ray could warn a rat of a pending shock or arouse a sleeping rat. Probing the rat's head with a 45-mm beam through a tiny homemade collimator indicated that the most sensitive spot was the olfactory area (Garcia, Buchwald, Feder, Koelling, & Tedrow, 1964). Surgical tests by Chester D. Hull verified this implication (Hull, Garcia, Buchwald, Dub-rowsky, & Feder, 1965). Tests with my most marvelous and wacky in-vention, an x-ray tachistoscope, indicated that a blip of less than 10 milliroentgens resulted in odor detection (Garcia, Schofield, & Oper, 1966).

Radiation scientists, like psychologists, are often resistant to new facts and oblivious to historical facts. Circa 1967, I was invited to present a seminar at the National Radiation Facility at Oak Ridge, Tennessee. A radiologist treating patients with low doses of ionizing radiation dis-counted their comments of olfactory sensations. That was several years after we reported such olfactory effects in *Science* and *Nature*. As I took the podium, my audience of radiation experts was buzzing about the news that astronauts on an Apollo mission reported visual effects from solar flares. That was several years after visual effects caused by cosmic hits on the retina were reported in *Nature* and about 70 years after visual effects of x-ray were historically recorded by Wilhelm Roentgen and others (Garcia y Robertson & Garcia, 1985).

Dual Data for a PhD

In 1965 at age 46, I filed a psychology thesis designed to awaken behaviorists from their dogmatic slumbers. The experimental set-up was simple. The touch of a rat's tongue on a waterspout produced a bright noisy flash and a sweet taste. Rats punished by immediate shock to the feet feared the noisy flash but ignored the sweet taste. Rats punished by delayed nausea ignored the noisy flash but rejected the sweet taste. Two behavioristic "laws" were abrogated: the law of effect, declaring that signals and reinforcers were transitional, and the law of contiguity, declaring that immediate reinforcement was necessary. Two reports based on my thesis were rejected by the *Journal of Comparative and Physiological Psychology*. One reviewer intimated that I did not know what was going on in Europe, so I sent copies to Jerzy Konorski in Poland and Konrad Lorenz in Austria. Konorski said that they were very pleased to see my data; Lorenz said that we had demonstrated what he had merely postulated. Then I sent abbreviated versions to *Psychonomic Science*, which accepted them without review (Garcia, Ervin, & Koelling, 1966; Garcia & Koelling, 1966). *Radiation Research* accepted a report on the ancillary thesis data (Garcia & Koelling, 1967).

A storm of criticism ensued. It was said that the CTA experiments lacked proper controls; were due to conditioned stimulus–unconditioned stimulus (CS–US) similarity; and would be of little use to wild rats, ruminant grazers, or carnivorous predators. All these allegations were proven false when CTA was demonstrated in various species ranging from mollusk to human. I was accused of being the instigator of CTA, but in fact CTA had been reported in 1538 by Juan Luis Vives, in 1690 by John Locke, in 1871 by Charles Darwin, and in 1887 by E. B. Poulton (Garcia & Riley, 1998).

Dual Brain Systems

Soon after I published my thesis data I discovered that the behavioral duality is subserved by a neuroanatomical duality described by C. Judson Herrick (1961). Auditory and cutaneous stimulation converge to a dorsal brain system to evoke motor responses in defense of the skin.

Taste and nauseous stimulation converge to a ventral brain system to evoke autonomic reactions in defense of the gut. Olfaction and vision can access either system through a gating system controlled by the attention of the animal (Garcia, 1990).

My thesis study may have been the most replicated experiment since Pavlov used tone-sour to elicit conditioned salivation in the dog. We conducted several dozen replications ourselves in which we changed conditions radically. Brenda McGowan substituted the size of food pellets for the noisy flash and substituted the flavor of the dry pellet for the sweet water confirming the original results (Garcia, McGowan, Ervin, & Koelling, 1968). Ken Green used a brief bout of illness preceded by one flavor, and followed by a second flavor before recuperation, obtaining a CTA for the first flavor and a conditioned taste preference (CTP) for the second flavor (Green & Garcia, 1971).

The most dramatic use of CTA was initiated by Carl Gustavson, who had a keen mind tuned to the ways of foraging wild animals in his native Utah. Carl essentially fed coyotes mutton paired with nauseous treatment to induce a mutton CTA, which caused coyotes to avoid living lambs (Gustavson, Garcia, Hankins, & Rusiniak, 1974). Carl went on to test baits formed of mutton and sheepskin laced with lithium chloride to reduce lamb predation by wild coyotes on the range (Gustavson, Jowsey, & Milligin, 1982). Mutton CTA was validated by Stuart Ellins in a pristine study completely blocking coyote predation on lambs in Antelope Valley, California (Ellins, Catalano, & Schechinger, 1977). On the flip side, Fred Provenza used CTA theory to study the feeding behavior of goats foraging on pastoral lands, where poisonous plants abound, thereby discovering a subtle form of CTA developed by domestic stock without exhibiting overt signs of toxicosis (Provenza, 1995).

The most fishy use of CTA was by experimental psychologists who aped our experiment in which we gave rats a choice between sweet water in the white arm of a T-maze and tap water in the black arm. After the rats habitually ran to the white arm for the sweet reward, we imposed a CTA for sweet in the home cage. When they recovered, we returned them to the T-maze and they persisted in choosing the white arm as if they were unaware that the sweet water was now disgusting (Garcia, Kovner, & Green, 1970). CTA was renamed "instrumental responding for devaluated reinforcers," a tacit admission of the neural duality, but the perpetrators did not discuss Herrick's neuroscientific explanation (Garcia, 1990).

Dual Learning Systems

When I returned to UCLA in 1973, I recalled Tolman's (1949) distinction of two kinds of learning, which corresponded to Herrick's dual brain systems: (a) cognitions, wherein animals acquire spatiotemporal maps of the environment to acquire needed objects, and (b) cathexes, wherein animals adjust the hedonic values of objects according to the feedback (FB) from object consummation. Tolman used *cathexes* broadly, including hedonic evaluations of food, drink, and sex objects (Garcia, 1989). His choice of a psychoanalytic term that implied the unconscious was prophetic. CTA is produced even when the nauseous FB is injected into an anesthetized animal. Similarly, pain induces an endogenous analgesic FB in anesthetized animals. In thermal regulation, where core temperature provides an FB, our bedmates hog all the blankets on cold nights and kick them off on hot nights without waking up. As for sex, who can say that sleeping with our mates does not increase our attachment to them (Garcia, 1990)?

Many good graduate students were attracted to my UCLA laboratory. With all that youthful energy available in the lab, I spent time in my office doodling on paper attempting to synthesize Darwin, Pavlov, and Tolman into coherency. First I had to abandon a popular opinion, to wit, a US is merely the second term in a CS–US pair and the essential difference between a US and a CS is merely intensity. For example, an extremely loud sound evoking avoidance is a US, whereas a soft sound evoking attention is a CS. This view may seem reasonable, but it is a behavioristic evasion of neuroscience. Auditory sounds of any and all intensities project to the dorsal brain system concerned with skin defense. And all taste stimuli of whatever intensity or quality project into the ventral brain system concerned with gut defense.

Pavlov chose taste as his US and an external stimulus as his CS because he was interested in studying "psychical experience,"or as Tolman labeled it, "cognitions" (Kaplan, 1966). On the other hand, Darwin was interested in affective processes, more akin to Tolman's cathexes. I doodled a three-element combination, CS–US–FB, joining Pavlovian CS–US and Darwinian US–FB; another way of expressing this is that I joined Tolmanian conscious cognitions and unconscious cathexes. UCLA students, particularly Kenneth Rusiniak and Claire Palmerino, provided substantiation for my CS–US–FB doodle. They demonstrated that odor alone is a weak cue for nausea but that odor attended by taste becomes a powerful potentiated cue for nausea. The prime function of a US is to convert an irrelevant stimulus into a relevant CS (Palmerino, Rusiniak, & Garcia, 1980). They also demonstrated that a pain US can block a food odor US by urgently gaining the animal's attention, thus neurally gating the food odor into the skin defense system where it is unavailable for gut defense (Rusiniak, Palmerino, Rice, Forthman, & Garcia, 1982).

Linda Philips Brett took on the daunting task of testing buteo hawks. These large, powerful avian predators were of special interest because they hunt from far above with their keen vision and seize prey with taloned feet without tasting their prey. Black and white mice were used, but the hawks could not use color to avoid the black mouse repeatedly paired with nauseous injections, presumably because lab mice taste alike regardless of color. However, when the black mouse was marked by a distinctive taste, the hawks avoided it from a distance after a single trial, indicating that the taste US had potentiated the color CS (Brett, Hankins, & Garcia, 1976).

Debra Forthman won a Fulbright award and ventured to test CTA as a deterrent to baboons raiding vegetable crops in Kenya, Africa. Under experimental conditions, Forthman achieved CTA for specific vegetables, but the political problems of getting permission from farmers and authorities for a broad program were as formidable as those encountered by Gustavson and Ellins on coyote control on United States sheep ranges (Forthman Quick, 1984).

Three graduates pushed our program into neurophysiology and endocrinology. Stephen Kiefer brought his expertise on odor stimulation to our lab as a postdoctoral fellow. Kiefer placed rats in a glass wind tunnel where odors could be presented and whisked away with the same precision as visual and auditory stimuli (Kiefer, 1985). Janet Coil studied the contributions of the vagus nerve and blood circulation to CTA (Coil, Rogers, Garcia, & Novin, 1978). Coil also showed that antiemetic agents would attenuate CTA. Anne Rice, working with an estrogen-induced CTA demonstrated by Carl and Joan Gustavson, showed that antihistamine reduces estrogen CTA (Rice, 1988). Taken altogether, the Gustavsons, Coil, and Rice provided evidence that the anorexia most prevalent in adolescent girls may be due to premature estrogen onset.

Finally, Federico Bermudez-Rattoni, who earned his PhD in our lab with his research on the roles of the hippocampus and the amygdala on odor potentiation by taste, pushed the program into brain research. In his own lab at the University of Mexico, Bermudez-Rattoni and his students blunted the CTA capacity of adult rats by scooping out tissue from the gustatory neocortex. Subsequently, they implanted homotopic fetal tissue in the lesion and restored the CTA capacity of the brain-damaged adults. Recently, Federico and two other international scientists published a book on CTA emphasizing brain research (Bures, Bermudez-Rattoni, & Yamamoto, 1998).

Aversions and Affinities

I rebelled specifically against the exclusion of neuroscientific explanations advocated by a triumvirate of learning theorists circa 1947 to 1959.

K. W. Spence (1947) wrote, "In the case of learning phenomena, a number of theoretical interpretations have been offered which make little or no use of neurophysiological concepts." W. K. Estes (1959) concurred, "all empirical independent variables (causal variables, antecedent conditions or determinants of behavior) which enter into behavioral laws influence behavior by way of stimulation." B. F. Skinner (1959), displaying cumulative lever presses by three different hungry animals working for their food delivered on a fixed-interval schedule, asked, "Pigeon, rat, monkey, which is which? It doesn't matter." It mattered very much to me! (A more complete discussion with references can be found in Garcia, McGowan, & Green, 1972.)

I cling to an older more inclusive way of thinking. In 1690, physician John Locke asked, "Let us then suppose the mind to be, as we say, white paper void of all characters, without any Ideas. How comes it to be furnished?" (1690/1975, p. 104). Locke's response to his own question was that two sources were involved: (a) sensations of external objects and (b) reflections stemming from internal effects (p. 105). He distinguished associations acquired by chance or custom from natural associations dependent on our "constitution." Later, Locke gave this example: An emetic substance acting on the palate is sweet; when it subsequently acts on the gut it is sickening, a natural association now called a CTA (p. 138). (For more on the neuroscience of Locke, see Garcia, 1981b.)

In 1904 at the end of his Nobel Prize address, Pavlov explained his reason for studying the brain:

> In point of fact, only one thing in life is of actual interest for us —our psychical experience. But its mechanism has been and still remains wrapped in mystery. All human resources—art, religion, literature, philosophy, and historical science—have combined to throw light on this darkness. Man has at his disposal yet another powerful resource—natural science with its strictly objective methods. (cited in Kaplan, 1966, pp. 56–57)

Pavlov's message is as timely today as it was a century ago. Psychology and neuroscience are conjoined twins at the center of the seamless science of life, and the psychologist must follow his empirical path wherever it may lead.

Irks, Quirks, and Perks

The psychological establishment is not a monolith; it is more like a parliament made up of small fractious parties. When I started out it was said that there were 7 psychologies, but now I guess there must be 14 or more. If one journal does not accept a contribution, another one might, or someone editing a book might accept a chapter. That was ever my strategy. I just kept hammering away with more evidence. It was great fun! Circa 1980, a grotesque fate befell me! I was an author on 15 articles in *Science* or *Nature*! Plaques on my walls flaunted establishment status! A perennial dropout made it all the way to the National Academy of Sciences!

In one year, the *American Psychologist* invited me twice to submit articles. In the first review, I tried to defuse the ruckus about my rejections with humor (Garcia, 1981b). That was my most requested article. Many requesters commented that they had also been rejected unfairly. I came to abhor anonymous reviews. I insisted on signing my critiques and met some interesting people in the bargain.

My second review was about mental aptitude testing. That has been my very least cited article (Garcia, 1981a). The notion that any behavior can be divided into two additive components with the main part attributed to heredity is biological nonsense; environment overpowers heredity. The most genetically gifted infant cannot flourish in a dark closet. Evolution teaches us that the environment selects the genes for survival. Paleontology teaches us that genetic constitutions cannot withstand vast environmental changes. Those who attribute performance on tests made up of cultural bits to genetic bits have an overweening faith in genetics, where they know too little, and a pathetic lack of faith in psychology, where they should know much more (Garcia, 1981a).

References

Brett, L. P., Hankins, W. G., & Garcia, J. (1976). Prey-lithium aversions. III. Buteo hawks. *Behavioral Biology, 17*, 87–98.

Bures, J., Bermudez-Rattoni, F., & Yamamoto, T. (1998). *Conditioned taste aversions: Memory of a special kind.* Oxford, England: Oxford University Press.

Coil, J. D., Rogers, R. C., Garcia, J., & Novin, D. (1978). Conditioned taste aversions: Vagal and circulatory mediation of the toxic US. *Behavioral Biology, 24*, 509–519.

Ellins, S. R., Catalano, S. M., & Schechinger, S. A. (1977). Conditioned taste aversion: A field application to coyote predation on sheep. *Behavioral Biology, 20*, 91–95.

Estes, W. K. (1959). The statistical approach to learning theory. In S. Koch (Ed.), *Psychology—A study of a science: Vol. 2. General systematic learning, formulations, and special processes.* New York: McGraw-Hill.

Forthman Quick, D. L. (1984). *Reduction of crop damage by olive baboons (Papio anubis): The feasibility of conditioned taste aversion*. Unpublished doctoral dissertation, University of California, Los Angeles.

Garcia, J. (1981a). The logic and limits of mental aptitude testing. *American Psychologist, 36,* 1172–1180.

Garcia, J. (1981b). Tilting at the papermills of academe. *American Psychologist, 36,* 149–158.

Garcia, J. (1989). Food for Tolman: Cognition and cathexis in concert. In T. Archer & L.-G. Nilsson (Eds.), *Aversion, avoidance, and anxiety* (pp. 45–85). Hillsdale, NJ: Erlbaum.

Garcia, J. (1990). Learning without memory. *Journal of Cognitive Neuroscience, 2,* 287–305.

Garcia, J., Buchwald, N. A., Feder, B. H., Koelling, R. A., & Tedrow, L. (1964). Sensitivity of the head to x-ray. *Science, 144,* 1470–1472.

Garcia, J., Buchwald, N. A., Feder, B. H., & Wakefield, C. (1962). Habituation as a factor in radiation-conditioned behavior. In *Effects of ionizing radiation on the nervous system* (pp. 145–153). Vienna, Austria: International Atomic Energy Agency.

Garcia, J., Ervin, F. R., & Koelling, R. A. (1966). Learning with prolonged delay of reinforcement. *Psychonomic Science, 5,* 121–122.

Garcia, J., Ervin, F. R., & Koelling, R. A. (1967). Toxicity of serum from irradiated donors. *Nature, 213,* 682–683.

Garcia, J., Kimeldorf, D. J., & Hunt, E. L. (1961). The use of ionizing radiation as a motivating stimulus. *Psychological Review, 68,* 383–395.

Garcia, J., & Koelling, R. A. (1966). The relation of cue to consequence in avoidance learning. *Psychonomic Science, 5,* 123–124.

Garcia, J., & Koelling, R. A. (1967). A comparison of aversions induced by x-rays, drugs and toxins. *Radiation Research Supplement, 7,* 439–450.

Garcia, J., Kovner, R., & Green, K. F. (1970). Cue properties vs. palatability of flavors in avoidance learning. *Psychonomic Science, 20,* 313–314.

Garcia, J., McGowan, B. K., Ervin, F. R., & Koelling, R. A. (1968). Cues: Their relative effectiveness as a function of the reinforcer. *Science, 160,* 794–795.

Garcia, J., McGowan, B. K., & Green, K. F. (1972). Biological constraints on learning. In M. E. P. Seligman & J. L. Hager (Eds.), *Biological boundaries of learning* (pp. 21–43). New York: Appleton-Century-Crofts.

Garcia, J., & Riley, A. L. (1998). Conditioned taste aversions. In G. Greenberg & M. M. Haraway (Eds.), *Comparative psychology: A handbook* (pp. 549–561). New York: Garland.

Garcia, J., Schofield, J., & Oper, D. (1966). A tachistoscope for x-rays. *American Journal of Psychology, 76,* 318–320.

Garcia y Robertson, R., & Garcia, J. (1985). X-rays and learned taste aversions: Historical and psychological ramifications. In T. G. Burish,

S. M. Levy, & B. E. Meyerowitz (Eds.), *Cancer, nutrition and eating behavior: A biobehavioral perspective* (pp. 11–41). Hillsdale, NJ: Erlbaum.

Green, K. F., & Garcia, J. (1971). Recuperation from illness: Flavor enhancement in rats. *Science, 173*, 749–751.

Gustavson, C. R., Garcia, J., Hankins, W. G., & Rusiniak, K. W. (1974). Coyote predation control by aversion conditioning. *Science, 184*, 581–583.

Gustavson, C. R., Jowsey, J. R., & Milligan, D. N. (1982). A 3-year evaluation of taste aversion coyote control in Saskatchewan. *Journal of Range Management, 35*, 57–59.

Herrick, C. J. (1961). *The evolution of human nature.* New York: Harper.

Hull, C. D., Garcia, J., Buchwald, N. A., Dubrowsky, B., & Feder, B. H. (1965). The role of the olfactory system in arousal to x-ray. *Nature, 205*, 627–628.

Kaplan, M. (Ed.). (1966). *Essential works of Pavlov.* New York: Bantam Books.

Kiefer, S. W. (1985). Neural mediation of conditioned food aversions. In N. S. Braveman & P. Bronstein (Eds.), Experimental assessments and clinical applications of conditioned food aversions, *Annals of the New York Academy of Sciences, 443*, 100–109.

Locke, J. (1975). *An essay concerning human understanding* (P. H. Nidditch, Ed.). Oxford, England: Clarendon Press. (Original work published 1690)

Palmerino, C. C., Rusiniak, K. W., & Garcia, J. (1980). Flavor-illness aversions: The peculiar roles of odor and taste in memory for poison. *Science, 208*, 753–755.

Provenza, F. D. (1995). Postingestive feedback as an elementary determination of food selection and intake in ruminants. *Journal of Range Management, 48*, 2–17.

Rice, A. G. (1988). *Estrogen produces conditioned taste aversion.* Unpublished doctoral dissertation, University of California, Los Angeles.

Rusiniak, K. W., Palmerino, C. C., Rice, A. G., Forthman, D. L., & Garcia, J. (1982). Flavor-illness aversions: Potentiation of odor by taste with toxin but not shock in rats. *Journal of Comparative and Physiological Psychology, 96*, 527–539.

Skinner, B. F. (1959). A case history in scientific method. In S. Koch (Ed.), *Psychology—A study of a science: Vol. 2. General systematic learning, formulations, and special processes.* New York: McGraw-Hill.

Spence, K. W. (1947). The role of secondary reinforcement in delayed reward learning. *Psychological Review, 54*, 1–8.

Tolman, E. C. (1949). There is more than one kind of learning. *Psychological Review, 54*, 189–208.

A lawyer, a book editor, a musical composer, an arranger, or a nightclub pianist—all were possible career avenues for a young Howard Gardner. Lucky for intelligence theory aficionados, Gardner received enough intermittent reinforcement early in his foray into psychology to stay the course. Forty years later, Gardner continues to, as he says, read, experiment, observe, teach, and write about intriguing human behaviors and thought. He is perhaps best known for his theory of multiple intelligences and is the author of such seminal works as *Frames of Mind: The Theory of Multiple Intelligences* and *Multiple Intelligences: The Theory in Practice.*

My Way | 5

Autobiographers have numerous choices. It is not difficult for anyone so approached to conjure up a number of stories. One can give an account of Pilgrim's Progress, where steady work and virtuous behavior are ultimately rewarded. One can offer humble pie, either denying success altogether or attributing it largely or wholly to others or to fate. One can allude to the sudden breakthrough (the road to Damascus), the series of insights (lucky batting streak or good eye), or regular plugging away (99% perspiration). One can say it was all in a day's (or night's) work. Or one can depict oneself as struggling against mighty and perhaps malevolent forces.

Without attempting to characterize my path, I'd like to give the autobiographical account that seems most authentic and that might be helpful to others. In what follows, I give a brief chronology of my youth and mention six major influences on my early career. I then mention those lines of my own work that I consider most significant. I conclude by drawing some general lessons, which I hope will prove helpful to others.

Youth and Training

I am quite certain that I did not have a passion for psychology as a child, nor do I think that psychology was necessarily the destined career choice for me. As a youngster growing up in Scranton, Pennsylvania, in the 1940s and 1950s, I assumed that I would become a lawyer or perhaps a teacher. At Harvard College in the early 1960s, I toyed with a number of careers, ranging from law to medicine to teaching.

Ultimately, I was attracted to the social sciences, probably because of the powerful influence of an eclectic collection of brilliant professors in the Social Relations Department, an interdisciplinary social sciences department that included David Riesman, Talcott Parsons, Gordon Allport, Henry Murray, David McClelland, Laurence Wiley, and Erik Erikson, just to name a few. Erikson's work and his charisma drew me to developmental psychology. When I worked on a summer educational project with Jerome Bruner, I discovered that I was more interested in cognitive than in personological or affective facets of development. Reading Jean Piaget and getting my hands involved in empirical work with Bruner, Roger Brown, and Jerry Kagan as gadflies, I soon found myself in the ranks of empirical developmental psychology, a contributor to journals like *Child Development* and *Developmental Psychology* (the chief publishing outlets at the time).

Six Career Influences

Many of my graduate student cohort at Harvard and elsewhere ended up as writers and editors of such influential gatekeeping journals. I found myself taking quite a different path. Reflecting on my strengths and on historical accidents, I can point to six factors that influenced my career choice.

MY INTEREST IN THE ARTS

As a youngster I was a serious pianist, and as an adolescent, I became an aficionado of several art forms. Turning to psychology, I was surprised to discover that the arts were virtually invisible in most texts. I noted that Piaget, along with other developmental theorists, saw "scientific knowledge" as the end-state of cognition. My initial attempts to publish articles about artistic cognition and development were routinely thwarted. Ignoring signals from "the field," I was determined to pursue the nature of creation, particularly in the arts, and searched for opportunities to do so. My first scholarly monograph, *The Arts and Human Development* (1973/1994), was an effort to examine the processes of human development using the artist, rather than the scientist, as the end-state toward which development was directed.

NELSON GOODMAN AND PROJECT ZERO

At the end of my first year in graduate school (spring 1967), I learned that a distinguished philosopher, Nelson Goodman, was planning to start a research project in artistic cognition at the Harvard Graduate School of Education. I knew almost nothing about Goodman (or the Education

School) but was intrigued by the idea. With David Perkins and several others, I became a founding member of Harvard Project Zero, and in 1972, I joined Perkins as a codirector of that institution. I have now been affiliated with Project Zero for more than a third of a century and have found it to be a stimulating intellectual home. Working at Project Zero has allowed me to pursue my interest in the arts and cognition as well as many other related (and not-so-related) issues with valued colleagues, many of whom have become friends, one of whom became my wife (Ellen Winner). At Project Zero, I conducted a long series of studies of the development of artistic capacities in children (style sensitivity, understanding of metaphor, story production, and comprehension; Gardner, 1980, 1982) and collaborated on an ambitious study of symbolic development in children, more generally (Gardner & Wolf, 1983). I also had the pleasure of helping to launch others in careers in research; younger colleagues like Winner, Dennie Wolf, Mindy Kornhaber, Tom Hatch, and Mara Krechevsky have contributed significantly to our understanding of knowledge, particularly in the arts.

PASSION TO WRITE

Since primary grade school, I have been an enthusiastic reader and writer. I edited my high school newspaper and continued to write steadily in college and graduate school. I discovered that, although I liked writing articles, the book was really my preferred form of communication, and, with little talent in the creation of fiction, my genre became the social sciences book. In graduate school, I coauthored a textbook in social psychology (with the now anachronistic name *Man and Men*; Grossack & Gardner, 1970) and also drafted two other monographs: the aforementioned scholarly tome, *The Arts and Human Development* (1973/1994), and a popularized account of French structuralism, *The Quest for Mind: Piaget, Levi-Strauss and the Structuralist Movement* (1973/1981). My teachers and fellow students looked somewhat askance at this nonempirically oriented writing facility—"write books after you get tenure, Howard," they advised—but some 20 books later, it is clear that writing has been an important part of my professional identity.

It has been noted that many of my books have the word *mind* in them. That choice of word is overdetermined, but my four children tease me by saying that my last book should be *Never Mind*.

INTELLECTUAL CURIOSITY (AKA READILY BORED BY REMAINING WITH A SINGLE TOPIC)

In graduate school, one of my professors was criticized because he went on to a new branch of psychology every decade or so. Without having any such master plan in mind, I find that I also have moved on at regular intervals to new areas, both within and beyond psychology. In college and graduate school, I regularly audited courses in various fields. I read widely although not systematically; last time I counted, I subscribe to and at least skim more than 30 publications. Most of those are not even in psychology! I marvel at those scholars who probe the same topic, deeper and deeper, for many years. Whereas I can certainly trace a continuity in my own intellectual and professional development, it includes excursions in many directions—quite possibly in too many directions. At present, I am deeply involved in a collaborative study on professional ethics (Gardner, Csikszentmihalyi, & Damon, 2001). Certainly, I could never have predicted this particular career turn 10 years ago.

A CHANCE MEETING WITH THE NEUROLOGIST NORMAN GESCHWIND

As a graduate student, I happened to attend a session given by Norman Geschwind, a brilliant behavioral neurologist and equally brilliant student of the history of neurology. Geschwind's approach to problems fascinated me, and I undertook postdoctoral work with him at Harvard Medical School and the Aphasia Research Center at the Boston University School of Medicine and the Boston Veterans Administration Medical Center. My 20-year excursion into neuropsychology constituted my most steady (and probably most significant) input to the experimental psychology literature (Gardner, 1975). Whereas most researchers were focusing on the left hemisphere, with its dominance in linguistic and conceptual matters, my colleagues and I investigated the right hemisphere's role in language and in artistic activities and published some 60 empirical articles (e.g., Gardner, Brownell, Wapner, & Michelow, 1983). My work at the Aphasia Research Center also gave me enough familiarity with the brain that I have been able to continue following discoveries in the neurosciences and to chronicle the area of cognitive science, including cognitive neuroscience, in my book *The Mind's New Science* (1985). At present, I am helping to launch a new area of study, which we at Harvard call *Mind, Brain, and Education*.

SUPPORT WAS AVAILABLE FOR UNUSUAL LINES OF RESEARCH

It is difficult for individuals my age (born 1943) or younger to appreciate that there was little or no support for empirical social sciences until the 20th century and that significant government grants became available only in the 1960s. Because of government grants, I was able to attend graduate school, to secure postdoctoral support for several years, and to carry out empirical work in developmental psychology and neuropsychology during the first crucial years of my career. That joint work eventually led to the positing of the theory of multiple intelligences (*Frames of Mind*, 1983/1993b), the work for which I am most widely known. I did not teach regularly until 1987 and could therefore dedicate two decades largely to research and writing.

By the 1980s, it became more difficult to secure support for the issues that I had become interested in. However, by this time I had become better known, and I was able to attract support from private foundations and, more recently, from generous individuals. My career could not have been possible without this continuing support, and I have gratefully acknowledged that support in all of my writings. Being a tad superstitious, I have never tried to tote up the amount of money that I have received for research, but I am sure that I would be quite affluent if I had kept it all for myself! I can categorically say that I am far happier that the sum went into research.

Three Contributions to Psychology

To the best of my reconstruction, those six factors catalyzed whatever modest success I have enjoyed. If asked to list my contributions to psychology, I would say that I have sought to broaden our conception of what the human mind is, to determine what the mind at its best can accomplish, and to outline how the young mind might be better educated.

BROADER CONCEPTION OF THE HUMAN MIND

Perhaps because their backgrounds are in the hard sciences, perhaps because they aspire for psychology to become a hard science, most psychologists in the United States have thought of cognition as the forms of thought of the scientist. From the beginning of my work, I have sought to broaden that conception, and in particular, to include artistic and creative thought as central to the functions of the mind. This mission impelled my propounding of the theory of multiple intelligences. It also accounts for my predilection to bring to bear insights from a variety of fields, ranging from the study of unusual populations, to the examination of the effects of brain damage, to the inclusion of evidence from different cultures and eras (Gardner, 1989).

STUDIES OF EXCELLENCE IN VARIOUS DOMAINS

Having laid out a theory of human intelligence, I began to ponder the nature of human accomplishment at its limits. My chosen vehicle for this study was intensive case studies of extraordinary individuals, through both interviews and library research. I studied exemplary creative figures from a variety of domains (Gardner, 1993a, 1997b), leaders (Gardner, with Laskin, 1995), and professionals who carry out work that is excellent and ethical (Gardner et al., 2001). I believe that the science of psychology is incomplete until it can explain the highest and most varied kinds of accomplishment; case methods remain the best vehicle for such research at the present time (Gardner, 1997a).

CONSTRUCTING EDUCATION ON A FIRM PSYCHOLOGICAL BASIS

As a cognitive developmental psychologist, I always had a peripheral interest in education. This interest grew significantly in the 1980s for two reasons. The first reason was idiosyncratic—the enthusiastic response among educators to the theory of multiple intelligences; the second was societal—widespread concern in the United States about the mediocre quality of precollegiate education. For 15 years I both wrote about educational issues and became active in school reform. My goal has been to forge stronger links between what is known about the nature and development of the human mind and how such knowledge can best be marshaled for educational ends. My major levers have been the positing of different modes of mental representation (Gardner, 1993c, 1999b); the examination of the powerful theories that children develop without explicit tutelage (Gardner, 1991); and the pursuit of education that develops a deep and enduring level of understanding in and across disciplines (Gardner, 1999a).

Reflections

In keeping with the theme of this book, I should describe some of the struggles, defeats, and victories I have experienced. I would have no trouble chronicling the dozens of bad peer reviews I received for scholarly articles; the equally nasty (and numerous) public reviews I received for books; the dozens of grant applications that were turned down; and the many dismissive comments I heard directly about my work or that were passed on to me by caring friends or by colleagues who may or may not have been experiencing *Schadenfreude*. Like many others, my memory for slights is quite good, if not elephantine. I can also cite honors and positive reviews, but frankly those don't really compensate for the criticism and insults; rather, it is as if they are stored in two quite separate files that cannot be merged.

It would be wrong to say that I have been uninfluenced by the criticism; certainly it has shaped my behavior in various ways. However, it would be equally wrong to say that it has deterred me from my major missions as a researcher, scholar, and writer. I am impelled by my curiosity about the world of human beings and human nature; I want to observe, study, read, and write about that world, and the fact that someone (or even many ones) may not like what I have done cannot dampen that curiosity or alter that course.

Now, had I been steadily rejected for my efforts at an early enough point in my career, I might quite well have gone to law school or become a book editor, musical composer, arranger, or nightclub pianist. (These are actually the career lines that I think I might have been able to follow without sinking into poverty.) Fortunately, as B. F. Skinner would put it, I received enough intermittent reinforcement (occasional praise, occasional prizes) that I did not lose heart. Such encouragement is important for almost everyone, and I try to provide it to younger colleagues, along with apt critiques.

By this time in my career (late mid-career), I doubt that any negative reaction would be enough to alter what I do. Perhaps I have become tough skinned; perhaps I have heard it all before; perhaps there are now enough awards that they can tip the balance; or perhaps my curiosity is as strong as ever, and that is what has impelled me throughout.

I have spent many years studying extraordinary people. From them, I have learned the importance of three inclinations: (a) reflecting regularly on one's goals and how one is fairing in pursuing them, (b) leveraging one's strengths and not worrying about areas of weakness, and (c) framing—confronting defeats and failures and trying to learn from them. As a youth, I was not as good at framing as I should have been, but I have been working steadily on training the framing muscle, and I believe that it is one of the most important parts of every thinking person's body.

My colleagues differ from one another in whether they head to the center of the fray or prefer to work in an untilled corner of the garden; whether they are energized or exhausted by confrontation; and whether they confront challengers directly, indirectly, or not at all. My own tack has been not to pay too much attention to what others are doing but to follow my own lights—in Frank Sinatra's memorable lyrics, to do it "my way." I rarely pick a fight but, then again, I don't run away from confrontations, either. This modest credo has served me pretty well in daily life, as well as in my professional career.

Probably the biggest honor that I will ever receive was the MacArthur Prize Fellowship that I was awarded in 1981, the first year that the prize was given. I remember being interviewed by the *APA Monitor* (then issued on newsprint) about the fact that I was the first psychologist to receive this distinction. I responded that I did not think I fit anyone's prototype as a psychologist but that I hoped to be on many people's list as a good psychologist. I have moved somewhat away from psychology in the succeeding 20 years, and so this latter hope is perhaps a bit forlorn. However, I continue to think of myself as a psychologist, and if I ever earn a tombstone in the graveyard of psychologists, I hope that it would recognize that I have helped to broaden our sense of cognitive activities and that I have served as a kind of ambassador between cognitive and developmental psychology on the one hand and among educators, policymakers, and the general public on the other.

Earlier I alluded to the other careers that I might have pursued had the world of "mainstream" psychology extinguished my enthusiasm rather than simply providing intermittent reinforcement. Were I to apply to myself a "profile of values," I would score high on writing (and only moderately on speaking or teaching), interest in human beings (and much less so in artifacts or other animals), the arts (although not sports or mass entertainment), and certain of the sciences (biology particularly). I believe that any career that I would have voluntarily chosen would reflect that profile, and so I could readily see myself as a scholar in several disciplines or as a journalist. I have some skills in administration but no lust for positions of authority. Personally, I doubt that I would go into psychology as a career if I were 21 years old again. Psychology has lost much of the luster that it had in the 1960s. Were I disposed to go into science, I would pursue developmental neuroscience. But I would continue to be interested in psychological issues and would attempt to approach them in other, less disciplined ways.

However, I have not a single regret. I am glad that I was born at the time when I was born; that I had the opportunity to pursue psychology and other social sciences as a student; and that I have spent almost 40 enjoyable years reading, experimenting, observing, teaching, and writing about intriguing human behaviors and thoughts. Still, I have a reason for indicating alternative careers: I believe that interests, passions, and intelligences endure across space and time but that the specific career options vary at particular historical moments. If there is reincarnation, and the discipline has a happier future than I can now envision, I will be only happy to return to earth as a psychologist and perhaps even a more loyal one than I have been this time around.

References

Gardner, H. (1975). *The shattered mind: The person after brain damage.* New York: Knopf.

Gardner, H. (1980). *Artful scribbles: The significance of children's drawings.* New York: Basic Books.

Gardner, H. (1981). *The quest for mind: Piaget, Levi-Strauss and the structuralist movement.* Chicago: University of Chicago Press. (Original work published 1973)

Gardner, H. (1982). *Art, mind, and brain: A cognitive approach to creativity.* New York: Basic Books.

Gardner, H. (1985). *The mind's new science: A history of the cognitive revolution.* New York: Basic Books.

Gardner, H. (1989). *To open minds: Chinese clues to the dilemma of American education.* New York: Basic Books.

Gardner, H. (1991). *The unschooled mind: How children think and how schools should teach.* New York: Basic Books.

Gardner, H. (1993a). *Creating minds. An anatomy of creativity as seen through the lives of Freud, Einstein, Picasso, Stravinsky, Eliot, Graham, and Gandhi.* New York: Basic Books.

Gardner, H. (1993b). *Frames of mind: The theory of multiple intelligences.* New York: Basic Books. (Original work published 1983)

Gardner, H. (1993c). *Multiple intelligences: The theory in practice.* New York: Basic Books.

Gardner, H. (1994). *The arts and human development: A psychological study of the artistic process.* New York: Basic Books. (Original work published 1973)

Gardner, H. (with Laskin, E.). (1995). *Leading minds: An anatomy of leadership.* New York: Basic Books.

Gardner, H. (1997a). Extraordinary cognitive achievement. In W. Damon (Series Ed.) & R. Siegler & D. Kuhn (Vol. Eds.), *Handbook of child psychology* (Vol. l, pp. 415–466). New York: Wiley.

Gardner, H. (1997b). *Extraordinary minds: Portraits of exceptional individuals and an examination of our extraordinariness.* New York: Basic Books.

Gardner, H. (1999a). *The disciplined mind: What all students should understand.* New York: Simon & Schuster.

Gardner, H. (1999b). *Intelligence reframed: Multiple intelligences for the 21st century.* New York: Basic Books.

Gardner, H., Brownell, H. H., Wapner, W., & Michelow, D. (1983). Missing the point: The role of the right hemisphere in the processing of complex linguistic materials. In E. Perecman (Ed.), *Cognitive processing in the right hemisphere* (pp. 160–192). New York: Academic Press.

Gardner, H., Csikszentmihalyi, M., & Damon, W. (2001). *Good work: When excellence and ethics meet.* New York: Basic Books.

Gardner, H., & Wolf, D. (1983). Waves and streams of symbolization. In D. R. Rogers & J. A. Sloboda (Eds.), *The acquisition of symbolic skills* (pp. 19–42). London: Plenum Press.

Grossack, M., & Gardner, H. (1970). *Man and men: Social psychology as social science.* Scranton, PA: International Textbook.

The introduction to Jerome Kagan's essay might at first lead you to believe you've stumbled on the musings of a psychoanalyst, not those of a noted child psychologist. Kagan's assessment of his own early childhood reads like a good Freudian case study. Kagan, who has made significant strides in the study of cognitive development of children by using a variety of novel methodologies, writes a piece that combines the best of philosophy, morality, religion, nature, literature, and psychology to form an opinion on the importance of the social sciences.

An Unwilling Rebel | 6

The events of my childhood years and a temperamentally based predisposition to avoid excessive uncertainty made me unfit for the role of rebel. As a firstborn with a protective mother who used guilt with unusual effectiveness to gain her socialization goals, I was reluctant to risk rejection from adults or children. Fortunately, this timidity, which favored conformity to consensual beliefs, was balanced by a father so preoccupied with the pain of his chronic arthritis that he represented an anguished human being who deserved sympathy rather than an authority to be held in awe. The combination of my father's compromised potency and my mother's emotional dependence on her adolescent son during the long periods of her husband's hospitalization made it easier to treat authority figures realistically rather than award them halos of unsullied virtue and extraordinary competence. These conditions freed me from the insatiable desire to be in positions of power, a trait that often develops in sons whose fathers appear to be impregnable. Thus, my occasional challenge of popular psychological positions did not represent a chronic hostility to or envy of authority, as is occasionally true of some later borns, but was allowed expression because of the absence of intimidation.

Childhood

Growing up Jewish in the 1930s in a small New Jersey town 20 miles south of New York City with a large blue-collar population that held antiSemitic attitudes fostered a vigilance toward the majority peer group, whom I regarded as alien. The feeling of separateness, and the conviction that their beliefs were irrational, inoculated me against caring too much about group acceptance as I entered adolescence. Although I rarely offended others, I understood the price that such a need exacted. I wished to be creative in some intellectual endeavor and understood that excessive worry over the opinions of others made achieving that goal less likely.

The linchpin in the construction of my character was early success in elementary school. Of equal significance were my mother's values, her adoring worship of her bookish father (whom I never knew), and the absence of any other talents. This profile rendered me eager for achievement, and being the best reader in the first grade was probably interpreted as a sign that intellectual work was the vocation fate had intended. Every adolescent has a rough conception of the perfect self. This Kantian imperative can award salience to a desire to be helpful, loved, attractive, strong, rich, famous, or respected. For a small number, the goal is to be wise. I do not understand the complex biological and experiential factors that lead 15-year-olds to pick one of these ideals rather than another to guide a life. But a scientific insight satisfies those who set wisdom as the prize. It helps, of course, if the person is a trifle uncertain over his or her ability to meet that standard. The novelist Flannery O'Connor once told an interviewer that to write a great novel one should not understand the plot too completely; uncertainty over the final form supplies the psychic energy required for the creative product.

Choosing Psychology

As my senior year at Rutgers University began, I could not decide whether to apply for graduate work in biochemistry or psychology, and so I applied to both departments. The letter of acceptance from the Yale University psychology department informed me that, should I decide to go to New Haven, I would be a research assistant to Frank Beach. By chance, I was reading Donald Hebb's (1949) *Organization of Behavior* that week in early April and noticed that F. A. Beach's name filled almost the entire first page of the bibliography. The opportunity to work with a famous scientist combined with my inchoate attraction to the study of human nature accelerated my heart more than the elegant objectivity of biochemistry. Furthermore, I believed that wisdom required an understanding of the mind, not molecules.

The First Decade

Although the laboratory work with Beach on the sexual behavior of rats and dogs was interesting, I had decided to become a child psychologist.

In the 1950s, that choice was uncommon but praiseworthy. I blush to admit that my cohort believed that the early causes of neuroses, criminality, and psychosis would be discovered in our lifetime and that we would be able to tell an eager, appreciative community how to prevent those outcomes. Thus, when Lester Sontag, the first director of the Fels Research Institute, invited me to direct a National Institutes of Health project designed to exploit the longitudinal corpus at the institute and relate the childhood evidence to the adult's personality, the decision to go to Yellow Springs, Ohio, in early 1957 was easy. I was the grateful recipient of 20 years of empirical data by many careful investigators. All I had to do was assess the adults and put the two pieces of the puzzle together. The 1962 publication of *Birth to Maturity,* with my collaborator Howard Moss, brought a small measure of fame because it was the first time any group had integrated extensive behavioral observations on a large group of infants and young children with interview and laboratory information on adults. Moreover, our conclusions supported the popular assumption of preservation of individual differences in development. Although the strongest signs of preservation did not emerge until ages 6 or 7 and the stability profiles interacted with gender and social class, these caveats were ignored by most readers because Moss and I had affirmed a fundamental axiom in developmental science.

The Rebel Emerges

The first article that angered some of my peers, and a few of the *éminences grise* in the American Psychological Association's Division of Developmental Psychology, was the 1973 article in the *American Psychologist,* written with Robert Klein, that challenged the view that an environmentally produced retardation in infancy was permanent. The origin of that seemingly bold assertion was the decision to spend a sabbatical year observing the conditions of third world children. I did not care where that knowledge was gained, and it was my good fortune that Klein, a Minnesota PhD working in Guatemala, made it possible to work in the small isolated Mayan village of San Marcos La Laguna, on the shore of cobalt blue Lake Atitlan in the northwest part of the country. I did not know, as I prepared for this trip during the summer of 1971, that the observations in that village would change my mind about the power of early experience. I saw cognitively retarded young infants wrapped in old rags and restricted to the inside of the hut during their first year because of the belief that infants were vulnerable to the evil eye. But I also observed high levels of competence in the 6-year-olds because, after their first 12 to 18 months, the children were allowed to leave the hut to encounter trees, stones, and other children. It was obvious by late spring that the serious cognitive retardation of the first year was temporary.

I thought, ingenuously, that this fact would be greeted with applause and was therefore surprised by the pockets of resistance the article aroused. The problem, which Klein and I had not anticipated, was that our conclusions were interpreted as inconsistent with the popular assumption that infants required a stimulating environment. Without adequate variety through adult handling, reciprocal play, and speech, the child's future competences would be compromised permanently. Some developmental psychologists feared that our article would motivate government agencies to reconsider their support of programs in early education.

We realized that our inferences went beyond the evidence, but if these claims had been radically unreasonable the *American Psychologist*, hardly a terrorist organ, would not have published the article. The reaction to the 1973 article eroded a little more of the concern with majority opinion. I had irritated some colleagues but continued to receive grant support and felt freer to respect intuitions about evidence and to worry a little less about others' views.

The Maturation of Cognitive Abilities

The research summarized in *Birth to Maturity* strengthened my curiosity about the infant origins of the adult differences Moss and I had discovered. Therefore, following the move to Harvard University in 1964, my students and I initiated a longitudinal study of the first year. The selection of variables revealed a premise that was influenced by undergraduate courses in biology and chemistry. Most biological research is motivated by a desire to understand a robust observation rather than to confirm or refute the implications of a theory or operationalize a hypothetical construct. By contrast, much psychological research, and especially work on personality and development, is designed to test a prediction that originates in an abstract idea, like attachment, intelligence, anxiety, or the concept of an object. I have always been suspicious of abstract concepts that originate in intuition rather than evidence and especially constructs that are value laden. The task is to understand ethically neutral phenomena. For example, human infants differ in the duration of attention they devote to varied events, but the reasons for those differences were—and continue to be—not well understood. Thus, we coded duration of attentiveness to varied events with the hope that the data would permit a theoretically important inference. That hope was realized. The evidence revealed a qualitative increase in the duration of attention to discrepant events between ages 8 and 10 months. We used that fact, which was unexpected, to infer a major enhancement in retrieval memory during the last half of the first year, the time when stranger and separation fear appear in all infants. The possibility that separation fear might be due to the enhanced memory generated a hypothesis that separation fear occurred when maturational events linked the medial temporal lobe with the prefrontal cortex and permitted the infant to retrieve representation of the parents' prior presence, to hold that representation and the current context in short-term memory, and finally to compare the two representations in the service of assimilation. The inability to reconcile the two representations (i.e., the mother was present moments earlier but is not present now) provoked a state of uncertainty and, in some infants, crying.

After students working in other cultures found that crying as a result of separation from the caretaker occurred between ages 8 and 14 months, whether in Botswana or Guatemala, I suggested that separation fear did not reflect quality of attachment to the caretaker (a consensual assumption at the time) but was the result of brain growth that permitted a new cognitive ability (Kagan, 1984). Because the index of a secure or insecure attachment to the caretaker in Ainsworth's strange situation (Ainsworth, Blehar, Waters, & Wall, 1978) was based on intensity of separation distress and ease of being soothed when the mother returned to the infant, I became skeptical of the inferences drawn from the evidence this procedure produced. A decade later, when my laboratory was studying inhibited and uninhibited children, I suggested that an infant's temperamental vulnerability to becoming fearful in an unfamiliar context made a contribution to the 1-year-old's behavior in the strange situation. Many infants who were classified as Type C (insecurely attached) were temperamentally vulnerable to becoming extremely fearful when the mother left them alone in the room and, as a result, were hard to soothe.

A Study of the Second Year

Because discovery of the enhancement in retrieval memory was based on detailed behavioral observations rather than on parental verbal reports, my students and I used the same strategy in a longitudinal study of the second year. These data permitted us to infer the first signs of a moral sense and of self-awareness in the middle of the second year (Kagan, 1981). In my book *The Second Year*, I argued that both of these competences were maturationally inevitable and would emerge in all but the most isolated or deprived children. I felt relatively certain of these claims because I had watched the children rather than being told what they did by research assistants. The verbal descriptions given by assistants often distort what film reveals because the semantic summaries are guided by a requirement for consistency among the sentences and between the sentences and the speaker's beliefs. Watching every child, live or on tape, can be tedious and occasionally boring, but it has a major advantage. If these observations invite a novel interpretation, one is more confident having seen the evidence on which it rests. The representations created by perceptual structures are not constrained by demands for semantic consistency. When graduate students made similar observations on children living on Pacific atolls, villages in Guatemala, and Vietnamese immigrant communities, I became persuaded that the ancients were correct in their belief that a human moral sense is universal—a claim contained in the tree of knowledge allegory and the fact that the terms *good* and *bad* appear in every human language.

Temperament

Two observations motivated study of the temperamental groups we call *high-* and *low-reactive infants* and their derivatives in inhibited and uninhibited children. First, the evidence in *Birth to Maturity* indicated that the only infant variable preserved from the first 3 years of life through early adulthood was a tendency to approach or to avoid unfamiliar events or challenging contexts. In addition, a prior study of the effects of day care on Chinese American infants living in Boston's Chinatown and White infants of the same social class revealed that the two groups were different in their reactions to unfamiliarity even though all infants attended the same day care center that Richard Kearsley, Phillip Zelazo, and I were directing (Kagan, Kearsley, & Zelazo, 1978). It was important that our measures were behavioral observations rather than parental report. Although most investigations of infant temperament at that time relied primarily on parental questionnaires, I was critical of that strategy because of the distortions that semantic constructions induce. Investigators who use only parental questionnaires do not posit the constructs *high* and *low reactivity* to unfamiliarity because parents are not sensitive enough to detect the infants who combine vigorous motor activity with crying to unfamiliar events. I believe that the constructs *high* and *low reactive*, which have been fruitful, would not have been discovered if we had relied on parental report alone (Kagan, 1994).

High-reactive infants are biased to become shy, timid, emotionally subdued, dour children; low-reactive infants are biased to display the opposite profile of spontaneity and optimism. Nathan Fox of the University of Maryland has affirmed these generalizations. Furthermore, both Fox's laboratory and our own have found interesting physiological correlates of the two infant temperaments. For example, children who had been high-reactive infants and fearful in the second year are more likely to show right frontal activation in the electroencephalogram; low-reactive infants, who usually become fearless, are more likely to show left frontal activation. I was initially troubled by the fact that some infants inherited a temperamental bias that made it difficult for them to become exuberant, joyful, optimistic adults. Although I have accepted that fact of nature, I remain saddened by its injustice.

Challenging Dogma

A skeptical stance toward sole reliance on questionnaire or interview data motivated exploration of the power of less direct methods to measure parental attitudes toward child rearing. Direct questioning of parents about their child's behavior is plagued by parental desire to avoid acknowledging beliefs that might violate the parents' or the examiner's ideals. Therefore, we used a technique in which differential recall of prose arguments containing opposing ideals for child rearing might reveal parents' deeper prejudices. We created 300-word essays containing balanced arguments for two opposing sides on three themes: the advantages and disadvantages of physical affection to the infant, loyalty to the family versus emotional independence from the family, and a restrictive versus a permissive socialization regimen. Robust social class differences in the recall of the opposing themes in each essay were in accord with theory but were not revealed by direct questioning. To my surprise, this article was rejected by four journals that publish research on attitudes because the reviewers argued that selective recall was not an index of attitudes. The *International Journal of Behavioral Development* published this article in 1986 (Kagan et al., 1986).

The longitudinal corpus on the high- and low-reactive infants permitted us to challenge a popular hypothesis regarding the meaning of Stroop interference. We administered a Stroop procedure to 7-year-old inhibited and uninhibited children because most investigators believed that selective interference to threatening content should differentiate the two groups. The children saw schematic pictures varying in affective valence. The pictures were outlined in different colors, and the children had to name the color and ignore the meaning of the picture. Although the pictures symbolic of harm and danger produced the most interference, as expected, there was no relation between the child's past or current level of fear or anxiety and the magnitude of interference to the pictures symbolic of harm or danger, implying that Stroop interference to threatening content may not be an index of the emotional state of the child. The article in which we described this experiment was rejected by three journals because reviewers resisted the suggestion that Stroop interference might not be a sensitive reflection of an affective state.

We also administered a standard startle procedure to the 7- and 10-year-old inhibited and uninhibited children in our longitudinal sample because it is generally believed that magnitude of potentiated startle to aversive stimuli reflects an aversive affect state and therefore should differentiate inhibited and uninhibited children. The children heard brief bursts of white noise while they saw pictures symbolic of positive, neutral, or aversive events or a blue light that signaled that an aversive air puff was about to be delivered to their throat. Although the aversive pictures and blue light produced the largest eye blink startles, there was no difference between the inhibited and uninhibited children in magnitude of potentiated startle to either the unpleasant pictures or the light.

Our habit of examining groups with extreme scores and forming categories rather than continua has also been criticized. The central tension in empirical studies of individual differences is whether people differ quantitatively on a set of dimensions, and therefore each person is best described as a set of values on factor scores, or whether some individuals belong to qualitatively distinct groups. Although some phenomena are best understood as products of linear continua, at least for certain ranges, others are not continuous.

Psychological data often display nonlinear functions, with categorical phenomena emerging for specific ranges. Popular statistical procedures, including regression analyses, often fail to reveal important nonlinear relations. The behavior of a single ant, or a few ants, appears to be random and without coherence. But rhythmic activity emerges when the number of ants in a colony reaches a critical density. A large colony has distinct qualities that cannot be predicted from, or explained by, an additive model that sums the behavior of an increasing number of ants.

The data on the 10-year-olds in our longitudinal study of temperament reveal, repeatedly, that comparisons of children in the top and bottom quartiles or terciles of the distribution separate the high- and low-reactive children, whereas mean scores do not. It is often useful to reflect on the possibility of small, qualitatively distinct groups when exploring psychological evidence (Kagan, Snidman, & Arcus, 1998). Only some individuals in a household come down with winter flu, even though all are exposed to the virus. Each organism has a biology and a history that influences its reaction to an incentive event; in psychiatry, *diathesis* captures this meaning. Hence, all psychological outcomes are derivatives of interactions of genes with environment. Few, if any, behavioral events are only genetic or only environmental in origin.

Summing Up

The occasional moments of sadness that trail the knowledge that some of my colleagues were critical of my conclusions were often replaced by longer periods of satisfaction that grew from the illusion that I had seen a tiny pearl disguised in one of nature's shadows. My highest moments form when I glimpse a phenomenon no one else has seen before or when a scatter plot reveals an unexpected relation that suddenly makes a set of disconnected facts coherent. The intention is critical to the pleasure extracted. If one is free of secular hopes and suppresses excessive arrogance, the moment can be beautiful.

I suspect there are two bases for the special pleasure scientists feel when their curiosity leads them to an original discovery. All humans wish to be morally virtuous agents with a touch of spirituality. For most, acts of kindness, empathy, and honesty are sufficient. A small proportion, because of life history, require more substantial proof. Growing up in a religious home where moral values are taken seriously can create a high standard of virtue. Jean Piaget was raised in such a home. Many creative natural scientists, more than one would expect by chance, grew up in homes where a parent or close relative was a clergyman. Ivan Pavlov, Robert Millikan, Alfred Wegener, and Luis Alvarez are examples from the 20th century.

A second basis for a link between creative scientific work and a moral concept of self occurs in those who believe they possess properties that the majority regards as less virtuous. Membership in a minority group is one way to create this state of uncertainty. A disproportionate number of 20th-century Nobel laureates, including Julius Axelrod, Rosalyn Yalow, Albert Einstein, Salvador Luria, Neils Bohr, Otto Loewi, Joshua Lederberg, Isidor Rabi, Francois Jacob, and Rita Levi-Montalcini, were members of a victimized minority group in their society. The latter two wrote about the dysphoric sense of difference they felt as Jews in Catholic countries with a streak of anti-Semitism.

Additionally, the selection of science as a life activity has a special meaning for victims of prejudice who are convinced that the oppressing majority holds a false, irrational belief. The replacement of incorrect beliefs with correct ones is the goal of science; hence, those who have been targets of prejudice always hope that when the truth is known the community will replace the old, ragged ideas with more valid ones. Einstein wrote that "one of the strongest motives that lead men to art and science is flight from every day life with its painful harshness" (cited in Holton, 1988, p. 395).

A different basis for a persistent curiosity about nature bears a superficial resemblance to Freud's (1933) notion that intellectual work can be a sublimation of sexual preoccupations. The concept of nature in Western society, as in most cultures, is semantically closer to the category *female* than to the category *male*. For example, *flower, earth, moon,* and *ocean* are usually referred to with a female pronoun. Thus, it is likely that, in the minds of most adolescents, natural events lie closer to the idea of female than to the idea of male.

A second assumption necessary for the argument, but more difficult to support, maintains that some boys develop an intense, affectively laden curiosity about girls and women that rests on more than the desire to know the details of the female genitalia. It is a motive to penetrate the mysteries of conception, pregnancy, birth, nursing, and the unquestioning nurturance women show toward their children and loved ones. Jacob (1988) recalls his mother,

> tender, sweet perfumed, warmth. Safe harbor from all fears and all violence . . . Maman, who rocked me to sleep, bathed me, wiped me, blew my nose, disciplined me, tucked me in, caressed me, scolded me, watched over me . . . Maman, who for years launched me into the day each morning. And waited at her window to welcome me home from school each afternoon. (pp. 21–22)

Children are so self-interested that they find the unselfishness of mothers puzzling. The desire to understand this enigma could provoke an intense curiosity over nature's secrets.

Every discipline contains at least two types of scholars. One group, more often represented in physics and mathematics, celebrates the mind and treats it as a revered object to be probed gently in a quiet room until it reveals its abstract beauty. The joy comes from using the mind to invent a set of logically coherent ideas that solves a conceptual problem. A second group, found more often among life scientists, celebrates nature, especially her interrelatedness, concreteness, and specificity. These scholars find satisfaction in the discovery of something new about real events in a real world. For the young Ernst Mayr it was birds; for Linus Pauling it was rocks. Unlike the formalists who are excited by the freedom of playing with impossible ideas, the empiricists heed Peter Medawar's advice to work on soluble problems. Axelrod (1981) wrote, "the important thing is to ask a question that is realistic" (p. 27). Jacob (1988) confessed, "biologists abhor distraction . . . I saw nature as a good girl. Generous, but a little dirty. A bit muddle-headed. Working in a hit or miss fashion" (p. 320).

No natural phenomenon has the bright pristine quality of a universal law woven from a logically commanding mathematical or formal argument. Bertrand Russell captured the difference between the two types of scholars. In a passage from *Portraits From Memory and Other Essays*, Russell (1963) commented on the differences between Alfred North Whitehead and himself:

> It was Whitehead who was the serpent in this paradise of Mediterranean clarity. He said to me once: "You think the world is what it looks like in fine weather at noon day; I think it is what it seems like in the morning when one first wakes from deep sleep." (pp. 39–40)

For reasons I do not understand, I derive more delight from discovering a novel aspect of nature, even one that must be hedged, than from formal arguments because I am deeply skeptical of the mind's susceptibility to settling on simple solutions that are aesthetic. I also confess to a flaw that may be fatal. I so revere nature that I may not want to understand her too completely; if I am successful she will lose all of her mystery. I poke her, but with e.e. cummings, smile privately in celebration of her perennial answer—spring.

I suspect that 9 of every 10 novel claims in the social sciences will turn out to be wrong, some wildly so, especially when based on a priori premises and abstract concepts rather than a rich set of reliable observations. Thus, when graduate students seek counsel I tell them to be self-critical of a priori notions in the social sciences. The energy required to study a trivial or improper question is not much less than the effort needed to work on a profound one. Investigators should pick a question they believe must be answered, gather the best data possible, and analyze it with the meticulous care an archaeologist would devote to a jaw bone believed to be the first mammal. If the observations imply that a popular notion is flawed, do not waffle.

Young faculty find it more difficult to follow this advice than my cohort did 50 years ago. Historical changes since 1954 have made many younger scholars acutely aware of the competition for research funds and professorial chairs. It is also relevant that the explosion in the number of doctoral degrees in psychology has led to a fragmentation into many subspecialties to which loyalty is primary. As a result, there is indifference to knowledge in other domains. This intellectual isolation makes it much more difficult to discover a novel relation between phenomena that originate in adjacent domains that use different vocabularies and methods. Perhaps it is unfair to judge younger scientists too harshly, for job security and peer acceptance are at high risk. I did not worry about job security and did not think my colleagues would be annoyed by the 1973 article with Klein. Hence, I do not deserve a shiny badge of courage.

What Have I Learned?

When I left New Haven 47 years ago, I was certain that the major determinants of psychological variation were due to the behaviors of parents with children during the opening decade. I now believe with the same certainty that these experiences play a much smaller role than the child's temperament; identification with family members; social categories, especially gender, class, and ethnicity; and the historical era in which adolescence is spent.

One premise remains unchanged. The interpretation of experience, not the encounters recorded on film, determines the older child's psychological response. Each mind, like a lens with a unique curvature, interprets the world in ways that are consonant with the person's network of schemata and semantic structures created by past history and the feeling tone that the body–brain creates. The unfinished task is to invent procedures that can detect these interpretations. I have tried many times to discover such methods but have failed. However, because physicists gained insight into the elements that determine the inorganic world, and biologists came to understand the structure of genes, surely the next generation of psychologists will enjoy their victorious moment.

References

Ainsworth, M. D. S., Blehar, M. C., Waters, E., & Wall, S. C. (1978). *Patterns of attachment: A psychological study of the strange situation.* Hillsdale, NJ: Erlbaum.

Axelrod, J. (1981). Biochemical pharmacology. In W. Shropshire (Ed.), *The joys of research* (pp. 25–77). Washington, DC: Smithsonian Institution.

Freud, S. (1933). *New introductory lectures on psychoanalysis.* New York: Norton.

Hebb, D. O. (1949). *The organization of behavior: A neuropsychological theory.* New York: Wiley.

Holton, G. (1988). *Thematic origins of scientific thought* (rev. ed.). Cambridge, MA: Harvard University Press.

Jacob, F. (1988). *The statue within.* New York: Basic Books.

Kagan, J. (1981). *The second year.* Cambridge, MA: Harvard University Press.

Kagan, J. (1984). *The nature of the child.* New York: Basic Books.

Kagan, J. (1994). *Galen's prophecy.* New York: Basic Books.

Kagan, J., Kearsley, R., & Zelazo, P. (1978). *Infancy*. Cambridge, MA: Harvard University Press.

Kagan, J., & Klein, R. E. (1973). Cross-cultural perspectives on early development. *American Psychologist, 28*, 947–961.

Kagan, J., & Moss, H. A. (1962). *Birth to maturity*. New York: Wiley.

Kagan, J., Reznick, J. S., Davies, J., Smith, J., Sigal, H., & Miyake, K. (1986). Selective memory and belief. *International Journal of Behavioral Development, 9*, 205–218.

Kagan, J., Snidman, N., & Arcus, D. (1998). The value of extreme groups. In R. B. Cairns, L. R. Bergman, & J. Kagan (Eds.), *Methods and models* (pp. 65–79). Thousand Oaks, CA: Sage.

Russell, B. (1963). *Portraits from memory and other essays*. New York: Simon & Schuster.

When Elizabeth Loftus published *Memory* in 1980, she had no idea that her interest in memory and its merits and flaws would lead her to the center of a maelstrom. Twenty years ago, Loftus postulated a future world in which people could go to a special kind of psychologist or psychiatrist, "a memory doctor," and have their memories modified. In the 1990s, Loftus's dream came true, although it quickly turned into more of a nightmare. The sudden appearance of "repressed-memory doctors" led to a wave of accusations levied by individuals—accusations of such offenses as child rape, incest, and even baby sacrifice. Loftus braved the enormous backlash created by her public condemnation of the many dubious practices used by repressed-memory doctors to "retrieve" the lost memories of their patients. Her dedication to exposing the problems of repressed-memory therapy eventually led to its downfall as a valid theory.

Elizabeth F. Loftus

The Dangers of Memory

7

Twenty years ago, I wrote a book with a simple title: *Memory* (Loftus, 1980). There I invited readers to imagine a future world in which people could go to a special kind of psychologist or psychiatrist—a memory doctor—and have their memories modified (p. xiv). The setting for this "thought experiment" was a world that preceded the election of Ronald Reagan to the presidency. It was a world in which the chairman of Digital Equipment Corporation had recently made a prediction about computers when he addressed the World Future Society: "There is no reason for any individual to have a computer in their home" (Celente, 1997, p. 20). Because futurist thinking is known to have some beginner's errors, my readers shouldn't have expected much better from me. But here's what I "predicted" and how I was eventually partly right and partly wrong.

Back in 1980, I invited readers to imagine a place where one could go once a week or once a month to have some particularly difficult memory altered. Why would anyone do this? I asked. Purely speculating, I suggested that depressed people might find it of therapeutic value. If a patient were plagued by feelings of deep sadness or worthlessness, the memory doctor could simply modify the memories leading to the feelings. If patients were having marital problems, the memory doctor might be called on to enhance pleasant memories of past events involving the spouse. On a larger scale, such doctors might even be useful for curing societal ills such as social prejudice. To the extent that prejudice is based on a few incidents involving a unique group of people, the memory doctor could wipe out or alter memory of these incidents. "These memory modification specialists would be omnipotent," I mused. "They would hold the key to total mind control" (Loftus, 1980, p. xiv).

I admitted at the time that all this might have sounded far-fetched because we obviously couldn't at that time modify memory on command. But I used this metaphoric notion to lead into the then-contemporary work on memory distortion, which showed that memory could be at least partially modified. There was ample evidence at that time that our memories of past events can change in helpful ways, leading us to be happier than we might otherwise be. But memory also changes in harmful ways and can occasionally land us in serious trouble. The research that prompted my musing about the memory doctors consisted of a sizable body of work showing that new, postevent information often becomes incorporated into our memory, supplementing and altering our recollection. The new information invades the mind, like a Trojan horse, precisely because we do not detect its influence. At the time I speculated about memory doctors, scores of studies on memory distortion had been conducted with a wide variety of materials. With many collaborators, I showed that people could be induced to recall nonexistent broken glass and tape recorders, a clean-shaven man as having a mustache, straight hair as curly, and even something as large and conspicuous as a barn in a bucolic scene that contained no buildings at all.

Taken together, these findings revealed that misleading postevent information can alter a person's recollection in powerful, predictable ways. In the real world, such misinformation was often available when people who experienced the same event talked to one another or gained access to information from the media, interrogators, or other sources. After years of investigating the power of misinformation, I and many other psychological scientists had unearthed a fair amount about the conditions that made people particularly susceptible to its damaging influence. People were particularly prone to having their memories modified when the passage of time first allowed the memory to fade. In its faded, weakened condition, memory—like the disease-ridden body—becomes especially vulnerable to misinformation.

While musing about the hypothetical memory doctor in 1980, I could not have known that a version of the memory specialist was in the making. These "repressed memory therapists" would go out and prospect for early childhood memories of trauma, and in the process they inadvertently created false memories of the most unimaginable kind. The memory doctors I had speculated about in 1980 were supposed to use their talents to help people. The memory doctors of the 1990s went in the wrong direction.

In the 1990s concerns were raised (by me and others) about some of the memories that were being created in psychotherapy, particularly memories that emerged in adulthood after extensive "memory work." Popular techniques for "recovering" memories included age regression, body memory interpretation, suggestive questioning, guided visualization, sexualized dream interpretation, aggressive sodium amytal interviews, misleading bibliotherapy, and more. These techniques were leading patients to "memories" of childhood molestation that were supposedly totally repressed. In some cases, what surfaced was an endless number of violent traumas spanning years of the patient's life. In other cases, the de-repressed memories were from the first 6 months of life or even from the prenatal period. On the basis of these newfound "memories," people were falsely accused of abuse, families were destroyed, and more than a few individuals went to jail (Johnson, 1997; Lindsay & Read, 1994; Loftus, 1993). It was exactly the sort of try-it-and-see-if-it-works approach that medicine had often relied on—but the hazards are well known, at least in medicine. What happened with the repressed memory doctors appeared to be another example of the "cure" being worse than the disease.

Battling the "Establishment"

My role in this controversy began when I was asked to consult on a court case in which a man was accused of a 20-year-old murder (and years of sexual abuse) based on "de-repressed" memories of his daughter (Loftus & Ketcham, 1994). It was the first time that I made a serious investigation into the evidence for the repression folklore—the idea that memories of severe, repeated brutalization are repressed into the unconscious, that they can be reliably excavated, and that this must be done in order to cure the patient. I could find not a shred of credible scientific support for this claim. I said so. As a result I began to hear from hundreds of desperate people. A woman from Maryland wrote,

> We were suddenly and inexplicably accused four years ago by our
> now 28-year-old daughter of having sexually . . . molested her,
> i.e., her father raped her as of age 2 months, I raped her
> repeatedly as of a very young age, one of her two older brothers
> raped her consistently. It is like a nightmare situation, where I
> feel that my daughter's mind has been replaced with another's.
> (Loftus & Ketcham, 1994, p. 6)

"Please help us," a woman from Canada wrote. "I am not a baby-raper . . . how could my daughter say these things about me?" an accused father asked me, tears running down his cheeks. I became overwhelmed with hundreds of anguished appeals for help.

The public exposure of false-memory cases, and the fascination with bizarre memories expressed by some litigants, helped lead to a new kind of study of the power of suggestion to influence memory. Instead of merely distorting memory for the details of a past event that was in fact experienced (changing a stop sign into yield sign or adding barns to memory), the 1990s researchers asked about the planting of entirely false memories. We convinced people that they had been lost in a shopping mall at the age of 5 for an extended time and rescued by an elderly person (Loftus & Pickrell, 1995). We convinced people that they had been born left-handed (Kelley, Amodio, & Lindsay, 1996), that they spilled punch over the parents of the bride at a wedding (Hyman, Husband, & Billings, 1995), or that they were victims of a serious animal attack (Porter, Yuille, & Lehman, 1999). It took a fairly strong form of suggestion to plant these memories. But even with simple encouragement to engage in imagination, people could be led to be more confident that they had childhood experiences that they probably did not have, for example, that they broke a window with their hand (Garry, Manning, Loftus, & Sherman, 1996) or that they fell off a bicycle and got stitches in their leg (Heaps & Nash, 1999) or that they witnessed demonic possession at a young age (Mazzoni, Loftus, & Kirsch, 2001). The newer studies showed that suggestions, strong and subtle, could be powerful in terms of making people believe that they had experiences in childhood that they almost certainly did not have. These sorts of findings enhanced our understanding of the many documented case histories in which therapy patients, at the hands of unwitting 1990s-style memory doctors, may have developed full-blown false memories for excruciatingly violent episodes (including rapes, animal torture, baby breeding, baby sacrifice, and more).

Through the combination of research and case histories, we have learned a great deal about the flimsy curtain that separates our memory from our imagination, and we are on our way toward being able to write the exact recipes for creating false memories of almost any size and shape. We know more than ever about the steps that are involved in creating false memories. We know, for example, that the recipe probably involves a multistage process (see Mazzoni & Loftus, 1998). Planting a false memory might first require making a person believe that a suggested event is a plausible one. The next step involves convincing the person to believe that the suggested event happened. From there, one can engage the person in various activities (e.g., visualization) that lead them to subjectively "remember" the suggested experience. Pressure for details often produces extensive and idiosyncratic elaborations. Thus, from this collective effort, we almost have a recipe for false memories in the making.

The Opposition and the Response

As I expressed doubts about the repression theory, spoke up about the dubious forensic cases, and presented and published my new research findings, I encountered opposition that I was not used to. People wrote to warn me that my reputation and even my safety were in jeopardy if I continued along these lines. People completely misinterpreted my writings and put words in my mouth that I had never spoken. People filed ethical complaints and threatened to sue organizations that invited me to speak. People spread defamatory falsehoods in writings, in newspapers, on the Internet, and in myriad other arenas. The fighting was not the clean, intellectual type that I was used to; it was downright dirty. It became impossible to respond to every assault and hard to know which ones to overlook and which ones to spend time on. After all, every minute, every hour spent responding to some irritated true-believer was an hour taken from the activities I truly valued: research, teaching (which I began to see, in part, as a way of creating new warriors), and helping the falsely accused.

When nasty comments and other verbal assaults come my way, I face the question of whether to respond. That is the same question faced by those who have become victims of a different sort of verbal attack: the peculiar literary genre known as the "revenge memoire." According to Merkin (2000), these memoires are often written by unhappy and lonely children who look back on their earlier life in anger and express it by exposing various skeletons, some real and some make-believe, from the family closet. Is it healthy or destructive? Is it motivated by candor or by greed? Should the person at the heart of the recollection respond? Should the person being attacked remain silent as though it were beneath her to join in such a transparently contemptible enterprise?

It was one thing when the attacks came from the recovered-memory patients themselves. After all, they were experiencing real pain, even if perhaps they didn't have the cause quite right. They were feeling disbelieved and had perhaps had few ways of expressing their hurt. But it was quite another thing when the attacks came from individuals who were supposed to be respectable professionals. For example, two colleagues, who made a considerable contribution to the repressed-memory movement in North America, wrote a piece in the Harvard Mental Health Letter, referring to my recently published essay as "social backlash" (Herman & Harvey, 1993). They claimed that academic researchers "have questioned the veracity of delayed memories of childhood sexual abuse and speculated on the possibility that these memories might be fictions inculcated by naive or manipulative psychotherapists" (p. 4). Furthermore, they stated,

> The notion that therapists can implant scenarios of horror in the minds of their patients is easily accepted because it appeals to common prejudices. It resonates with popular fears of manipulation by therapists and popular stereotypes of women as

irrational, suggestible, or vengeful. It appeals to the common wish to deny or minimize the reality of sexual violence. (p. 4)

Nothing could be further from the truth, as my revelations about my own abuse in childhood should have made evident (Loftus & Ketcham, 1991).

Another colleague thoroughly misrepresented my views:

Loftus uses theoretical constructs and methods that were developed from research on adults, whose memories and other cognitive functions do not follow the same developmental patterns as those of children, to demonstrate that children's memories can be altered by new information. . . . She then concludes that children are so confused by their suggestible or malleable memories that their accusations cannot be trusted. (Walker, 1994, p. 83)

By the time her critical remarks had been published, I had already published at least a half dozen studies on children's memory and had never reached a conclusion that even resembled her claim. After explicit reference to my work, this dissenter then asked why people like me would contradict the clinical or research evidence for memory problems and invoked such motivations as "personal biases, such as distrust of therapists, desire to support male perpetrators, . . . enjoyment of the recognition provided by groups that rally around men who are allegedly falsely accused" (Walker, 1994, p. 85). She then insinuated that "adult memory researchers" like me are overly gullible in accepting stories of accusations of abuse that are presented by "poorly trained therapists or, for whatever reason, by female abuse victims" (p. 85). She insinuated that we were part of a profession that chose denial over accuracy, just as Freud "turned away from the truth" (p. 85).

A Bosnian War Crimes Trial

The attacks from a few entrenched professionals continued throughout the decade, even insinuating themselves in unexpected ways. In the mid-1990s I consulted on a number of cases arising out of the Bosnian war crimes trials. The first was a consultation for the prosecution in the trial of Dusan Tadic, a Bosnian Serb and former café owner accused of killing two policemen and torturing Muslim civilians. The accusations involved the rape of a woman and a charge that he forced one prisoner to emasculate another with his teeth. The relevant psychological issue concerned the ability of witnesses to identify people who were not simply strangers, but acquaintances (Loftus, 1997). Tadic became one of the first individuals to be convicted by the Yugoslav War Crimes Tribunal.

My involvement for the prosecution in the Tadic case was not cited in a recent attack on me by another irate professional. Instead, she focused on a later case. Here are the facts. Back in 1993 a Muslim woman (known as Witness A), who lived in a once-peaceful part of Bosnia, was kidnapped and spent months in a house where numerous soldiers raped her over and over. Not surprisingly, this nightmarish incident left her in shock, depressed, and plagued with physical symptoms such as skin rashes and stomach pains (Simons, 1998). The actual rapists had not been captured, but one man, Anto Furundzija, was captured and charged with aiding and abetting one of the rapes. Furundzija was accused of being present at the time Witness A was first interrogated and doing nothing to stop an attack on her. The issue at trial was not whether Witness A had been horribly victimized—no one doubted that she had. The only issue was whether Furundzija was present briefly at the beginning of her ordeal and whether he was aware of the beginning of one of the first assaults.

I testified at Furundzija's trial in The Hague in the summer of 1998 on the subject of eyewitness identification. I agreed to do so after a thorough examination of the specific eyewitness statements and out of a belief that psychological science could shed important light on the eyewitness issues in the case. Diana Russell (2000), author of a well-known book on incest, took exception to my decision to even consult on the case, calling me "one of the major hired guns of the false memory movement" (p. 13). In her article, she stated that I "served as an expert witness for the defense of Anto Furundzija, a member of the Croat armed forces, who was accused by a woman referred to as Witness A, of being her principal interrogator and torturer" (p. 13). She reiterated the horrors that Witness A had endured but misrepresented Furundzija's participation. She went on to claim that I told the court that "those who suffer from post-traumatic stress disorder (PTSD) are more likely to be 'especially vulnerable to post-event suggestions'—i.e., false memories" (p. 13) and that I "cited no research to support this conjecture" (p. 13). When referring to my service in this case, Russell wrote, "yet she is willing to contribute her expertise to create doubt about the validity of the memories of a known torture/rape victim in an infamous genocidal and femicidal war" (p. 13).

What's the real story? Witness A's nightmare began in May of 1993. She endured horrific abuse, and sometime after she was interviewed she reported that a particular individual had been present on the first day. At first (2 years later), she described him as 172 cm, with blond hair and small features. At trial (3 years after that day in May 1993), she described him as 180 cm with chestnut to black hair, a description that resembled the defendant. In between providing the two descriptions, Witness A had seen a photograph of the accused showing clearly his dark hair. I testified about the phenomenon of postevent information, that postevent information can contaminate one's recollection, and that the impact of postevent information can be even greater when the memory has faded significantly. I pointed out that viewing a photograph of someone after an event is the kind of postevent information that can be absorbed by a witness and can cause a distortion "in the memory of a witness who is otherwise trying to be as honest as she can be" (*Furundzija case*, 1998, p. 614).

As for my alleged testimony about people who experience PTSD being especially vulnerable to false memories, here is exactly what I said:

> When someone has experienced a horribly traumatic event, there are sometimes, many times, very serious consequences from that experience. And post-traumatic stress disorder is usually diagnosed when certain symptoms are present, such as depression, anxiety, suicidal ideation or thoughts about suicide, nightmares, and so on. (p. 614)

I was then asked, "Do you have an opinion. . . as to the relationship between post-traumatic stress disorder and post-event information?" (p. 614). After acknowledging the clear evidence for Witness A having a strong reaction to a very horrible set of circumstances and clear evidence of symptoms of PTSD, I answered,

> Now, there has been no explicit study of comparing a PTSD patient's susceptibility to post-event information to a person without PTSD. But based on other considerations, based on the fact that we know that when people are not processing information particularly well, are not able to notice discrepancies between what is being suggested to them and what is part of their memory, and to defend against these discrepancies, under those conditions, people are more susceptible to suggestive influences or to post-event information. In my opinion, this would be a situation where someone would be vulnerable to post-event suggestions and, perhaps, especially vulnerable. (p. 615)

There was other "indirect evidence" to support the possibility that people with PTSD might be more susceptible to suggestion than those without it. Although not explicitly mentioned in my court testimony, I am referring to evidence from the dissociation literature that shows a connection between dissociation and the production of false memories (e.g., Winograd, Peluso, & Glover, 1998).

Numerous publications now report research that shows that people who experience PTSD are more vulnerable to false memories. One study, for example, compared traumatized individuals with PTSD with traumatized individuals without PTSD and with nontraumatized control individuals. Those with PTSD generated more false recalls of nonpresented information than did the other groups (Zoellner, Foa, Brigidi, & Przeworski, 2000). Another study showed that abused women with PTSD had a higher frequency of false-recognition memory than did abused women without PTSD, nonabused women without PTSD, or nonabused men without PTSD (Bremner, Shobe, & Kihlstrom, 2000). Thus, if testifying today on the same issue, I would modify the caveat that I was careful to include ("there has been no explicit study . . . but based on other considerations . . .").

I would have enjoyed Russell's (2000) essay if she had not misrepresented me. Much of the rest of her piece is an astounding recognition that the battle fought by many of us over the past decade has not been in vain. This heroine of the child abuse community, who once revealed that 16% of randomly interviewed women in her study reported being sexually abused by a relative before age 18 and brought attention to the very real problem of incest, was now acknowledging that both sides of the "Great Incest War" have some validity. She couldn't have been clearer when she wrote, "retrieved memories cannot be assumed to be authentic" (p. 5). But her otherwise thoughtful essay was diluted by misunderstanding comments from an expert witness about a case that was not about incest.

Costs, Benefits, Advice

The costs of being a soldier in the repressed-memory war have been great: nasty letters, calls, and e-mails, defamatory utterances that sometimes cannot be ignored, complaints to address, and even one instance of being swatted with a newspaper by a woman on an airplane when she learned my identity. Sometimes I wish my skin were thicker. I stumbled into this controversy rather than deliberately choosing it, and I am often asked whether I would do anything differently if I'd known about this side of it. My first response is, probably not. So if the costs have been great, I say to myself, there must be some rather large benefits. What are those benefits? New research paradigms were developed, new findings in the area of memory were discovered, all of which greatly enhanced our understanding of memory and its enormous malleability. Not only were many behavioral studies conducted that were inspired by the controversy over false memories, but also interest was increased in the neural events that underlie remembering things that never happened (e.g., Gonsalves & Paller, 2000). I got the big benefit of joy that comes when one can join in the contribution to scientific advancement.

Many innocent people were freed from prison, and fewer new questionable cases were being brought to trial. Women who had been badly damaged by their false beliefs brought successful lawsuits for compensation, such as occurred in the case of Joan Hess of Wisconsin, who received a jury award of $850,000 from her former psychiatrist who helped her create memories of molestation by her father and gave her multiple personalities in the process (AP Wire, 1999). Prestigious organizations stepped forward as well; the American Psychiatric Association (2000), for example, published a revised Fact Sheet titled "Therapies Focused on Memories of Childhood Physical and Sexual Abuse" in which they warned about the problem of false memories. To educate members to the fact that "memories can also be altered as a result of suggestions particularly by a trusted person or authority figure" was a huge step in the right direction.

The world began to see the repressed-memory folklore for what it was worth. The media began using the term *myth*, as occurred in an obituary for Peggy McMartin Buckey (Talbot, 2001). Buckey was a middle-aged woman who worked in a day care center run by her family. She was indicted, along with her son Ray and others, and served 2 years in prison before she was freed. The *New York Times* obituary suggested that she was one of the many victims of the satanic abuse scare that gripped the United States, describing it as "the myth that Devil-worshippers had set up shop in our day-care centers, where their clever adepts were raping and sodomizing children, practicing ritual sacrifice, shedding their clothes, drinking blood and eating feces, all unnoticed by parents, neighbors and the authorities" (p. 51). The change in public attitude also became evident in "cartoons" and commentary such as one *New York Times Magazine* item subtitled "Things that are puzzling." Number 5 was on point: "Can those 'recovered memory' psychiatrists get you to remember high school French, or is it just sexual abuse?" (Viladas, 1999, p. 55). Even Ann Landers now understood. She published a letter from a Canadian man named "Floyd," who wrote, "Norma's odd behavior and hostile accusations sound a lot like those false recovered memories that were so popular a few years ago. This now-discredited type of therapy was based on the flaky theory that all adult problems are the result of some childhood trauma, the memories of which have been repressed. . . ." Landers (2000) pulled no punches when she responded, "I go along with every word you have written. Thanks for another opportunity to unmask those charlatans who destroy families" (p. C9).

Aside from a benefit to society, I also derived some personal benefits, primarily stemming from an enhanced sense of purpose in life, corny as that might sound. A few years ago, when the attacks had mounted, I created a "When Blue" file on my computer where I could store electronic communications. Then, and now, I access the file periodically when the skin needs thickening. One of my recent favorites is from the sister of a falsely accused man who is now in prison in Texas. She wrote to me in November 2000:

> I just wanted to take the time to tell you how much I appreciate all you are doing to help . . . I am grateful and appreciative for your wisdom and education and research in your field of expertise. But most of all your kindness in sharing with us and others who need you as desperately as we do. My Mother and I often discussed your kindness and wondered how you had the time to help. I just wanted you to know how much our Mother appreciated all you are doing for her son. She died claiming his innocents (sic) and his name was her last word. I hope no other Mother has to suffer as she did. May God bless you and keep you safe.

When the enemies are acting particularly nasty, a "When Blue" file is handy, indeed.

I never planned to immerse myself in this or any controversy. Especially when it came to the repressed-memory controversy, I made no deliberate decision to embark on such a controversial path. When I found myself in it, I tried to take steps to be something of a peacemaker. I wrote what I felt were highly balanced pieces (e.g., my first large essay on the topic in the *American Psychologist*; Loftus, 1993). But peaceful it was not to be. The attacks began right away and continued for years. Surely this hasn't been easy, and it certainly is not the path for everyone.

On his deathbed, Cecil Rhodes, who a century ago built railroads, created empires, and became a leading ruler of his day, was said to have muttered, "So little done, so much to do" (cited in Tierney, 2000, p. 18). Whatever he meant, the little quotation raises the question of what it is a person wants to be sure to do before he or she dies. The story of Rhodes begins a lovely essay in *Forbes* magazine entitled "Ten Things to Do Before You Die." One of them caught my eye: "Make an enemy for life." Part of the entry reads, "Stand up to a bully, speak out against fraud. . . . Care enough about something to make someone mad. An enemy helps you define yourself." Then there is a quote from Schopenhauer: "We can come to look upon the deaths of our enemies with as much regret as we feel for those of our friends, namely when we miss their existence as witnesses to our success" (cited in Tierney, 2000, p. 84).

Okay, so maybe I'm not there yet. I'll miss my friends far, far more than my enemies. But I have come to appreciate that it might be a real gift to care about something so much that you are willing to make someone very mad.

References

American Psychiatric Association. (2000, June). *Therapies focused on memories of childhood sexual abuse* [Fact sheet]. (Available from American Psychiatric Association, 1400 K Street, NW, Washington, DC 20005)

AP Wire. (1999, September 2). Jury reaches verdict in negligence trial focusing on memories. *Milwaukee Journal–Sentinal.*

Bremner, J. D., Shobe, K. K., & Kihlstrom, J. F. (2000). False memories in women with self-reported childhood sexual abuse: An empirical study. *Psychological Science, 11,* 333–336.

Celente, G. (1997). *Trends 2000.* New York: Warner Books.

Furundzija case: Hearing before the International Tribunal for the Former Yugoslavia (Case No. IT-95-17/1; 1998) (testimony of Elizabeth Loftus).

Garry, M., Manning, C., Loftus, E. F., & Sherman, S. J. (1996). Imagination inflation. *Psychonomic Bulletin & Review, 3,* 208–214.

Gonsalves, B., & Paller, K. A. (2000). Neural events that underlie remembering something that never happened. *Nature Neuroscience, 3,* 1316–1321.

Heaps, C., & Nash, M. (1999). Individual differences in imagination inflation. *Psychonomic Bulletin and Review, 6,* 313–318.

Herman, J. L., & Harvey, M. R. (1993, April). The false memory debate: Social science or social backlash? *Harvard Mental Health Letter,* pp. 4–6.

Hyman, I. E., Husband, T. H., & Billings, J. F. (1995). False memories of childhood experiences. *Applied Cognitive Psychology, 90,* 181–197.

Johnson, M. (1997). *Spectral evidence.* Boston: Houghton-Mifflin.

Kelley, C., Amodio, D., & Lindsay, D. S. (1996, July). *The effects of "diagnosis" and memory work on memories of handedness shaping.* Paper presented at the International Conference on Memory, Padua, Italy.

Landers, A. (2000, October 2). Also-"crushed" readers offer their own advice. *Washington Post,* p. C9.

Lindsay, D. S., & Read, J. D. (1994). Psychotherapy and memories of childhood sexual abuse: A cognitive perspective. *Applied Cognitive Psychology, 8,* 281–338.

Loftus, E. F. (1980). *Memory.* Reading, MA: Addison-Wesley.

Loftus, E. F. (1993). The reality of repressed memories. *American Psychologist, 48,* 518–537.

Loftus, E. F. (1997). Dispatch from the (un)civil memory wars. In J. D. Read & D. S. Lindsay (Eds.), *Recollections of trauma: Scientific research and clinical practice* (pp. 171–198). New York: Plenum Press.

Loftus, E. F., & Ketcham, K. (1991). *Witness for the defense.* New York: St. Martin's Press.

Loftus, E. F., & Ketcham, K. (1994). *The myth of repressed memory*. New York: St. Martin's Press.

Loftus, E. F., & Pickrell, J. (1995). The formation of false memories. *Psychiatric Annals, 25,* 720–725.

Mazzoni, G. A. L., & Loftus, E. F. (1998). Dreaming, believing and remembering. In J. DeRivera & T. R. Sarbin (Eds.), *Believed in imaginings: The narrative construction of reality* (pp. 145–156). Washington, DC: American Psychological Association.

Mazzoni, G. A. L., Loftus, E. F., & Kirsch, I. (2001). Changing beliefs about implausible autobiographical events: A little plausibility goes a long way. *Journal of Experimental Psychology: Applied, 7,* 51–59.

Merkin, D. (2000, October). Betrayal by memoire. *Brill's Content,* pp. 78–80.

Porter, S., Yuille, J. C., & Lehman, D. R. (1999). The nature of real, implanted, and fabricated memories for emotional childhood events. *Law and Human Behavior, 23,* 517–538.

Russell, D. E. H. (2000, Spring). The great incest war: Moving beyond polarization. *Coalition Commentary: A Publication of the Illinois Coalition Against Sexual Assault,* pp. 1–14.

Simons, M. (1998, July 29). Landmark Bosnia rape trial. *New York Times,* p. A3.

Talbot, M. (2001, January 7). The devil in the nursery. *New York Times Magazine,* pp. 51–52.

Tierney, J. (2000, September 18). Ten things to do before you die. *Forbes,* pp. 83–84.

Viladas, P. (1999, February 21). Grand illusions. *New York Times Magazine,* p. 55.

Walker, L. E. A. (1994). *Abused women and survivor therapy*. Washington, DC: American Psychological Association.

Winograd, E., Peluso, J. P., & Glover, T. A. (1998). Individual differences in suggestibility to memory illusions. *Applied Cognitive Psychology, 12,* S5–S27.

Zoellner, L. A., Foa, E. B., Brigidi, B. D., & Przeworski, A. (2000). Are trauma victims susceptible to "false memories?" *Journal of Abnormal Psychology, 109,* 517–524.

When William McGuire, the "father of the social cognition revolution," is asked why he tends to study neglected topics, he often argues that more researchers should study topics because of, not in spite of, their being neglected. He studies underrepresented topics not to play the rebel but to avoid the overcongregation of researchers at current fads. Among underrepresented topics rescued from neglect by McGuire are immunization-against-persuasion research and a theory of the content, structure, and functioning of thought systems, describing work of his that eventually helped end the long domination of experimental psychology by stimulus–response behaviorism.

William J. McGuire

Doing Psychology My Way | 8

O ften when I give a colloquium talk describing some line of my research, a member of the audience asks a disturbed and disturbing question that I seldom hear put to other colloquium speakers. My questioner usually struggles to put his or her inquiry, the very asking of which sounds hostile, in as gracious a form as possible. "I enjoyed your talk," this member will say, "and I found your work quite interesting. I mention my pleasure at the outset so you will appreciate the spirit in which I am asking my question."

"Je vous ai compris," I encourage the speaker, repeating General Charles de Gaulle's enigmatic 1958 reassurance to the revolting *pied noirs* of Algeria.

"My question is," the critic continues, "Why are you doing this research?"

I counter this annoying question with the annoying tactic of answering the question with a question. "Why," I ask, "Do you raise this question?"

The inquirer typically responds with a popularity explanation, "Well, . . . I wonder because no one else seems to study the topic."

"Just so," I shoot back. "Your answer to my question also answers yours."

(Over)Congregation at Optimal Points: Popularity and Payoff

I do not advocate taking a knee-jerk contrarian stance, studying only topics that everyone else is neglecting and standing on its head, as Karl

Marx did G. W. F. Hegel, every explanation that anyone else suggests. Indeed, I admit that a topic's popularity is a presumptive sign of its high promise for payoff and that low research attention often indicates a well-deserved neglect. What I am urging is correction of a tendency of researchers to overcongregate at optimal points.

Such overconcentration tendencies are exhibited over a wide range of phenomena, from the biological to the cognitive. As a biological illustration, consider pouring a dense colony of paramecia into a beaker of distilled water and then letting a nutrient solution drip into one localized spot in the beaker. The paramecia's distribution in the beaker tends to match the variation in nutrient richness, most of these protozoa congregating in the food-rich area right under the nutrient drip, but with a quantitative peculiarity: The paramecia crowd into the richer areas even more than the nutrient gradient would justify. The protozoa that do best are the peripheral feeders who forage at the less rich areas that most members of the colony neglect even more than its lower nutritional richness warrants.

Conceptual domains also exhibit overconcentration at optimal points. The popularity of hypotheses and explanations tends to reflect their intellectual promise less powerfully than would justify their overwhelmingly greater popularity. Researchers contribute more when they study the slightly less rich but disproportionately neglected unpopular topics rather than joining the crowd studying the current fad.

Multiplicity of Less-Traveled Roads

Excessive crowding of researchers on overpopular issues can be observed in many aspects of scientists' work including the topics chosen for study, the types of dependent–independent variable relations predicted, the kinds of explanatory theories used to account for these hypothesized relations, and the metatheories used to orient oneself to one's subject matter. Overcongregation occurs also in that a historical cohort tends to restrict itself too narrowly to current establishment methods, to orthodox styles and to the criteria used to judge validity. Below I give examples of needed establishment-disturbing diversity in these various aspects of research, drawing mostly on my own work because this volume is intended to emphasize personal testimonies.

Anti-establishment deviationism probably has a general-trait component such that a researcher who is unorthodox in one regard is likely to be unorthodox in others as well. However, there are probably also a number of specific deviation factors in that some researchers who take a stand against the establishment in one aspect of their research may well be upholders of orthodoxy in other aspects (e.g., some researchers may select popular topics but investigate them by unusual methods). My own research corpus shows this mixed pattern. Overall I may be more of a maverick than average, but I have been unconventional in some regards more than others. My choice of topics for study tends to be quite unorthodox, but the research styles I use to study them have been more conventional, except perhaps in making more than average use of multiple methods in studying any one topic. I have been decidedly unorthodox in my metatheorizing, in reconciling the contending forces in psychology's perennial antinomies, and in using multiple criteria in appraising hypotheses and theories.

How have my colleagues responded to my heterodoxies? In general they have been admirably permissive, encouraging and even rewarding me for taking roads less traveled. On the other hand, few colleagues have tendered me the sincerest form of flattery, imitation, leaving me a well-regarded but lonely traveler. Some of my anti-establishment deviations are specified below. As usual, the devil and the divine are in the details.

Orthodox and Heterodox Research Styles: Linear (Divergent vs. Convergent) and System Styles

A scientist's "style" of doing research is an underappreciated distinctive aspect of how science is done (McGuire, 1983). By researcher's *style* I refer to the pattern of choices that the investigator makes at the successive steps of carrying out a research project, extending at least from topic selection to application of the findings. At each step the researcher has many alternatives among which to choose, although choices made at earlier steps tend to reduce the alternatives available at later steps. With a dozen choices available at each of 10 to 15 successive research steps there are an astronomical number of potential research-style paths that could be adopted, but actually at any given period in a discipline's history few styles are in active use, perhaps including one dominant style, a mainstream alternative style, and two or three tolerated aberrant styles. Because a style affects research so pervasively and because at any era most potential styles are neglected, style innovations offer rich opportunities for creative departures from the establishment way of doing research.

DIVERGENT, THEORY-FOCUSED
LINEAR STYLES

In the past half-century, two linear styles, divergent and convergent, have dominated psychological research, the divergent being slightly in the ascendance. More recently a third, deviant "systems" style has been gaining popularity. Divergent versus convergent styles differ most basically in where the investigator enters his or her research program. Divergentists are independent-variable oriented, drawn to a topic by a theory that provides explanations. Convergentists are dependent-variable oriented, drawn to a topic by the relations to be explained. A given topic (e.g., how self-esteem is related to persuadability) may be approached either divergently or convergently. The divergent, theory-oriented stylist approaches the topic from an independent-variable perspective (e.g., the divergentist may be a self-esteem theorist predicting a wide range of self-esteem effects, one of which is susceptibility to persuasion). The divergentist uses self-esteem programmatically as an independent variable to account for a little of the variance in each of a wide variety of dependent variables.

CONVERGENT, RELATION-FOCUSED
LINEAR STYLES

A convergentist might arrive at a similar self-esteem/persuadability hypothesis from the other direction, while trying to account for the dependent-variable persuadability variance in terms of a wide spectrum of independent personality variables (one of which is self-esteem). The two styles contrast in many regards (McGuire, 1983). The divergentist tends to use powerfully manipulated independent variables but poorly scaled (often only dichotomously) dependent variables, whereas convergentists tend to use weak independent-variable manipulations but elegant dependent-variable scaling. To the basic independent–dependent variable main-effect research design, the divergentist tends to add mediational variables, whereas the convergentist adds interactional variables. As regards inferential statistics, the divergentist tends to use analyses freer of parametric assumptions, whereas the convergentist tends to use more sensitive analyses. The divergent theorist looks more for theory relevance and the convergent for practical relevance. Other contrasts between these two linear styles are described in McGuire (1983).

Neither style is inherently superior. Depending on the researcher's proclivities and the nature of the topics studied, one or the other style might be better in a specific situation, but the two are supplementary rather than opposed. However, belligerent adherents of one style may disparage the other: Theory-oriented divergent stylists (Clark Hull, Leon Festinger) may regard the convergent stylist as a plodding dust-bowl empiricist, whereas convergent stylists (B. F. Skinner, Carl Hovland) may regard the divergent stylist as a superficial, hit-and-run dilettante. I myself have been eclectic in style and so may have annoyed both sides. Divergent stylists may regard my word-order research (McGuire & McGuire, 1992b) as too convergently eclectic in using seven classes of explanatory theories; convergentists may regard my inoculation-against-persuasion work (McGuire, 1964) as too divergent, using a single biological-immunization theoretical analogy for generating hypotheses.

SYSTEMS STYLES

Both divergent and convergent research styles were popular choices in the mid-20th century when I began my doctoral studies in experimental psychology. Were I starting out now in the 21st century I would probably be drawn more to "systems" styles. Divergent and convergent research styles are both "linear" in that their theorizing and their research designs in any study use few variables, each predesignated as an independent, mediational, interactional, or dependent variable, with the causal flow perceived as going unidirectionally, from independent through mediational to dependent variables. In the emerging systems style a study's research design includes many variables, each of which is allowed to covary naturalistically without rigid predesignation as independent or dependent variables, with a time-series of scores on each variable. These longitudinal data are then subjected to causal analyses like LISREL, capable of detecting bidirectional causal links, multiple causal paths between any two variables, and feedback loops.

My Deviating From Establishment Orthodoxies by Choice of Neglected Research Topics

MY RESEARCH ON INOCULATION AGAINST PERSUASION

Although my choice of research styles has been somewhat unorthodox, at least by its eclecticism, my choices of topics for investigation have been much more aberrant. The earliest deviant line of my work to receive recognition was the immunization-against-persuasion research published in the early 1960s (McGuire, 1964). In the preceding 1950s decade, social psychology's liveliest topic had been attitude change, investigating how various classes of communication variables enhance persuasive impact. The military metaphor that bigger guns evoke thicker armor, which evokes still bigger guns, suggests that all this research on inducing attitude change should have evoked considerable compensatory work on inducing resistance to persuasion, but actually this latter immunization topic remained neglected.

My switch in 1960 from producing to preventing attitude change was well received, both as a correction of past neglect and perhaps also because it is more appealing to train people to resist attacks than to make attacking messages more effective. Some of my colleagues may have been attracted also by my use of an easily grasped and powerful inoculation analogy as the theoretical underpinning. The resulting research showed that one's beliefs tend to be overprotected by being insulated in an ideological germ-free environment which, as predicted, leaves them vulnerable when exposed to strong attacks. Pre-exposure to weakened belief-attacking arguments (analogous to vaccination), strong enough to stimulate without overcoming the believer's defenses, conferred more resistance to subsequent strong attacking arguments than did prior bolstering with supportive arguments. As with vaccination there are delayed action build-up effects of this pre-exposure, and there is temporal decay of immunity calling for "booster shots." My immunization reaction to the establishment attitude-change preoccupation received awards and coverage in the mass media but evoked little imitation, with most attitude-change researchers continuing to investigate production rather than prevention of persuasion.

MY RESEARCH ON COGNITIVE SYSTEMS

A line of work that I began even earlier (in my graduate student days), and continued much longer (up to the present, 50 years later), was also off the beaten trail and yet received wide if delayed acceptance, even prompting my being called the father of the social cognition revolution. My theory of the content, structure, and functioning of thought systems takes as its basic postulate that people maintain connectedness and coherence among their thoughts (McGuire & McGuire, 1991b). I postulated that thought systems operate in accord with formal logic, elaborated to include a probabilistic (rather than two-valued) scale for the truth of propositions and to include both logical consistency (e.g., syllogistic reasoning, the principle of sufficient reason) and hedonic consistency (e.g., keeping wishes and expectations congruent, as in rationalization and wishful thinking). The theory makes numerous predictions about (a) interrelations within the person's thought systems at any moment in time; (b) resistance to new information as a function of whether its acceptance would raise or lower internal consistency; (c) persuasion from within, that is, changing attitudes not by providing new information from an outside source but by Socratic questioning or directed-thinking tasks that increase the salience of related attitudes already in the person's belief system; and (d) remote ramifications such that persuasive communications change attitudes, not only on their explicit issues but also on unmentioned related issues.

My thought system theory and my methods for studying it were heterodox when proposed in the mid-20th century and even now seem deviant to some. When I introduced this theorizing at mid-century, experimental psychology was still in its long domination by stimulus–response reinforcement theory (learning theory, behaviorism), whose metatheoretical depiction of thought as epiphenomenal subvocal speech could not handle complex thought processes. My approach deviated also from the opposite mid-century philosophical orthodoxies (e.g., symbolic logic, British word quibbling) that also focused on phenomenal systems but only in their logical or intellectual aspects, whereas my "probabilogical" theorizing gave as big a role to affective as to cognitive processes (McGuire & McGuire, 1991b).

MY FOCUS ON THE ORGANIZED PHENOMENOLOGICAL

How is my early switch from the establishment's simple stimulus–response behaviorism to this unorthodox complex phenomenology to be accounted for on personal and Zeitgeist considerations? Furthermore, why was this aberrant work received so well that it became a major impetus to the 1960s cognitive consistency movement (McGuire, 1966) and to the subsequent social cognition movement (McGuire, 1986b)? My master's thesis and doctoral dissertation were both behavioristic, so why was I contemporaneously pursuing the phenomenological thought systems research that should have been stunningly objectionable on several grounds to behaviorists like my establishment instructors and myself? My aberrant wrestling with phenomenological complexity may derive from my having entered psychology from an intellectual tradition much underrepresented in the great secular research universities that set the research agenda. I attended and taught at a Catholic Jesuit college (Fordham University) whose curriculum was shaped by Aristotelian–Thomistic theorizing within which my phenomenological work seemed quite appropriate for a psychologist.

In addition to my being pulled toward complex phenomenological systems, there may also have been some push away from the stimulus–response (S-R) habits of establishment behaviorism. By mid-century

S-R behaviorism had had a long run of a couple of decades, so it was time for a change. That the change took the form of a 180-degree reaction follows the pattern of a true-believer conversion (Weiss, 1963). Also, some intrinsic shortcomings of behaviorism imposed limits on its run as the dominant ideology: Behaviorism could be elegant (in its Hullian form) or provocative (in its Skinnerian mode), but its meta-theoretical depictions of thought as subvocal speech or movements of the vocalization organs were deficient in evoking new hypotheses or explanations.

On the other hand, approaches like behaviorism should not now be condemned for their commonsensicality, lest our call for more exciting un-commonsensicality be mistaken as a call for common-nonsensicality. There were giants in those days, and in considering the yin-and-yang progress of science their day may dawn again. At the heart of S-R habit behaviorism was simplistic physiologizing suggested by Sherrington's (1906) reflex arc, but such austere theorizing is appealing in its parsimony and provides a fertile analogy. My switch to phenomenological cognitive systems may have been a corrective whose time had come in 1950, but the 21st century may be the time for a return to an alternative austere physiologizing of psychology, which will generate hypotheses from neuroscientists' computer analogies and test them with evidence from positron-emission tomography and functional magnetic resonance imaging (fMRI) scans.

MY STUDIES OF THE PHENOMENAL SELF

The self has been heavily investigated, as befits the topic that a century ago the founding father William James (1890, chap. 8) considered to be psychology's central concept. Unfortunately, the yield of this self research has been distinguished more by its quantity than its quality. The disappointing yield of so much research on so fascinating a topic by so many talented psychologists I attribute to the narrowness and superficiality of the approaches traditionally taken. My own research (McGuire & McGuire, 1988) moves the topic out of its well-worn ruts by asking novel, more interesting questions and using new, more powerful methods to answer them.

Prior to my research program (e.g., McGuire & Padawer-Singer, 1976), at least 90% of self research was focused on the reactive self and only a negligible amount on the spontaneous phenomenal self. In the conventional reactive-self approach the researcher chooses a dimension on which selves are perceived to differ and asks the participants whose self-concepts are being studied to report where they fall on this researcher-chosen dimension. This provides information on only a hypothetical "as-if" self, on where the person would perceive the self on this dimension if he or she ever thought about it. It provides little salience information on the as-is self, that is, how prominently the dimension looms in the person's actual sense of self. The yield of the conventional reactive approach is further limited by a second narrowness: More than 90% of reactive self researchers present the same dimension, self-evaluation, as the one on which the participant is asked to describe the self. It is as if people's self-concepts vary only on self-esteem, on how good or bad they perceive themselves to be. Evaluation is indeed an important dimension of the self as experienced, but I find that only 5 or 10% of spontaneous self-descriptors are explicitly evaluative.

My spontaneous self-concept approach departs radically from this conventional approach. Departing from psychologists' obsession with reactive measures and with the evaluative dimension, I use open-ended probes (e.g., "Tell me about yourself," "Tell me about your family") and then extract self-descriptions from the free associations so evoked. By allowing people to describe themselves in their own terms and in various contexts, I obtain salience information that indicates not only where people would see themselves on the researcher's dimension if they ever thought about it but also on which dimensions people characteristically do perceive themselves.

By providing information on the neglected salience dependent variable, my open-ended approach allows me to answer new questions about the content of the spontaneous sense of self. For example, my distinctiveness theory postulates that people think of themselves in terms of and to the extent of their being peculiar, becoming aware of personal characteristics by their absence (as in the maxim that the fish will be the last to discover the ocean). People are conscious of their physical characteristics to the extent that they are odd (e.g., atypically thin and atypically fat people are more likely than average-weight people to mention their weight in describing spontaneous self-concepts). As regards ethnicity, members of minority groups spontaneously describe themselves in terms of their ethnicity more often than do members of the majority group, and minority-group ethnicity declines in salience as the minority group becomes larger. As regards gender, children are more likely to describe themselves in terms of their gender as the other gender becomes more predominant in their households. For example, boys are more conscious of their being males when their fathers are absent from the home than when fathers are present, and children in general become more conscious of their gender as the other gender predominates among their siblings.

My investigations of differences between the affirmational self ("Tell me what you are") and the negational self ("Tell me what you are not") show, for example, that people are twice as likely to mention their ethnicity and three times as likely to mention their gender in their negational than affirmational selves. That is, people are much more likely to think of the other ethnicities and the other gender as something they are not than of their own ethnicity and gender as something that they are (McGuire & McGuire, 1991a, 1992a).

Another line of my open-ended self research derives from the postulate that in language meaning is carried especially by verbs. It uses a tree-diagram classification of the verbs that appear in free self-descriptions to show a variety of basic ways in which the child's school self differs from his or her home self, how concepts of self differ from concepts of other people, and how the spontaneous self-concept changes during childhood and adolescence (McGuire & McGuire, 1988).

MY RESEARCH ON WORD-ORDER REGULARITIES

Whereas my cognitive-systems research received considerable recognition and even some imitation, my research on pervasive word-order regularities in natural speech has evoked little praise and no emulation from establishment colleagues (McGuire & McGuire, 1992b). Almost all native English speakers say commonly paired words in the same order, for example, in noun pairs like *apples and oranges, ham and eggs, aunt and uncle, knife and fork,* and *shoes and socks* and in adjective series like *dirty old man* and *old oaken bucket,* even though the preferred orders seem to serve no obvious purpose nor can they be accounted for by a few general rules such as Panini's law (that one says the easier—e.g., shorter—word first).

I have explained word-order regularities by five diverse types of theories that are easy to investigate and yield rich nonobvious interaction predictions. Two of these five types of explanations are phonological (encoding ease of articulation and decoding accuracy of recognition) and three are semantic (cognitive salience, affective involvement, and social status). I have investigated these explanations in diverse domains in which word-order regularities are ubiquitous (e.g., kin pairs, food lists, sets of common objects, series of adjectives) and by a variety of methods (e.g., natural speech, reactive ratings, concordances to the historical literary canon). A general explanation may emerge in terms of language acquisition (e.g., that toddlers learn multiword expressions before the component words), with the delight being in the details.

My investigation of word-order regularities remains a lonely undertaking. The vigor of my own investigations may have frightened some off. My diversity of explanations may have turned off some divergent-style researchers who prefer a single theory. Perhaps the timing is wrong so that this topic has not yet grabbed the attention of the critical mass of investigators that are needed to sustain steady growth. Conceivably this word-order topic seems facetious in lacking theoretical or applied relevance. Some other research topics admittedly do cry louder to heaven for investigation (e.g., the nature of the chemical bond, the origin of the universe, the periodic table of the elements, mapping the genome), but advances have come also from noticing and accounting for trivial regularities or aberrant fluctuations, such as the legendary "Eureka!" of Archimedes, the falling apple of Isaac Newton, or perhaps these frozen word orders. Cute word-order regularities may seem trivial or slight like the precession of Mercury, but once understood they may become a powerful tool for understanding more important relations.

REBALANCING ANTINOMIES AS A TOOL FOR DRIVING THE EVOLUTION OF PSYCHOLOGY

Dialectical oppositions characterize both the world as we find it and our conceptualizations of this world. Both involve dynamic interpenetrations of opposites whose contradictions must be kept in a balance that retains much of the driving impetus of each component. The thesis and antithesis in each antinomous pair (e.g., basic vs. applied research, inductive vs. deductive inferences, creative vs. critical thinking) are not mutually exclusive in the sense that the researcher must accept one and reject the other. Rather, they are mutually supplementary and call for a balanced choice that incorporates aspects of each that correct and complement deficiencies in the other. Each operates more effectively in coordination with the other. The establishment's balance of major pairs of such antinomic forces shapes psychology in any era by defining its limits, its directions, and its potential to construct a higher synthesis on the basis of each thesis and antithesis. In every era some attention must be paid to each of the antinomously paired forces, but from era to era the preferred balance shifts and within any era there are considerable individual differences among psychological researchers as to where the balance is struck between the attractive thesis–antithesis alternatives. In general, vive la différence: Although these antagonisms make for heated contention, they also fire progress.

Thesis–antithesis antinomies characterize the choice both of topics and of methods (McGuire, 2000). Here I mention five of psychology's perennial methodological antinomies. Heterodoxies of individual psychologists, including my own, often involve shifting the balances within antinomous pairs away from the given era's establishment positioning. Psychology, like other sciences, tends to advance in a zigzag course, like a ship tacking before the wind, its direction and progress often directed by successive rebalancings of the contending forces in these various antinomous pairs.

Preoccupation With Research Strategy vs. Research Tactics

One methodological antinomy pits tactics against strategy. Tactical issues are those that arise in designing individual experiments, whereas strategic issues are those that arise in planning systematic multi-experiment programs of research. Today's establishment methodology as expounded in textbooks, courses, and journals focuses almost entirely on within-experiment tactics (e.g., manipulating, measuring, and controlling variables; calculating the size and significance of relations between these variables; selecting and testing participants). Almost completely neglected are programmatic, across-experiments strategic issues (e.g., selecting problems, deciding where to begin one's investigations, dividing the research program into manageable individual experiments, setting priorities for ordering experiments).

I have been a methodological maverick on this antinomy in that I have dealt (McGuire, 1983, 1999) more with strategy than tactics. I have described (McGuire, 1989) strategies for developing a program of research on three levels: (a) on the initial hypothesis's own level of abstraction (e.g., clarifying the rich meaning of the variables, expressing relations between these variables in multiple modalities, specifying the limits of these relations); (b) on a more abstract level (e.g., generating multiple explanations of these hypothetical relations and of the contrary relations and analyzing the mediational variable implied by each theory and adding that variable to the experimental design); and (c) on a more concrete level (e.g., exploring the logical structure of each theoretical explanation and deriving hypotheses from each premise of each explanation for testing dispositional and situational interactions).

Preoccupation With Creative Hypothesis Generation vs. Critical Hypothesis Testing

Another antinomy seriously imbalanced in current psychological methodology is that our textbooks, courses, and journals on method overfocus on critical hypothesis testing to the almost complete neglect of creative hypothesis generating. Most researchers recognize that hypothesis creation is at least as important as hypothesis testing; the neglect may derive from despair of its teachability or even its describability. Therefore I have long been describing (McGuire, 1973, 1997) dozens of diverse creative heuristics that can be taught to and used by researchers to generate nonobvious hypotheses, theories, and methods. These creative heuristics range from simply enhancing one's sensitivity to provocative natural occurrences to sophisticated modes of reanalyzing old data or collecting new.

Preoccupation With Using Empirical Confrontation for Discovery vs. for Evaluation

Humanistic scholars settle for formulating and illustrating their propositions; the social and behavioral scientists go further in subjecting their propositions to some kind of validation or clarification through an empirical confrontation that puts the proposition at risk of disconfirmation or explores its need for revision. A major imbalance in current psychology is that the potential of the confrontation is largely lost as a result of the establishment's treating the confrontation as if it serves only to falsify or confirm a rigid, a priori hypothesis.

I have urged (McGuire, 1989, 1999) that the higher mission of the empirical confrontation is to serve as a discovery process that reveals the fuller meaning of the hypothesis, that is, the pattern of circumstances (often expressed in interaction hypotheses) in which the hypothesis does (or does not) hold in various degrees and for a variety of theoretical reasons. Our "perspectivism" (earlier, "contextualism") epistemology (McGuire, 1989) provocatively argues that testing the truth of propositions is supererogatory because (as epitomized by William Blake) everything possible to be believed is an image of truth. All hypotheses and their contraries are true (as all are false) at least occasionally, depending on ascertainable circumstances. Empirical testing being a defining distinctive feature of the scientific process, researchers naturally exaggerate its importance. My perspectivist psychology of science shows how to develop and use the empirical confrontation for its higher purpose of discovering new understanding and not simply for its modest purpose of testing whether a rigid a priori hypothesis is valid in some special set of circumstances.

Preoccupation With Open-Ended vs. Reactive Measures

Most social psychological researchers measure where a person is located on some psychological variable such as sources of anxiety by presenting the person with a list of dangers and asking the person to react by indicating how much he or she worries about each of these dangers. This provides as-if information on how fearful the respondent would be of a given danger if he or she ever thought of it, but does not provide information on salience, on how often the respondent actually does worry about the danger. The neglected alternative open-ended measures involve presenting participants with low-restrictive probes like "What are some of the dangers you worry about these days?" which provide relative salience information on how often the respondent does spontaneously worry about various dangers.

Open-ended measures serve also as discovery procedures, particularly in the early stages of research on a topic. Allowing the participants to express their thoughts and feelings in their own terms is often revealing. For example, in measuring the public's anxieties, use of open-ended probes (e.g., "What worries you about life today?") often reveals a hierarchy of worries quite different from a reactive measure that presents a long list of dangers and asks the respondents to indicate how often they worry about each danger. Open-ended and reactive measures each have their advantages, but too few of us exploit the open-ended.

Preoccupation With a Diversity of Validating Criteria

Establishment scientific researchers are likely to declare that "survival of disconfirmation when put in empirical jeopardy" is hypotheses' main validity criterion. In actuality a wide range of additional criteria, intrinsic and extrinsic to the knowledge itself, are and ought to be used if our canon of scientific knowledge is to go beyond the obvious. Often both of a pair of mutually contradictory criteria are desiderata of scientific knowledge, revealing further antinomies that characterize science and keep it vital. Elsewhere (McGuire, 1986a, 1999) I have described many intrinsic and extrinsic criteria of scientific validity.

Numerous antinomous pairs of intrinsic criteria can be mentioned as illustrations. Scientific propositions should be (a) novel but also (b) banal (in not being outside the current respectable explanatory range as would be, say, a parapsychological explanation). Scientific hypotheses should be (c) stable across conditions but also (d) sensitive to context; they should be (e) parsimonious, and yet (f) a rococo extravagance can be provocative as when the cabala, psychoanalysis, or Marxism is attractive because of, rather than in spite of, its complexity. (g) Common sense, in the form of a priori plausibility, is attractive but so also is (h) counterintuitiveness. In the case of such pairs of antinomous intrinsic desiderata, establishment orthodoxy often overuses one to the neglect of the other.

Many extrinsic desiderata for evaluating scientific knowledge also deserve use, although some are frowned on by the purist. Among extrinsic desiderata besides the popular one of (a) survival of empirical jeopardy are (b) the hypothesis' creative provocativeness; (c) the past track records of its originator or proponents; (d) the subjective feeling of correctness it evokes; (e) its practical utility; and (f) its supportiveness of the status quo or, for contrarians, (g) its divergence from establishment orthodoxy, as discussed further in McGuire (1999).

Personal and Social Origins of Innovations in Psychology

I have argued that a moderate degree of unorthodoxy is good for the progress of psychology as a body of knowledge. Here I mention some personal and societal factors that promote innovations in the discipline. Evolutionary metatheorizing suggests that some anti-establishment deviationism may be useful for the improvement of the science, analogous to mutations being good for the species by diversifying the gene pool and facilitating selective improvement.

PERSONAL FACTORS PROMOTING OPTIMAL LEVELS OF INNOVATION

Psychologists have accorded generous recognition to my work and its unorthodox innovativeness, even overlooking its possible links to my Catholic ethnic background which, when I entered the field, was vastly underrepresented. However, although colleagues forgave (and even encouraged) my deviationism, they have been slow to incorporate my innovations into their own work. Perhaps this is as it should be. A field's evolution requires innovations (like mutations) to enhance diversity and adaptation. Rewards for innovation (especially periodic reinforcement) increase the expression of creativity. Just as the process of mutation is a good thing even though most specific mutations may be aversive, so innovativeness should be encouraged even though most specific innovations should not be generally adopted. The optimal level of innovation is probably modest. A psychology without innovation would be banal, but a psychology in which everyone is continuously innovating would be weak in maintaining sustained progress in any direction. Rampant anti-establishment deviationism is as maladaptive as rigid orthodoxy. The accepted ways tend to be the winners that have emerged from past challenges and so will tend to emerge triumphant in future contests. Psychological deviations might be best left to peripheral players, although gatekeepers (e.g., department chairs, journal editors, grant awarders) should deliberately nurture some deviators.

SOCIOSTRUCTURAL FACTORS PROMOTING INNOVATIONS IN THE DISCIPLINE

Innovation (at least in moderation and subject to demanding scrutiny) being adaptive for psychological progress, it is not surprising that psychology and other sciences are so organized that deviations inevitably arise and are occasionally widely adopted. My bullish stance on the role of innovation in the evolution of sciences derives from my perception that psychology and its subdisciplines advance by successive waves of enthusiasm. My own field, social psychology, has grown from attaining maturity around 1920 to the present time, 2002, in five such successive creative waves, each promoting a faddish hegemony lasting about 20 years and overlapping somewhat with the preceding and subsequent hegemonies (McGuire, 1986b). These five waves of 20th-century social psychology were dominated successively by (a) attitude measurement and relation to behavior, 1920–1940; (b) group dynamics, 1935–1955; (c) persuasive communication, 1950–1970; (d) social cognition, 1965–1985; and (e) organized cognitive systems, 1980–present. Each of the five eras began as a deviation, implicitly or explicitly rejecting some of the predecessor establishment ways of doing social psychology and substituting for the rejected ways new content and methods.

During each successive orthodoxy's two decades of hegemony, deviations gradually emerge until their accumulation weighs down the current hegemonous orthodoxy. Two basic questions arise: (a) What is it that dampens enthusiasm for a prevailing orthodoxy after a couple of decades of hegemony, and (b) what are the factors that shape the new orthodoxy that replaces it, selected out of numerous innovations that contend during a transitional period? I argue (McGuire, 1986b) that the stifling of the old orthodoxy comes from forces intrinsic to the discipline itself, often excesses of the old orthodoxy's own virtues. The shaping of the new orthodoxy I attribute to forces from outside the discipline.

Internal Forces Bringing Down Old Orthodoxies

Each establishment orthodoxy during its 20-year run of dominance is maintained by various virtues, three of which are increasing quantification and rigorous methodology, enhanced conceptual elaboration, and greater practical application. Each of these three is a Good Thing but tends to become a victim of its own successes, increasingly weighing the orthodoxy down with inertial baggage. For example, the first flourishing of social psychology, the attitude-measurement era (1920–1940), involved giant leaps forward in quantification and scaling by statisticians like Lewis Thurstone, Edgar S. Bogardus, and Rensis Likert, advances that were elegant in themselves but burdensome to average researchers and made elites become disdainful of entering into hypothetical relation with the less elegantly scaled variables from other domains.

Also in this first, attitude-measurement, establishment ascendancy there developed an elegant but eye-glazing conceptual analysis and nomenclature (Gordon Allport, Quinn McNemar). Clarification of what one is talking about is desirable, but for psychologists newly entering the field the need to learn the 20-year accumulation of distinctions and definitions imposes a heavy initiation fee. A third virtue of this 1920–1940 attitude-measurement ascendancy is that it tended increasingly to be mined for practical applications. Again this is a Good Thing in that a Mandarin stance of science for science's sake, however claimed by the high-table elite, would lose support from other segments of society, including funding agencies. Nevertheless, as a dominant orthodoxy moves increasingly into the practical arena (as did the 1920–1940 attitude-measurement movement with its studies of conservatism, racial relations, birth control, etc.), elite researchers tend to move to other topics, possibly to avoid political pressures and distractions.

External Forces Shaping New Orthodoxies

Thus the old hegemony's decline, essential if room is to be left for innovations to flourish and diffuse, is due to internal forces, namely, excesses of the old orthodoxy's own virtues like quantitative rigor, conceptual elaboration, and practical application. In contrast, the new orthodoxy is shaped by forces outside the field. As the old orthodoxy becomes more encumbered, innovative psychologists pay increasing attention to developments in other disciplines that can be adapted to psychology. These psychological borrowings from neighboring disciplines can include conceptual insights (e.g., evolutionary theory, brain physiology, the computer analogy), methodological data-collecting tools (e.g., galvanic skin response, fMRI, data archives), or modes of analyses (e.g., multivariate analysis, structural equation modeling, longitudinal designs). Other external inputs come from sociopolitical realities in society such as its economic trends, international conflicts, and technological innovations. Still other outside influences come from cultural innovations in contemporary art and literature and from changes in popular culture and lifestyle, such as structuralism, feminism, and postmodernism.

Thus, every couple of decades the aging establishment's orthodoxy begins to slow down, mostly from the weight of its own virtues (quantifications, conceptualizations, applications). Then middle-level innovators (e.g., associate professors) struggle to synthesize a new orthodoxy out of fashionable concepts and tools inspired by kindred disciplines, the arts, and political and economic developments in the broader society. How much acceptance is given to an innovation depends on where the discipline is in the 20-year generational cycle when the innovation is proposed.

References

James, W. (1890). *Principles of psychology* (Vol. 1). New York: Henry Holt.

McGuire, W. J. (1964). Inducing resistance to persuasion: Some contemporary approaches. In L. Berkowitz (Ed.), *Advances in experimental social psychology* (Vol. 1, pp. 191–229). New York: Academic Press.

McGuire, W. J. (1966). Current status of cognitive consistency theories. In S. Feldman (Ed.), *Cognitive consistency* (pp. 1–46). New York: Academic Press.

McGuire, W. J. (1973). The yin and yang of progress in social psychology: Seven koan. *Journal of Personality and Social Psychology, 26,* 446–456.

McGuire, W. J. (1983). A contextualist theory of knowledge: Its implications for innovation and reform in psychological research. In L. Berkowitz (Ed.), *Advances in experimental social psychology* (Vol. 16, pp. 1–47). New York: Academic Press.

McGuire, W. J. (1986a). A perspectivist looks at contextualism and the future of behavioral science. In R. Rosnow & M. Georgoudi (Eds.), *Contextualism and understanding in behavioral science: Implications for research and theory* (pp. 271–301). New York: Praeger.

McGuire, W. J. (1986b). The vicissitudes of attitudes and similar representational constructs in twentieth century psychology. *European Journal of Social Psychology, 16,* 89–130.

McGuire, W. J. (1989). A perspectivist approach to the strategic planning of programmatic scientific research. In B. Gholson, W. R. Shadish, Jr., R. A. Neimeyer, & A. C. Houts (Eds.), *The psychology of science: Contributions to metascience* (pp. 214–245). New York: Cambridge University Press.

McGuire, W. J. (1997). Creative hypothesis generating in psychology: Some useful heuristics. In J. T. Spence, J. M. Darley, & D. J. Foss (Eds.), *Annual review of psychology* (Vol. 48, pp. 1–30). Palo Alto, CA: Annual Reviews.

McGuire, W. J. (1999). *Constructing social psychology: Creative and critical processes.* New York: Cambridge University Press.

McGuire, W. J. (2000). L'evoluzione dialettica psicologia tramite il riequilibrio delle sue antinomie (Psychology's dialectical evolution by means of shifting resolutions of its antinomies). *Rassegna di Psicologia, 17*(3), 29–43.

McGuire, W. J., & McGuire, C. V. (1988). Content and process in the experience of self. In L. Berkowitz (Ed.), *Advances in experimental social psychology* (Vol. 21, pp. 97–144). New York: Academic Press.

McGuire, W. J., & McGuire, C. V. (1991a). The affirmational versus negational self-concepts. In J. Strauss & G. R. Goethals (Eds.), *The self: Interdisciplinary approaches* (pp. 107–120). New York: Springer-Verlag.

McGuire, W. J., & McGuire, C. V. (1991b). The content, structure, and operation of thought systems. In R. S. Wyer, Jr. & T. K. Srull (Eds.), *Advances in social cognition* (Vol. 4, pp. 1–78). Hillsdale, NJ: Erlbaum.

McGuire, W. J., & McGuire, C. V. (1992a). Cognitive-versus-affective positivity asymmetries in thought systems. *European Journal of Social Psychology, 22,* 571–591.

McGuire, W. J., & McGuire, C. V. (1992b). Psychological significance of seemingly arbitrary word-order regularities: The case of kin pairs. In G. Semin & K. Fiedler (Eds.), *Language, interaction, and social cognition* (pp. 214–236). London: Sage.

McGuire, W. J., & Padawer-Singer, A. (1976). Trait salience in the spontaneous self-concept. *Journal of Personality and Social Psychology, 33,* 743–754.

Sherrington, C. S. (1906). *Integrative action of the nervous system.* London: Constable.

Weiss, R. F. (1963). Defection from social movements and subsequent recruitment to new movements. *Sociometry, 26,* 1–20.

Walter Mischel turned the field of personality psychology on its proverbial rear with his controversial 1968 monograph *Personality and Assessment*. Met first with a cold shoulder, the work later led to a hot debate, the so-called person versus situation debate. As Mischel notes, he was often referred to as the "devil" of the [personality] field who tried to destroy it. One extreme example of Mischel's infamy came in the form of an item on a major state examination: The correct answer to the question of which psychologist "did not believe in personality" was Walter Mischel. Since that seminal monograph went to press more than 30 years ago, Mischel has continued to challenge traditional paradigms with such theories as the cognitive affective personality system in an effort to push the science ever forward.

Walter Mischel

Challenging the Traditional Personality Psychology Paradigm

9

Contrary to many stories, I did not set out to topple any paradigms and my motivations at the start were mundane. I was a 30-year-old bottom of the academic ladder lecturer in Harvard University's Department of Social Relations in 1960, and used the early leave term available to junior faculty to prepare myself to teach a better course on personality and assessment. For this, I reviewed the state of the main existing personality theories and assessment methods, and the relevant empirical literature. The deeper I searched, the greater the discrepancies grew between what the theories assumed about the basic nature of personality and what the data showed—and the more perplexing the picture became.

Questioning the Core Assumptions: Identifying the "Personality Paradox"

The core assumption of the traditional personality psychology paradigm was (and is) that individuals are characterized by broad cross-situational personality traits (dispositions) that are expressed consistently in their trait-relevant behavior—a conscientious person, for example, will behave conscientiously across many different kinds of sit-

I am deeply grateful for the generous and constructive detailed comments on earlier drafts by many colleagues, most notably Ozlem Ayduk, Daniel Cervone, Tory Higgins, Rodolfo Mendoza-Denton, Carolyn Morf, and Yuichi Shoda. Preparation of this chapter was supported by National Institute of Mental Health Grant MH39349.

uations. As I reviewed the massive literature on consistency, I found that in the domain of social dispositions and interpersonal relations most central for personality, consistency across different types of situations (e.g., from home to school to work) was surprisingly low. A high degree of behavioral specificity or "discriminativeness" (Mischel, 1973) was found regularly in the behavioral referents for such traits as rigidity, social conformity, dependency, and aggression; for attitudes to authority; and for virtually any other personality dimension (Mischel, 1968; Peterson, 1968; Vernon, 1964). Personality dispositions began to seem much less global, much more situation-specific, than had been assumed: The person's response patterns even in highly similar situations typically were not strongly related.

As a clinically trained psychologist teaching at the time in clinical programs, I also became familiar with the personality assessments that were routinely made to go beyond surface trait descriptions to "deeper" unconscious levels. These efforts, mostly in the psychoanalytic or psychodynamic tradition, went beyond the mainstream academic trait approach to infer underlying motivations and conflicts. For this purpose it was standard clinical practice to use a variety of measures ranging from projective tests to situation-free questionnaires, all of which I was teaching my students—and all of which turned out to have little validity. Worst of all, they had even less utility when it came to making useful predictions about important life outcomes or to designing effective treatments.

Nevertheless, in both trait and psychodynamic approaches, even small samples of behavior were being treated as if they were a diagnostic X-ray to illuminate the core of personality. Rapid inferences were made routinely from a few signs observed by experts to broad generalizations about what the individual was like "on the whole." But in study after study, the results failed to support these assumptions when researchers, myself included, tried to predict social behavior in many domains and contexts from a variety of personality indicators or "signs" from which these dispositions were inferred.

The more I read the more I saw how many research articles and doctoral dissertations ended like my own: with a caveat at the end—an apology—that the tests used accounted for so little of the variance when one was trying to predict what people would actually do in particular situations. And always these disappointing results were seen as due to poor methods, bad judgments, and unreliable tests.

It was the increasing discrepancy between the establishment assumptions and the data that began to haunt me. I realized that I had become obsessed when I found myself completely submerged in trying to make sense of it, oblivious to my favorite Mozart opera while it was being performed on the stage in front of my eyes. After the curtain came down, my family told me it had been a great performance: That night I began to write *Personality and Assessment* (1968).

For many years before I started to write my monograph, evidence had been reported indicating instability and lack of consistency across situations in domains of behavior expected to reflect generalized and stable traits (e.g., Hartshorne & May, 1928; Newcomb, 1929), and that undermined the utility of the then-dominant clinical practices (e.g., Peterson, 1968). Nevertheless, mainstream work simply continued, with some efforts to develop improved tests and methods and reduce measurement error.

The turmoil for me began when I asked myself, "What if the problem is not just with bad methods and poor data but also with wrong assumptions?" A 7-year-long internal dialogue followed, and it later became what Bem and Allen (1974) named the *personality paradox* of the field. On the one hand, the data indicated lack of consistency. On the other hand, human intuition, and a tradition dating to the ancient Greeks and the "four humors" of personality (blood, bile, cholera, phlegm), as well as personality psychology as a field, led to the conviction that the opposite was true. In my internal dialogue, one voice urged, "Just look at those data!" The other voice asked, "But what about the intuition of consistency in traits and personality?"

To resolve this dilemma, my hunch—and lifetime bet—was that the data were right—but so also were the intuitions that there is consistency in personality. What the data did suggest to me was that the locus and nature of personality consistencies must be fundamentally different from what had been assumed, and that the intuitions must be based on something other than cross-situational consistency. The resulting search to find the locus and nature of personality consistency and its underlying organization set the agenda for the rest of my career.

After reviewing in detail diverse lines of evidence undermining the utility of classic trait and state approaches to personality, I concluded,

> Global traits and states are excessively crude, gross units to encompass adequately the extraordinary complexity and subtlety of the discriminations that people constantly make. Traditional trait–state conceptions of man have depicted him as victimized by his infantile history, as possessed by unchanging rigid trait attributes, and as driven inexorably by unconscious irrational forces. This conceptualization, besides being philosophically unappetizing, is contradicted by massive experimental data. The traditional trait–state conceptualizations of personality, while often paying lip service to [the] complexity and to the uniqueness of each person, lead to a grossly oversimplified view that misses both the richness and the uniqueness of individual lives. (Mischel, 1968, p. 301)

The book made the case—and emphasized—that the meaningful expressions of personality depend importantly on the situation and context and that therefore the situation needed to be incorporated into the study of personality. It proposed that it consequently was time for personality psychology to study closely what people actually do in different kinds of situations and conditions, rather than focussing on asking "what they are like on the whole."

The Aftermath

THE FIRST WAVE OF REACTIONS

When *Personality and Assessment* was published in 1968, the initial reaction was silence: It was briefly reviewed on a back page of *Contemporary Psychology* and quickly dismissed as trivial and unjustified under the header "Personality unvanquished." But within less than a year it created a divisive debate that still reverberates and that changed the field's agenda. Although prepublication reviews, and my own concerns, had led me to expect strong reactions, I had no idea that the consequences would turn out to be so profound.

As a relative newcomer, confronting the field with the state of the data and the importance of the situation in personality had seemed like the reasonable thing to do in light of my literature review. I did not anticipate that it would have the impact it turned out to have perhaps because I did not take into account that my senior colleagues in personality had staked their professional identities and careers on assumptions that *Personality and Assessment*, in their eyes, assaulted. For them, the defiant part of this monograph was the proposal that the findings it reviewed might reflect not just poor methods and measurement noise but also the state of nature. Perhaps even worse, it suggested that they and their field were missing the complexity and finely textured nature of human beings and their remarkable variability across different situations and in different contexts and relationships recognized in literature, and philosophy, and human experience but bypassed by the establishment paradigm.

So initially *Personality and Assessment* was read and dismissed by many in the personality field as a "situationist" attack on personality itself and as an unjustified denial of the importance of individual differences (e.g., Bowers, 1973). Remarkably, the idea that personality dispositions were not expressed with high consistency across different kinds of situations, and that the situation needed to become part of the conception and assessment of personality, was seen at that time as a threat to the very existence of the personality construct and the viability of the discipline devoted to it. That became clear when, after the initial silence, for the next dozen years passionate discussions, debates, and confrontations on the topic proliferated in the journals and the agendas of the field's national and international meetings (e.g., Endler & Magnusson, 1976; Magnusson & Endler, 1977).

THE PARADIGM CRISIS

In retrospect, my interpretation of the data presented in *Personality and Assessment* was upsetting to the establishment because it violated the implicit set of assumptions underlying the then-standard science paradigm in personality psychology and in much of Western thought about human nature. Namely: People have stable traits and dispositions that should lead them to be consistent across many different situations over time. Given that the situation in the traditional personality paradigm was defined as a source of error and noise that obscured the consistencies that characterize the individual, to see the consistency of the person it was believed it was essential to remove the effect of situations. This was done either by making the situation completely ambiguous, as on an inkblot or a blank card on the thematic apperception test in projective testing, or by getting rid of it on situation-free global measures and ratings of what the person is like on the whole.

Furthermore, the academic domains and loyalties of the science were divided into subdisciplines in ways consistent with these beliefs. Thus, since its inception a century ago personality psychology was mostly devoted to studying the person apart from the situation. In contrast, the field of social psychology seemed mostly interested in understanding the general effects and power of situations regardless of individual differences. So here the person became the error variance, the noise, that had to be removed, or at best treated by throwing in some global measure in case the dissertation on the main effects didn't work out.

Given the way that the terrain and identity of personality and social psychology as disciplines was divided, a personality psychologist who argued for the importance of the situation was easily seen as trying to bury personality as a field and as a construct. And that is how *Personality and Assessment* was generally interpreted: Most personality psychologists condemned it as an assault to undo the field that trivialized "the power of the person" and the importance of personality. In contrast, most social psychologists hailed it as proving the importance and power of the situation and the relative insignificance of individual differences in personality. I thought both were equally wrong.

This zero-sum conception of the relationship between social and personality psychology (i.e., to the degree that the person was important, the situation was not and vice versa) led to the unfortunate person versus situation debate. It fueled a period of prolonged and heated controversy about personality dispositions and structure that consumed much attention throughout the 1970s and early 1980s. Again in retrospect, the extreme reactions and the long bitter debates had many of the defining characteristics of a Kuhnian paradigm crisis.

THE PERSON VS. SITUATION DEBATE

Situationism

Using the challenge of my 1968 book as a basis, many social psychologists amassed evidence for the power of situational variables and proposed that humans have a persistent tendency to invoke dispositions as favorite (albeit erroneous) explanations of social behavior (e.g., Nisbett & Ross, 1980). Indeed, the tendency to focus on dispositions in causal explanations soon was seen as a symptom of a "fundamental attribution error" committed by laypersons in everyday life, as well as by the psychologists who study them (Ross, 1977). Evidence of systematic judgmental errors in personality assessment and inferences, of course, had been noted often in the past. Whereas before the limitations of judgments about personality had been dismissed as merely due to unreliable, imperfect methods, open to correction by improving the quality of measurement, now instead they were read as reflecting human nature (e.g., Nisbett & Ross, 1980). In its most extreme form, some critics argued that personality was mostly a fictitious construction in the mind of the perceiver (e.g., Shweder, 1975).

Return of the Traditional Paradigm and Status Quo

At the opposite pole, many personality psychologists renewed even more intensely their efforts to retain the traditional paradigm. For example, the case was made that global dispositions as traditionally conceptualized were "alive and well" if one simply aggregated multiple observations and measures across different situations, thereby again eliminating the role of the situation by averaging it out. This strategy now acknowledged that specific behaviors across different types of situations could not be predicted by such a model (e.g., Epstein, 1979) and simply continued to treat the situation as a source of noise by removing it as before.

In a related influential movement to resume the traditional trait paradigm, beginning in the early 1980s, a resurgence of the factor analytic approach occurred in personality psychology. It was based on an agreement to reach a consensus concerning the set of major traits or basic dispositions needed for a comprehensive taxonomy of personality using factor analyses based on traits ratings, in the form of the "Big Five" (e.g., McCrae & Costa, 1992). Many similar factor analytic studies and taxonomies had been done in earlier years, and their strengths and limitations had been duly noted, including in critiques like mine. The difference now was that the agreement about what those factors "really were" allowed the formulation of the Big Five with its own measurement scales, with the hope and claim that this constituted the fundamental reality about the basic structure of personality. This was greeted with great enthusiasm by personality psychologists eager to resume the status quo without having to deal with the challenges to the fundamental assumptions of the paradigm and returning to business as usual.

Consequences of the Debate

The hostile exchanges from a decade of the person versus situation debate that ensued widened the gulf between the fields of social and personality psychology. The debate unfortunately had further divided social and personality psychology as disciplines, each with its own roots, assumptions, and sociology of science, that polarized the issues rather than addressing them and moving toward a resolution. The result? On one side was a situationist bandwagon effect that indeed trivialized the role of personality, and on the other side was a fundamentalist conservative (if not reactionary) personality psychology that trivialized the role of context and the situation. At best, each discipline treated the other as irrelevant.

The effect was seen, for example, in the division of the premiere research publication, the *Journal of Personality and Social Psychology*, within which the two fields had been integrated since its founding at the start of the century. One of the sadder days in my career came in April of 1980 when the journal was split, within the same covers, into three separate entities, each with its own editors and boards. The split was as follows: Part 1. Attitudes and Social Cognition; Part 2. Interpersonal Relations and Group Processes; and Part 3. Personality Processes and Individual Differences. To me it seemed that this was a political division in which the phenomena of interest were carved not at their natural joints but on the basis of disciplinary and even political considerations. For a number of years the front piece for Part 3 described its mission as devoted to contributions on "personality psychology as traditionally defined"—a definition that might surprise a reader expecting that a science would hope for new research that might upset and revise the traditional definitions of a field!

PERSONAL AND PROFESSIONAL CONSEQUENCES AND COSTS

What was needed in my view was not a war between extremist views but an alternative paradigm that better captured the nature of personality consistencies. Until that paradigm was developed, however, the consequences of the crisis for me were substantial.

The crisis brought recognition for my work from many sources, but much of the fame was really infamy. During this time, in diverse personality publications, textbooks, and review articles, I was not infrequently described as the "devil" of the field who tried to destroy it—a reputation that endured for a long time and perhaps still lingers. For example, the 1992 *Annual Review* article on personality opened with this: "The budding personologist is likely to find both villains and heroes in forging his or her own personal identity . . . the early heroes were Henry Murray and Gordon Allport, and the first villain was Walter Mischel" (Wiggins & Pincus, 1992, p. 474). Indicative of the atmosphere was a test item on a major state examination that for years asked test-takers to identify the psychologist who "did not believe in personality," and while listing people like B. F. Skinner among the alternatives, considered Mischel to be the right answer. The test item captured the field's mood seen in articles like Goldberg's (1993) *American Psychologist* piece, which opened with "Once upon a time, we had no personalities," attributing this temporary loss of personality to "Mischel, 1968."

Beginning in the early 1980s, for the first time in my career my research grant applications were rejected by study sections dominated by traditional personality psychologists but given top priority by those with social and cognitive psychologists. Likewise, articles submitted by me and/or my students to the personality sections of the prime journals fared badly and were generally rejected. Often caustic critiques abruptly dismissed the research that showed the role of the situation in personality as, for example, "pseudoscience," but without reasoned explanations for the pejoratives and the rejection.

From Crisis to Resolution: Development of an Alternative Paradigm

MY REACTION TO THE CRISIS

The intended challenge of *Personality and Assessment* was not to compare the power of the situation to the power of the person to see which is more important. Rather, it was to understand how the interactions between the two play out in stable ways and reflect the characteristics of the person and the underlying system. The need was not to debate whether personality exists, but rather to conceptualize it in ways that allow those person–situation interactions to be understood and predicted more effectively and that do justice to their complexity. Although the 1968 book was more successful than I could have imagined in challenging the establishment, it did not provide a well-articulated alternative. It thus stirred a paradigm crisis without offering a new one. The development of such an alternative has been the goal my collaborators and I have continued to pursue over the many years.

A first step required rethinking dispositions to take account of the situations with which the personality system continuously interacts. I thought that dispositions needed to be conceptualized in terms of "psychological person variables" (rather than trait terms), but what should they be? In selecting the kinds of "cognitive social person variables" needed within a personality system, I tried to overcome the curious bifurcation that had developed between progress in the concepts and findings of the larger science and the regnant conceptions of personality that had long ignored them. I therefore turned to the variables—like expectancies and beliefs, and goals and values—that seemed most important from half a century of empirical research in psychology. I was encouraged by the fact that my 1968 research review had shown that, although the evidence for cross-situational consistency in personality domains was low, in fact there was a good deal of evidence for significant consistency in various kinds of cognitive variables and measures. For example, the cognitive constructions about oneself and the world (e.g., the personal constructs identified by George Kelly, 1955, who had been my mentor in graduate school), as well as the expectations, self-concepts, and theories that we have about ourselves and each other, had considerable consistency. Hence they seemed potential candidates for the kinds of person variables that might prove useful for understanding person–situation interactions.

The findings from my own research program were pointing directly to the importance of such variables. I was trying to understand how young children become able to delay immediate gratification for the sake of delayed but ultimately more valued outcomes and goals. In one laboratory situation that proved particularly informative, the child tries to delay taking an immediately available smaller reward (e.g., a little treat) in order to get a larger, more desired treat later. It became clear to me in these studies in the late 1960s that the crucial determinant of delay ability was not the rewards the child faced but how they were represented mentally, that is, how the child construed or encoded them. For example, if the children were primed to think about how "yummy and chewy" the marshmallow treats were, they could hardly wait at all. But if they thought about them as if they were puffy clouds, or pretended they were just pictures and "put a frame around them" in imagination, or distracted themselves mentally, they could wait easily. So what mattered was what was in their heads, and that was more important than what was in front of them. Although this now seems self-evident, at that time—when behaviorism prevailed and the cognitive revolution was in its infancy—it seemed startling. For me it meant that the personality system had to include how the individual represents different kinds of social situations cognitively.

Building on such findings, I proposed (Mischel, 1973) a set of person variables that included personal constructs (encoding strategies), expectancies, values–goals, self-regulatory systems/plans, and competencies (e.g., like those needed for delay of gratification). This article also outlined the underlying psychological processes that might lead people to interpret the meanings of situations in their characteristic ways and that could link their resulting specific patterns of behavior to particular types of conditions in potentially predictable ways (p. 278). The approach emphasized "the crucial role of situations but view[ed] them as informational inputs whose behavioral impact depends on how they are processed by the person" (p. 279). The focus thus shifted away from broad situation-free trait descriptors in semantic terms (e.g., conscientious, sociable) to more situation-qualified characterizations of persons-in-contexts, making dispositions situationally hedged, that is, "conditional" and interactive. A main message was then—as it still is 30 years later—that

> [t]he term "personality psychology" need not be preempted for the study of differences between individuals in their consistent attributes: it fits equally well to the study of the individual's cognitive and behavioral activities as he interacts with the conditions of his life. (p. 279)

My 1973 *Psychological Review* article with these proposals was widely cited by social psychologists, and in diverse ways seemed to facilitate the social cognitive revolution that co-occurred with the retrenchment of the traditional personality paradigm. Its influence may be seen for example in *Personality and Social Intelligence* (Cantor & Kihlstrom, 1987), which explored the relevance and implications for personality of the then-new social cognitive revolution. During the next three decades that revolution transformed social psychology. It opened new vistas, generating prolific research spanning from the nature and representation of the self, to self-regulation and self-control processes, to social perception. Interestingly, in one of these recent developments it has become clear that lay people are not just intuitive trait theorists as had long been assumed: When asked appropriate questions they also think about personality like social cognitive theorists; they take the situation into account and make inferences about the motivations and feelings that underlie the behavior of people who matter to them (Shoda & Mischel, 1993). Indeed the better the perceiver knows the perceived, the more inferences are made spontaneously that go beyond traits to such cognitive and affective underlying variables as goals, intentions, and beliefs (e.g., Chen Idson & Mischel, 2001).

In short, the fuzzy boundary between social and personality psychology became for me the locus for the kind of personality model and research most needed. It is at this boundary that the characteristic interactions of persons and situations unfold, and one begins to see in greater depth the complexity of the person. The findings from three decades of research and theory-building at this interface between social, cognitive, and personality psychology, in turn, paved the way—and have been waiting—to be incorporated into a more comprehensive conception of personality that could address the problems that my 1968 book had identified but not solved.

TOWARD A RECONCEPTUALIZATION OF PERSONALITY CONSISTENCY, STRUCTURE, AND THE ROLE OF SITUATIONS

In the development of this alternative approach to personality, several decades of work by many researchers were needed to go from the outlines and anticipations of my 1973 article to my 1995 *Psychological Review* article with Yuichi Shoda, "A Cognitive–Affective System Theory of Personality: Reconceptualizing Situations, Dispositions, Dynamics, and Invariance in Personality Structure." Shoda came to do graduate work with me at Stanford University in 1982, and he joined me in the move to Columbia University in 1983. Ever since, our joint work has been a genuine collaboration that reflects his contributions, insights, and efforts at least as much as mine.

RESOLVING THE CONSISTENCY PARADOX

The goal of the research program Shoda and I pursued together was to find and understand the nature and locus of personality consistency. We started with the basic personality paradox as the problem to untangle. To recapitulate, the construct of personality rests on the assumption that individuals are characterized by distinctive qualities that are relatively invariant across situations and over a span of time. The paradox was that in a century of personality research, evidence showed that individual differences in social behaviors tend to be surprisingly variable across different situations. The hypothesis that drove our own work was that the variability across situations seen as the person's behavior unfolds across different situations is not simply error variance but could provide a stable and meaningful window into the underlying system that produced them.

For instance, suppose two people on the whole display the same average amount of sociability. However, the first person is extremely sociable and warm with students but unfriendly and cold with colleagues, whereas the second person shows the opposite pattern and is unfriendly and disinterested with students but very sociable with colleagues. If such patterns are stable, they could be meaningful expressions of the personality system worth studying systematically. To test this possibility directly, in a project that absorbed us for more than 10 years, we conducted an extremely data-intensive set of studies. More than 150 hours of direct observation were recorded for participants in a camp setting as they lived their lives across a set of different situations and over many weeks.

We found that this type of variability (He does A if situation X, but B if situation Y) is not just a source of "error" that will disappear if enough observations are sampled as had been assumed in the long search for broad traits. On the contrary, we discovered that these "if–then" patterns or "profiles" of situation–behavior relationships were stable and yielded highly significant intraindividual stability coefficients. Indeed, such profiles seem to constitute a sort of "signature of personality" that does reflect some of the essence of personality coherence and promises to provide a route to glimpse the underlying system that generates them (Mischel & Shoda, 1995; Shoda, Mischel, & Wright, 1994). In short, we found stability not in cross-situational consistency, where the century-long search began, but rather in the intraindividually stable patterns of cross-situational variability that characterize the person. And we found it by taking account of the situation rather than eliminating it.

In the same set of studies we found that these patterns are also the behavioral locus for the self-perception of consistency with regard to a given domain (e.g., conscientiousness). Namely, people's impressions of the degree to which they are consistent is based not on the degree to which their behavior is cross-situationally consistent but on the degree to which their if–then pattern of variability is stable in that domain. Taken collectively, the results of these studies allowed a resolution of the personality paradox: The data reviewed in the 1968 critique were right, and so was the intuition of consistency. It's just that the locus of the consistency is found where it had least been expected.

To account for these findings required a theory of personality that would capture the fact that the individuals' expressions of consistency are seen both in the overall average levels of different types of behavior and also in their stable if–then patterns of variability across different situations. With that goal, we developed the cognitive affective personality system (or CAPS) theory (Mischel & Shoda, 1995). In CAPS theory, individuals are characterized not only by the particular subset of goals, ways of encoding the world, affects, and self-regulatory competencies that may be potentially accessible to them, but also—and most important—by the distinctive and stable organization of relationships among them in the personality system, that is, the person's distinctive "network." This unique organization guides and constrains the activation of the specific cognitions, affects, and potential behaviors when an individual processes situational features. It constitutes the basic structure of personality and reflects and underlies the individual's uniqueness. When the ifs posed by the situation change, so do the thens generated by the personality system, but the relationship between them remains stable. This type of system is intrinsically interactionist. And it has been shown, in formal modeling simulations as well as in empirical studies, to generate both overall mean differences in a given behavior, as well as the specific if–then profiles that are a person's behavioral "signature" (Mischel & Shoda, 1995; Shoda & Mischel, 1998).

The Present—and the Future?

At the time of this writing, two paradigms coexist in personality psychology and it remains to be seen whether or not they are compatible and can be integrated in the future. The first one provides a continuation of the traditional paradigm currently represented most strongly in the form of the Big Five. The approach can be very useful if the main question one wants answered is how people differ overall in their rated behavior tendencies and characteristics. It is, however, mute about some of the most important expressions of consistency that become visible in the meaningful variability of the person's behavior. The discovery of these signatures has opened the route to identifying the natural types and subtypes that they express and the characteristic organization of the underlying processing systems that generate each of these types.

To understand these signatures of personality requires a fundamentally different conception of personality invariance, as represented in the processing approach of the CAPS framework (Mischel & Shoda, 1995). Neither the underlying processes nor their expressions can be properly assessed unless the situation is incorporated into the conception and analysis of personality coherence. In this conception, personality is construed as a relatively stable system of social–cognitive affective mediating processes whose expressions are manifested in predictable patterns of situation–behavior relations. CAPS theory provides a general cognitive–affective processing framework for the analysis of personality types, sketching the outlines or terrain maps that need to be filled in with the particular organizations and signatures that distinctively characterize different personality types.

Examples of research into such personality types guided by a CAPS processing framework are already yielding exciting results. To illustrate briefly, in work on the narcissistic personality type, Morf and Rhodewalt (2001) are identifying the narcissist's distinctive personality signature—a paradoxical mix of grandiosity and vulnerability. This signature is played out in characteristic interaction patterns in the interpersonal arena, for example, by bragging or derogating the other when threat to self-esteem is perceived. Concurrently these researchers are uncovering the motivations and internal processes—the intrapersonal processing dynamics—that those signatures reflect and that make the narcissistic paradox explicable. Although their model of narcissism is unique and goes in new directions, it is also compatible with a CAPS framework and illustrates how a processing approach like this can yield a rich analysis of the personality dynamics of an extremely complex type.

In a second example, the work of Geraldine Downey and collaborators, in which I also have been involved, is revealing the characteristic personality signatures and processing dynamics of individuals who are anxiously oversensitive to interpersonal rejection cues, particularly in intimate relationships (e.g., Ayduk, Downey, Testa, Yen, & Shoda, 1999; Ayduk et al., 2000; Downey & Feldman, 1996). Theoretically, in the defining behavioral signature for this kind of rejection-sensitive disposition, the person is more prone than others to anger, disapproval, and coercive behaviors in certain types of situations in intimate relationships but not in many and even in most other situations. The specifics of when and why that does, or does not, happen are becoming increasingly clear. The theory views the individual's distinctive patterns of variability not as internal contradictions but as the potentially predictable expressions of a stable underlying system whose fascinating organization continues to be explored in the research program.

Examples like these show the utility of this kind of framework. They also are important steps toward forming a personality typology that takes serious account both of the situation and of the characteristic organization of the underlying system that distinguishes each type. Ultimately numerous research programs of this sort can help build a comprehensive triple typology of persons, situations, and behaviors. Such a typology should make it possible to attempt specific predictions that certain subtypes of individuals are likely to think, feel, and behave in certain kinds of ways in certain kinds of situations. This fundamental goal, articulated years ago (e.g., Bem, 1983), is now beginning to be actively pursued (e.g., Vansteelandt & Van Mechelen, 1998). It promises to provide a route to explore systematically the structural characteristics of the signatures of selected subtypes, and their consequences for flexible, adaptive behavior and coping. Theoretically, such a typology would make it possible to parse at relatively subordinate, situationally contextualized levels the taxonomies of personality and behavioral dispositions cast at the more molar, superordinate levels of analysis. Whether or not these different levels of analyses ultimately connect and allow integration among paradigms is still an open question, but one that should be worth examining.

There has long been a need for context-sensitive methods that incorporate the situation not only into the theory of personality but also into its assessment. Fortunately, the types of theory-driven, situation-specific assessments that are needed are becoming clear. They also seem increasingly possible to develop in practical terms, using methods that range from rigorously monitored daily diary studies to computer-presented and situation-specific assessments (e.g., Ayduk et al., 1999; Cervone, Shadel, & Jencius, 2001; Cervone & Shoda, 1999; Shoda & Tiernan, in press). Likewise, the CAPS framework is being used to reconceptualize critical clinical issues that have been difficult to study rigorously in the past. This is seen in ongoing work that is clarifying the nature of transference and tracing its implications for understanding the "relational self" and its contextualized expressions in different types of close relationships (e.g., Andersen, Reznik, & Chen, 1997; Chen & Andersen, 1999). In a related health-relevant direction, the consequences of contextualized behavior patterns for flexible, adaptive coping are being explored (Chiu, Hong, Mischel, & Shoda, 1995; Mendoza-Denton, Ayduk, Mischel, Shoda, & Testa, 2001).

Of course difficult challenges and a huge agenda of unanswered and even unasked questions are ahead. But to me it seems that the field has gone a long way since my review of its precarious health: The call for constructive change in the establishment approach to personality made in 1968 now seems to have been clearly heard—and it is well on the way to being richly answered. Although in retrospect the path I pursued turned out to create a crisis for establishment views and core assumptions, I was not motivated by that intention. I was driven by a commitment to say what I saw in the data that I cared about, even if it flew in the face of the existing wisdom of the field. If a message follows from my professional life it is to focus on the data and phenomena that matter, regardless of where they may lead.

References

Andersen, S. M., Reznik, I., & Chen, S. (1997). The self in relation to others: Cognitive and motivational underpinnings. In J. G. Snodgrass

& R. L. Thompson (Eds.), *The self across psychology: Self-recognition, self-awareness, and the self-concept* (pp. 233–275). New York: New York Academy of Science.

Ayduk, O., Downey, G., Testa, A., Yen, Y., & Shoda, Y. (1999). Does rejection elicit hostility in rejection-sensitive women? *Social Cognition, 17*, 245–271.

Ayduk, O., Mendoza-Denton, R., Mischel, W., Downey, G., Peake, P., & Rodriguez, M. (2000). Regulating the interpersonal self: Strategic self-regulation for coping with rejection sensitivity. *Journal of Personality and Social Psychology, 79*, 776–792.

Bem, D. J. (1983). Further deja vu in the search for cross-situational consistency: A response to Mischel & Peake. *Psychological Review, 90*, 390–393.

Bem, D. J., & Allen, A. (1974). On predicting some of the people some of the time: The search for cross-situational consistencies in behavior. *Psychological Review, 81*, 506–520.

Bowers, K. S. (1973). Situationism in psychology: An analysis and a critique. *Psychological Review, 80*, 307–336.

Cantor, N., & Kihlstrom, J. F. (1987). *Personality and social intelligence.* Englewood Cliffs, NJ: Erlbaum.

Cervone, D., Shadel, W. G., & Jencius, S. (2001). Social–cognitive theory of personality assessment. *Personality and Social Psychology Review, 5*, 33–51.

Cervone, D., & Shoda, Y. (1999). The coherence of personality: Social–cognitive bases of consistency, variability, and organization. New York: Guilford Press.

Chen, S., & Andersen, S. M. (1999). Relationships from the past in the present: Significant-other representations and transference in interpersonal life. In M. P. Zanna (Ed.), *Advances in experimental social psychology* (Vol. 31, pp. 123–190). San Diego, CA: Academic Press.

Chen Idson, L., & Mischel, W. (2001). The personality of familiar and significant people: The lay perceiver as a social–cognitive theorist. *Journal of Personality and Social Psychology, 80*, 585–596.

Chiu, C., Hong, Y., Mischel, W., & Shoda, Y. (1995). Discriminative facility in social competence: Conditional versus dispositional encoding and monitoring-blunting of information. *Social Cognition, 13*, 49–70.

Downey, G., & Feldman, S. (1996). Implications of rejection sensitivity for intimate relationships. *Journal of Personality and Social Psychology, 70*, 1327–1343.

Endler, N. S., & Magnusson, D. (1976). Toward an interactional psychology of personality. *Psychological Bulletin, 83*, 956–974.

Epstein, S. (1979). The stability of behavior: On predicting most of the people much of the time. *Journal of Personality and Social Psychology, 37*, 1097–1126.

Goldberg, L. R. (1993). The structure of phenotype personality traits. *American Psychologist, 48,* 26–34.

Hartshorne, H., & May, A. (1928). *Studies in the nature of character: Vol. 1. Studies in deceit.* New York: Macmillan.

Kelly, G. (1955). *The psychology of personal constructs.* New York: Basic Books.

Magnusson, D., & Endler, N. S. (Eds.). (1977). *Personality at the crossroads: Current issues in interactional psychology.* Hillsdale, NJ: Erlbaum.

McCrae, R. R., & Costa, P. T., Jr. (1992). Toward a new generation of personality theories: Theoretical contexts for the five-factor model. In J. S. Wiggins (Ed.), *The five-factor model of personality: Theoretical perspectives* (pp. 51–87). New York: Guilford Press.

Mendoza-Denton, R., Ayduk, O., Mischel, W., Shoda, Y., & Testa, A. (2001). Person × Situation interactionism in self-encoding (I am . . . when . . .): Implications for affect regulation and social information processing. *Journal of Personality and Social Psychology, 80,* 533–544.

Mischel, W. (1968). *Personality and assessment.* New York: Wiley.

Mischel, W. (1973). Toward a cognitive social learning reconceptualization of personality. *Psychological Review, 80,* 252–283.

Mischel, W., & Shoda, Y. (1995). A cognitive–affective system theory of personality: Reconceptualizing situations, dispositions, dynamics, and invariance in personality structure. *Psychological Review, 102,* 246–268.

Morf, C. C., & Rhodewalt, F. (2001). Unraveling the paradoxes of narcissism: A dynamic self-regulatory processing model. *Psychological Inquiry, 12,* 177–196.

Newcomb, T. M. (1929). *Consistency of certain extrovert–introvert behavior patterns in 51 problem boys.* New York: Columbia University, Teachers College, Bureau of Publications.

Nisbett, R. E., & Ross, L. D. (1980). *Human inference: Strategies and shortcomings of social judgment* [Century Psychology Series]. Englewood Cliffs, NJ: Prentice-Hall.

Peterson, D. R. (1968). *The clinical study of social behavior.* New York: Appleton.

Ross, L. (1977). The intuitive psychologist and his shortcomings: Distortions in the attribution process. In L. Berkowitz (Ed.), *Advances in experimental social psychology* (Vol. 10, pp. 174–221). New York: Academic Press.

Shoda, Y., & Mischel, W. (1993). Cognitive social approach to dispositional inferences: What if the perceiver is a cognitive–social theorist? *Personality and Social Psychology Bulletin, 19,* 574–585.

Shoda, Y., & Mischel, W. (1998). Personality as a stable cognitive–affective activation network: Characteristic patterns of behavior variation emerge from a stable personality structure. In S. Read & L. C.

Miller (Eds.), *Connectionist models of social reasoning and social behavior* (pp. 175–208). Mahwah, NJ: Erlbaum.

Shoda, Y., Mischel, W., & Wright, J. C. (1994). Intraindividual stability in the organization and patterning of behavior: Incorporating psychological situations into the idiographic analysis of personality. *Journal of Personality and Social Psychology, 67,* 674–687.

Shoda, Y., & Tiernan, S. (in press). Searching for order within a person's stream of thoughts, feelings, and behaviors over time and across situations. In D. Cervone & W. Mischel (Eds.), *Advances in personality science.*

Shweder, R. A. (1975). How relevant is an individual difference theory of personality? *Journal of Personality, 43,* 455–485.

Vansteelandt, K., & Van Mechelen, I. (1998). Individual differences in situation–behavior profiles: A triple typology model. *Journal of Personality and Social Psychology, 75,* 751–765.

Vernon, P. E. (1964). *Personality assessment: A critical survey.* New York: Wiley.

Wiggins, J. S., & Pincus, A. L. (1992). Personality: Structure and assessment. *Annual Review of Psychology, 43,* 473–504.

It might seem strange that the "father of cognitive psychology" treasures his some-time position on the fringes of the modern field, but such is the case for Ulric Neisser. Neisser spent his earliest years in the field struggling to find his niche. After a somewhat lengthy search, he found it—a discovery that prompted *Cognitive Psychology*, from which his honorary title of *pater familias* originated. Thrust into the spotlight, Neisser sought the familiar confines of the fringes, which took the form of ecological memory. Relative anonymity was short-lived however, as Neisser soon made waves with his distinction between academic and general intelligence. A subsequent American Psychological Association report on the idea of intelligence brought further success and notoriety. In his own estimate, Neisser has defied the establishment roughly half a dozen times, and he continues to champion the causes of psychology's greatest underdogs.

Ulric Neisser

Adventures in Cognition: From *Cognitive Psychology* to *The Rising Curve*

For most of my life—roughly since identifying myself as a psychology major in college—I have had strong convictions about the direction in which psychology should go. Whenever there seemed to be a chance, I've tried to push it that way. Those efforts have not always been consistent—I favored information-processing models in *Cognitive Psychology* (Neisser, 1967) and rejected them in *Cognition and Reality* (Neisser, 1976a)—but they have usually been vigorous. Not surprisingly, they have met with varied receptions. Some were so popular that I suddenly found myself in the middle of the mainstream, others so far out that I was a lonely prophet. Generally speaking, outside suits me best.

To be sure, there is an element of fantasy in all this. Psychology never moves in just a single direction: It is not coherent enough for that. Even if it were, no single person could push it very far alone. But there is at least this excuse: I have not been the only fantasist. Psychology in the mid-20th century was still host to a wide array of conflicting schools and ideologies, all trying to move it one way or another. To become a psychologist was (or so it seemed to this 20-year-old Harvard undergraduate) to choose sides in a sort of struggle for human nature. In that struggle I was not yet sure who the good guys were, but I could easily spot the bad guys: They were the behaviorists.

I chose sides against behaviorism for two main reasons. The first, of course, was my dislike of its assumptions. (Because I am still uncomfortable with those assumptions, I will not review them here.) But a second reason, equally important, was that I was then and still am an instinctive underdog lover, an *infracaninophile* (isn't that a great word?).

To my mind, the sheer dominance of behaviorism in America was reason enough to look for an alternative.

Against Behaviorism

The first alternative that I became aware of was Gestalt psychology. Rejecting the stimulus–response formulas of behaviorism, the Gestalt theorists insisted that what matters is not isolated stimuli but entire patterns and configurations. The whole, they said, is more than the sum of its parts. The reason that this principle applies to perception and memory and thought (and it really does, as they demonstrated in many ingenious experiments) was that it also applies to the brain itself. There may be holistic electrical fields in the cortex, fields that spontaneously organize themselves into coherent and elegant patterns, which are then reflected in conscious experience. That sounded pretty good to me, so when it was time for graduate school I applied to the master's program at Swarthmore College. I hoped to study there with Wolfgang Köhler, the last surviving founder of Gestalt psychology.

As it turned out, I learned more from other members of the Swarthmore faculty than from Köhler himself. One was Henry Gleitman, who had studied with the dissident behaviorist E. C. Tolman (even behaviorism had underdogs!). Gleitman and Jack Nachmias (another master's candidate) and I were soon writing an article that attacked Hull's behavioristic theory of extinction (Gleitman, Nachmias, & Neisser, 1954). I thought of it as a first stroke against the establishment.

The master's program at Swarthmore took only 2 years; what next? The most attractive possibility was to work with my old Harvard advisor George A. Miller, who had meanwhile moved to the Massachusetts Institute of Technology (MIT). Miller had already been exploring the psychological implications of linguistics and information theory for several years. (I had taken his course "The Psychology of Communication" while still an undergraduate.) He probably understood those implications more clearly than anyone else, certainly more clearly than I did. But it was obvious that information theory was becoming increasingly important, and at least it wasn't behaviorism. So I signed on and moved back to Cambridge.

There I became seriously confused. Some aspects of the new information psychology appealed to me very much, but I couldn't think of much to do with it. In a year and two summers at MIT, my only successful project was a visual priming study based not on information theory but just on my own antibehavioristic instincts. (It showed that visual priming of one member of a homonym pair like *kernel–colonel* does not change the visual threshold for the other member. The set is for a visual pattern, not a spoken response; Neisser, 1954.) I was discontent and took a year off from graduate school; when I returned it was to Harvard rather than MIT.

At that point my chief goal was to finish a doctoral degree, but with whom and on what? The arch-behaviorist B. F. Skinner was at one end of the building, so I moved to the other end, which was the domain of S. S. Stevens. There I did my thesis on Stevens's "quantal hypothesis" of auditory sensation, a quirky claim that perceived loudness can increase only in steps, not continuously. I didn't really believe it, which helped. (The hypothesis itself died quietly a few years later, with no help from me.) So I completed my degree in two years, stayed one more year for postdoctoral research (testing a hypothesis about pain thresholds that I also didn't believe), and was finished with Harvard. It was 1957: I was on top of all the latest developments and thought myself a clever fellow but still had no direction of my own.

Information Processing

That year I got my first real job, at Brandeis University. The pay was thin, and I had a family by that time, so I looked around for something extra. A friend introduced me to Oliver Selfridge, who was working on various computer and "artificial intelligence" projects at the MIT Lincoln Laboratory just down the road. We hit it off, and Selfridge suggested that I become a regular weekly consultant at the laboratory to continue our discussions. I had no idea what consultants did, but at the princely stipend of $50 a day I was sure I could learn it.

I did learn it, and much more besides. Selfridge was working on pattern recognition, and his ideas about feature detection and parallel processing seemed just as applicable to humans as to computers. They really were good ideas: His pandemonium model (Selfridge & Neisser, 1960) is still being taught to students today. I was especially fond of the concept of *parallel processing*: A coherent global result can emerge from the simultaneous activity of many small and independent units. Here was an informational theory with a Gestalt ring to it—just what I had been looking for. I began to think (and to talk with Selfridge) about how one might demonstrate parallel processing in the laboratory. The result was a series of experiments on visual search. The best of those experiments (Neisser, 1964) showed that (surprisingly) people can scan a column of random letters looking for any 1 of 10 different targets just as quickly as they can scan for a single target. I finally had a paradigm of my own.

The Brandeis department was an interesting mix of experimental, clinical, and "existential" psychologists, of whom Abraham Maslow was the most charismatic. Maslow insisted that psychology must be a science, but also that it should focus on the good in human nature as well as the bad; his own studies of "self-actualization" were an example (Maslow, 1962). I liked Maslow, who shared my feelings about behaviorism and also had little use (indeed, less than I did) for psychoanalysis. He often said that psychology needed a "third force" different from both. In retrospect it seems clear that cognitive psychology was to be that force, but I did not foresee it at the time. In fact, I was rapidly losing interest in all schools and systems. As the '50s gave way to the '60s, I had found something better to do.

Cognitive Psychology

What gradually became clear to me—without any "aha!" moment that I can recall—was that the concept of information could be applied to a wide range of interesting phenomena. Visual pattern recognition, short-term memory, selective attention, and many other things could all be regarded as (and indeed, were) processes of information pickup or storage or retrieval. This seemed to me not a mere theoretical claim but an obvious matter of fact, so I decided to put it all into a book. In the end, *Cognitive Psychology* (Neisser, 1967) took me $2^1/_2$ years to write. It is sometimes suggested that the rise of cognitive psychology led to the downfall of behaviorism. If this is true then *Cognitive Psychology* can probably claim some of the credit. Oddly, however, that was not one of my goals in writing it. The behavioristic tide seemed to be receding anyway, and explicit attacks on it would only have distracted the reader. I even said so: "A generation ago, a book like this one would have needed at least a chapter of self-defense against the behaviorist position. Today, happily, the climate of opinion has changed, and little or no defense is necessary" (p. 5). In fact, it was also I who had changed. No longer just a nattering nabob of negativity, I had something positive to say. This attitude—presenting a matter-of-fact argument instead of trying to refute other views—probably contributed to the success of the book.

My assignment in this chapter is to recount how I have "battled the establishment." But although I have indeed done so more than once, *Cognitive Psychology* is hardly a clear example. It did not attack behaviorism directly, as Gleitman, Nachmias, and I had done in 1954. Instead it laid out a different mode of thinking, a mode that many psychologists were already practicing and that they therefore welcomed with open arms. Indeed, the fact that *Cognitive Psychology* became popular so quickly is another reason not to credit it with "defying the crowd." In 1967, information processing was a sort of establishment-in-waiting: The people were already there, the research was already in progress. By supplying it with a name and a textbook, I became an instant charter member of a new and powerful establishment.

Second Thoughts

So I suddenly found myself famous. Accepting a professorship at Cornell University, I soon received offers to spend time in think tanks, to go abroad, to write other books, to edit journals, to present innumerable colloquia. For two decades I could hardly give a talk anywhere without sitting through a flattering introduction in which I was called "the father of cognitive psychology." (Even today I am still sometimes introduced in this way.) Doesn't that sound great? Shouldn't I have been happy? In fact, I was increasingly uneasy.

One problem was the direction in which the new field was moving. There was a spate of information-processing models, often illustrated with flow charts. Almost every issue of every cognitive journal (there were soon several cognitive journals) included one or more models of this kind, each reporting new reaction time data to show that last year's models were wrong. Of course this was partly my fault: I myself had presented such models in *Cognitive Psychology*. But there I had tempered them with other proposed mechanisms, particularly by the claim that perceiving and remembering were "constructive processes." Without some such mitigation, the flow charts were too mechanical for me.

I received a good deal of mail in those days, some of it disturbing. An eminent behaviorist wrote to say how much he admired *Cognitive Psychology* and how easily its argument could be adapted to behaviorism with just a few changes in terminology! Even worse was the psychiatrist who liked my account of perception as a "constructive process" because it fit the delusions of his schizophrenic patients so well. I had not meant to say that perception was just a form of hallucination! Even the notion of "construction," which once seemed so attractive, began to trouble me. Was it just an empty phrase? Or worse, actually misleading? I had written about "the continuously creative processes by which the world of experience is constructed" (Neisser, 1967, p. 11), but if those processes are really creative, why do all of us construct and experience pretty much the same world?

My musings on these issues were strongly influenced by James J. Gibson and Eleanor Gibson, who became my colleagues when I moved to Cornell. J. J. Gibson, America's most distinguished perception psychologist, denied the need for information processing altogether. The information that is available to moving, active perceivers—texture gradients, occlusion, optic flow—fully specifies both the layout of the environment and the position and motion of the observer. That information need not be processed because it is already there, available in the structured optic array that surrounds every observer.

If J. J. Gibson were alive today, he would certainly deserve a chapter in this volume. In his books—especially *The Ecological Approach to Visual Perception* (1979)—he "defied the crowd" more profoundly than any other psychologist of his generation. For a time, the cognitive science establishment seemed to tremble on its throne (Fodor & Pylyshyn, 1981). And although Gibson's challenge was eventually rejected, many of his radical concepts (optic array, occlusion, affordances, invariants, movement-produced information) are now accepted commonplaces in the profession. As I write this in 2001, a vigorous group of ecological psychologists continues to do elegant Gibsonian research (their journal is now in its 13th year) and a related position called *embodied cognition* is rapidly gaining adherents among philosophers of mind.

It took me several years at Cornell to understand what J. J. Gibson was all about. When his argument finally began to seem clear, it also began to seem right. And besides being right, Gibson was definitely the underdog in relation to cognitive orthodoxy, an orthodoxy that I had already found suspect for reasons of my own. For an infracaninophile like me, that made ecological psychology irresistible.

Cognition and Reality

Just the fact that cognitive psychology had become the mainstream was enough to make me suspicious; worse yet, it had become boring. The more I studied information processing, the less I liked it. In contrast, the more conversations I had with J. J. and Eleanor Gibson, the more interesting the ecological approach began to appear. Matters came to a head in 1973–1974, when I was a Fellow at the Center for Advanced Study in the Behavioral Sciences. (We lucky Fellows called it—as they still call it—"The Leisure of the Theory Class.") But leisure was not in the cards that year; my publisher insisted that the world was ready for an integrative second edition of *Cognitive Psychology*. For the first few months I worked on it dutifully, but there came a time when I couldn't read another reaction time information-processing article to save my life. I threw away my drafts and began to work on a different book, to be called *Cognition and Reality* (Neisser, 1976a).

The underlying premise of *Cognition and Reality* was that perceiving is an act that occurs over time. It is both bottom-up and top-down, cycling repeatedly through schema-driven expectations, active exploration, and the pickup of objective information. That new information revises the schema and thus leads to the formation of new expectations, new explorations, and so on. This "perceptual cycle" combined Gibson's idea of perception as information pickup with a new account of information processing based on Bartlett's (1932) concept of "schema."

Cognition and Reality had several goals besides the presentation of a new theory. I hoped to make Gibson's views more widely accepted and understood, and indeed to make a more general case for "ecological validity": Research is best when it focuses on variables that matter in real-world settings. With luck I might even redirect psychology a little, weaning my colleagues away from information processing by showing them what a more realistic approach had to offer. Less consciously, I may have been trying to make myself into an underdog again.

Cognition and Reality certainly did defy the crowd, but it was hardly a success. Reviews were negative; no one seemed to like it much, not even the Gibsonians. It was not widely read even when it first appeared, and—unlike *Cognitive Psychology*—is almost never cited today. A few people were intrigued by the concepts of *schema* and *perceptual cycle*, but their interest did not lead them to suggest any critical experiments. To be honest, I couldn't think of any either.

A major part of this failure can be attributed to the flaws of *Cognition and Reality* itself. Its overall attitude was negative and critical; its coverage of many topics was superficial and may have seemed glib; the term *schema* was used too freely everywhere. In addition, psychology itself was changing. The time for global theories of perception had passed, perhaps never to return. Young psychologists were no longer looking for banners under which to enlist, as I had done; they were looking instead for specific solvable problems. In the coming era of cognitive neuroscience and connectionism, perceptionists would find it more rewarding to seek concrete understandings of well-defined phenomena than to pursue vague and broad generalizations. Maybe they are right.

Although it never really caught on, *Cognition and Reality* did achieve some of its lesser goals. It did help make ecological psychology respectable: A number of people told me that my advocacy of Gibson's views was what first led them to read his *Ecological Approach to Visual Perception* (Gibson, 1979), and then of course how intriguing they had found it. Others may have had the same experience without telling me, so my Brownie points were well spent. As for me, I had successfully established a new position well away from the center. I was an outsider again, and it felt comfortable.

New Directions

When *Cognition and Reality* was finished, I needed a new project. Redirecting all of cognitive psychology had proved too difficult, so I looked for a smaller target. Was there not a subfield somewhere to which the underdog ecological approach could offer some relevant insights? I soon found three such domains. One of them was the study of various controversial issues in intelligence, in which I am still engaged. A second was attention, where my students and I uncovered several phenomena that are still occasionally cited: genuinely divided attention (Hirst, Spelke, Reaves, Caharack, & Neisser, 1980) and what I called *selective looking* (Bahrick, Walker, & Neisser, 1981; Neisser & Becklen, 1975). The third was the ecological study of memory, which has probably been the most establishment-defying as well as the most successful of all my enterprises.

The first century of memory research had relied mostly on rather dull list-learning methods; would it be possible to focus on practical everyday phenomena instead? To develop a kind of ecological approach to memory? In the mid-1970s I believed myself to be pretty much alone in this way of thinking. Then, to my great surprise, the mail brought an announcement of an international conference on the subject! It was to be called Practical Aspects of Memory and would be held in Cardiff in 1978. I was not so alone after all!

Responding to the conference announcement, Doug Herrmann and I submitted a paper (Herrmann & Neisser, 1978) on self-ratings of memory. The conference organizers responded in their turn by asking me to give the keynote address! (Sometimes it does help to be well-known.) This was an ideal opportunity to set out the ecological approach to memory, so I did. Because there was not yet much ecological research to describe, the tone of my address was rather negative: "If *X* is an interesting or socially significant aspect of memory, then psychologists have hardly ever studied *X*" (Neisser, 1978, p. 4). The conferees responded enthusiastically, and my newest defiance was under way.

The Ecological Study of Memory

Although I used the term *ecological* for this approach to memory, my enterprise was very different from Gibson's. His emphasis on ecological validity was driven by his own highly original theory of perception, whereas my advocacy of naturalistic memory research involved almost no theory at all. I was just sure that the study of memory in natural contexts would lead to new and interesting findings, and it did. Many ecological memory studies have appeared since the Cardiff conference, including a few of my own. These have mostly focused on confabulations in recall: "John Dean's Memory" (Neisser, 1981), "Phantom Flashbulbs" (Neisser & Harsch, 1992), "Remembering the Earthquake" (Neisser, Winograd, et al., 1996). This work still seems interesting, but I will not review it here. My chief concern in the 1980s was less with specific projects than with establishing the basic legitimacy of naturalistic memory research. That called for a new strategy.

Memory Observed

For a third time I tried to redirect psychology with a book, but this book was different. Technically I was not even its author, only its editor. *Memory Observed* (Neisser, 1982) was a sharply focused collection of readings designed to accompany undergraduate courses in memory. I knew how dull those courses were, and I was sure that both the students and their teachers would be happy to supplement them with something more lively. So I gave them whatever I had: Sigmund Freud, childhood amnesia, and flashbulb memories; John Dean, eyewitness testimony, and Sherlock Holmes; oral poetry, tribal history, astonishing mnemonic gifts. Just to make sure nobody missed the point, I tied the selections together with a running commentary. The naturalistic study of memory was portrayed as interesting and even amusing, but also as scientifically important.

One way or another, the point got across. Ecological memory research began to flourish: There were new methods, findings, a sense of excitement. Unsurprisingly, researchers committed to more traditional methods were not enthusiastic about this trend (especially given the unflattering account of their work in my Cardiff address!). In "The Bankruptcy of Everyday Memory" (1989), Banaji and Crowder responded by describing ecological memory research as a complete failure. I was delighted! They would hardly have bothered to mount such an attack unless the ecological movement was at least partially successful. So I wrote a confident response to their article (as did others) and kept on going.

By this time I was teaching at Emory University in Atlanta, having left Cornell in search of new challenges. During my 13 years at Emory (1983–1996) I organized several conferences on memory and related topics. The resulting edited volumes were useful but, like most conference books, they were not widely read. I was also working on a new (ecologically oriented!) theory of self-knowledge; to develop that theory, I held five conferences and published three edited volumes that focused on it (Neisser, 1993; Neisser & Fivush, 1994; Neisser & Jopling, 1997). Perhaps this was another act of "defiance": Once more I was trying to change how psychologists think about something. But defiant or not, my self theory has had little impact. Perhaps it is just not a good theory, or perhaps edited conference volumes are just not an effective way to move a field.

By the late 1990s, *Memory Observed* was out of date; a new edition was needed. In assembling that edition (with the help of Ira Hyman), I encountered a problem exactly opposite to the one I had faced 18 years before. Then, it had been hard to find enough naturalistic studies to fill up a book, even a small one. Now, Hyman and I confronted an embarrassment of riches: How to choose among so many good studies? We did choose, somehow (Neisser & Hyman, 2000).

Intelligence

The personal intellectual history recounted here did not occur in a vacuum: Real history was happening too. In the 1960s and 1970s, thousands of protestors took to the streets, hoping to make America a better place. Protesting is not my thing, but wasn't there something I could do? Some way to bring cognitive psychology to bear on a real social problem? Given my interests, intelligence testing was the obvious candidate. Unfortunately, I had never taken a course or even read a book on the subject. Then, in 1974, Lauren Resnick invited me to a conference on intelligence at the University of Pittsburgh. I accepted eagerly. It was the year in which I was writing *Cognition and Reality;* maybe there would be an ecological angle.

Such an angle was all too easy to find. The Pittsburgh conference was dominated by concepts derived from "artificial intelligence"; indeed, my nominal assignment was to comment on a paper by Herbert Simon. The puzzles that Simon and his colleagues used in their experiments certainly seemed artificial, as do many of the items on standardized tests of intelligence. With this in mind I made a distinction between *academic intelligence* (skill in solving artificial puzzles) and *general intelligence* (skill in dealing with everyday life). Although this distinction is hardly subtle or original, my comments (Neisser, 1976b) were soon widely quoted; apparently no one had put it just this way before. I had defied the establishment without even breaking a sweat!

School Achievement

So perhaps I might have something to contribute to social issues after all. But what, exactly? Apart from one offbeat idea about the definition of intelligence (Neisser, 1979), I was at a loss. Why, for example, is the mean IQ score of Black Americans so consistently below that of White Americans? I did not know, and none of my friends knew, either. In the hope of learning more, I invited a number of experts—including several Black scholars—to a 1983 conference on the subject at Cornell. It turned out to be a remarkable experience. Talks by John Ogbu, Wade Boykin, Ron Edmonds, Ann Brown, and others offered a whole range of ideas that were new to me; they made the notorious "Black–White difference" seem much more subtle and interesting than I had imagined.

Partly because of my move to Emory, that conference book did not appear until 1986. When it did appear, *The School Achievement of Minority Children: New Perspectives* had little impact. As a challenge to the establishment it was a flop—just another conference volume. To this day I have never met a White person who claims to have read it, although some of my Black friends say it was important to them. In the years after 1986 I continued to teach an undergraduate course on intelligence but saw no way to make a further contribution. Then, as Humphrey Bogart might have put it, destiny took a hand.

The American Psychological Association Task Force

In April 1995 I was serving the final year of a term on the Board of Scientific Affairs of the American Psychological Association (APA). Our spring meeting was dominated by talk about *The Bell Curve* (Herrnstein & Murray, 1994), which had appeared a few months earlier. Its pessimistic analysis of intelligence and group differences had ignited a sort of intellectual firestorm across the country. My own reaction was mixed. I did not think the facts justified Herrnstein and Murray's gloomy conclusions, but the vicious criticism directed at them did not seem justified either. Because these were clearly psychological questions, the media had been knocking on APA's door. Embarrassingly, there was no official report or position statement to give them. As the board discussed this situation, someone suggested setting up a task force to produce such a report now: not an item-by-item response to *The Bell Curve* but an authoritative review of the issues themselves. Who should lead such a task force? All of a sudden, everyone was looking at me.

In accepting this challenge, I was determined to present the scientific findings in an authoritative way while keeping the unresolved issues open and on the table. The composition of the task force itself would be crucial: Members would certainly represent different groups and views, but they all had to be sensible people committed to the scientific weighing of evidence. Here there could be no question of defying the establishment; we *were* the establishment. Happily, the members of the task force turned out to be realistic, open-minded, and industrious. In less than 2 years we were able to produce a unanimous report (Neisser, Boodoo, et al., 1996). I am very proud of it, especially because it drew sharp criticism from both left and right. We had evidently found the middle way.

The Rising Curve

One result of the APA report was that I became a de facto member of the intelligence establishment. Happily, that didn't last long. Working on the report had brought many findings to my attention, and one was particularly intriguing: the worldwide rise in mean IQ that is often called the *Flynn effect*. For nearly a century, some environmental factor or factors have been raising scores almost everywhere at a rate of about three IQ points per decade. On tests of abstract reasoning they are rising still faster, at six or seven points per decade. In that perspective, a 15-point difference such as the one between Black and White Americans no longer looms so large: The Black IQ mean today is about where the White mean was in 1950.

The size and systematicity of these gains was discovered by James A. Flynn, a likable American expatriate who lives in New Zealand. Neither a psychologist nor a statistician, Flynn is by profession a political philosopher. Talk about an underdog! It seemed to me that these gains deserved much more scientific (and public) notice than they had received. So it was like old times: I held a conference and assembled an edited volume. *The Rising Curve: Long-Term Gains in IQ and Related Measures* came out in 1998, and it still seems to be getting a reasonable amount of attention.

Roughly speaking, then, I have led the charge (against one establishment or another) about half a dozen times. Two of those efforts were notably successful: defining cognitive psychology in the 1960s and advocating the ecological study of memory in the 1980s. One characteristic of both cases was that I began the effort by preaching to the converted, that is, by appealing to a constituency that was already in place. Thus I was not only defying one crowd but giving voice to the aspirations of another. Where no such constituency existed, I have been less successful. The theory presented in *Cognition and Reality* found few takers, and my 1990s account of self-knowledge has had fewer still. Both theories have serious flaws, but so did *Cognitive Psychology*, and it went up like a rocket all the same.

To my mind, the lessons are clear. If you want your battle against the establishment to succeed, don't try to do it alone. Pick a fight where at least a small constituency is already on your side, ready to cheer you on and spread the good word. It's also wise to avoid negative rhetoric: Speak positively about your own cause instead of bashing the other guys. You'll get more listeners that way. To be sure, even both steps taken together do not guarantee success; there are no guarantees in this business. But so what? If you like a good fight, finding one is never hard. Enjoy it while it lasts! If you're the underdog, I'll be on your side.

References

Bahrick, L. E., Walker, A. S., & Neisser, U. (1981). Selective looking by infants. *Cognitive Psychology, 13,* 377–390.

Banaji, M. R., & Crowder, R. G. (1989). The bankruptcy of everyday memory. *American Psychologist, 44,* 1185–1193.

Bartlett, F. C. (1932). *Remembering.* Cambridge, England: Cambridge University Press.

Fodor, J., & Pylyshyn, Z. (1981). How direct is perception? Some reflections on Gibson's "Ecological approach." *Cognition, 9,* 139–196.

Gibson, J. J. (1979). *The ecological approach to visual perception.* Boston: Houghton-Mifflin.

Gleitman, H., Nachmias, J., & Neisser, U. (1954). The S–R reinforcement theory of extinction. *Psychological Review, 61,* 23–33.

Herrmann, D. J., & Neisser, U. (1978). An inventory of everyday memory experiences. In M. M. Gruneberg, P. M. Morris, & R. N. Sykes (Eds.), *Practical aspects of memory* (pp. 35–51). London: Academic Press.

Herrnstein, R. J., & Murray, C. (1994). *The bell curve: Intelligence and class structure in American life.* New York: Free Press.

Hirst, W., Spelke, E. S., Reaves, C. C., Caharack, G., & Neisser, U. (1980). Dividing attention without alternation or automaticity. *Journal of Experimental Psychology: General, 109,* 98–117.

Maslow, A. H. (1962). *Toward a psychology of being.* New York: Van Nostrand.

Neisser, U. (1954). An experimental distinction between perceptual process and verbal response. *Journal of Experimental Psychology, 47,* 399–402.

Neisser, U. (1964, June). Visual search. *Scientific American, 210,* 94–102.

Neisser, U. (1967). *Cognitive psychology.* New York: Appleton-Century-Crofts.

Neisser, U. (1976a). *Cognition and reality: Principles and implications of cognitive psychology.* San Francisco, CA: W. H. Freeman.

Neisser, U. (1976b). General, academic and artificial intelligence. In L. Resnick (Ed.), *The nature of intelligence* (pp. 135–144). Hillsdale, NJ: Erlbaum.

Neisser, U. (1978). Memory: What are the important questions? In M. M. Gruneberg, P. M. Morris, & R. N. Sykes (Eds.), *Practical aspects of memory* (pp. 3–24). London: Academic Press.

Neisser, U. (1979). The concept of intelligence. *Intelligence, 3,* 217–227.

Neisser, U. (1981). John Dean's memory: A case study. *Cognition, 9,* 1–22.

Neisser, U. (Ed.). (1982). *Memory observed: Remembering in natural contexts.* New York: W. H. Freeman.

Neisser, U. (Ed.). (1986). *The school achievement of minority children: New perspectives.* Hillsdale, NJ: Erlbaum.

Neisser, U. (Ed.). (1993). *The perceived self: Ecological and interpersonal sources of self-knowledge.* New York: Cambridge University Press.

Neisser, U. (Ed.). (1998). *The rising curve: Long-term gains in IQ and related measures.* Washington, DC: American Psychological Association.

Neisser, U., & Becklen, R. (1975). Selective looking: Attending to visually specified events. *Cognitive Psychology, 7,* 480–494.

Neisser, U., Boodoo, G., Bouchard, T. J., Boykin, A. W., Brady, N., Ceci, S. J., et al. (1996). Intelligence: Knowns and unknowns. *American Psychologist, 51,* 77–101.

Neisser, U., & Fivush, R. (Eds.). (1994). *The remembering self: Construction and accuracy in the self-narrative.* New York: Cambridge University Press.

Neisser, U., & Harsch, N. (1992). Phantom flashbulbs: False recollections of hearing the news about Challenger. In E. Winograd & U. Neisser (Eds.), *Affect and accuracy in recall: Studies of "flashbulb memories"* (pp. 9–31). New York: Cambridge University Press.

Neisser, U., & Hyman, I. E., Jr. (Eds.). (2000). *Memory observed* (2nd ed.). New York: Worth.

Neisser, U., & Jopling, D. (Eds.). (1997). *The conceptual self in context: Culture, experience, self-understanding.* New York: Cambridge University Press.

Neisser, U., Winograd, E., Bergman, E. T., Schreiber, C. A., Palmer, S. E., & Weldon, M. S. (1996). Remembering the earthquake: Direct experience vs. hearing the news. *Memory, 4,* 337–357.

Selfridge, O. G., & Neisser, U. (1960, August). Pattern recognition by machine. *Scientific American, 203,* 60–68.

When it comes to defying the establishment, Robert Perloff is all in favor, but he cautions against defiance for its own sake. Rather, he says, follow the advice Polonius gave to his son Laertes in that most famous of Shakespearean works, *Hamlet*: "This above all: to thine own self be true." Perloff emphasizes that the point is not to defy, the point is to stick to your guns, and if that means bucking the establishment, well so be it. He praises the power of failure as a much more powerful motivator than its antithesis, success. And Perloff should know—his self-titled failures have led to great success, including a term as president of the American Psychological Association and countless published papers.

Robert Perloff

Moving Forward by Sticking Your Neck Out | 11

This above all: to thine own self be true. And it must follow, as the night the day, Thou canst not then be false to any man.
—Shakespeare, *Hamlet*

Defiance of the crowd, constrained by caveats warning that at times defiance may not be warranted no matter how spiritedly defiant one feels, is an honorable and frequently efficacious strategy for audaciously breaking new ground in psychology, ground that needs to be broken. Opposing the mainstream and disassociating oneself from conformity are, in this chapter, supported metaphorically by celebrated essayists such as Henry David Thoreau, by public figures like James Madison, by notables in popular culture, and by the annals of great literature. Those who defy mainstream thinking boldly, and sometimes at great personal risk, rip asunder the chains of mediocrity and retrogression that block the pursuit of truth and the betterment of the human condition.

The person (identity unknown) who wisely exclaimed, "Watch the turtle: He only moves forward by sticking his neck out," said a mouthful or, rather, a "neckful." This anonymous sage's prescription for fueling individual and institutional progress is the keystone—even the very foundation—of this chapter. Paralleling the centrality of this aphorism on behalf of my plea for aggressive but responsible defiance in psychology is the compelling advocacy of nonconformity in the scientific enterprise persuasively articulated by the editor of this volume (Sternberg, 1998).

As several thumbnail case histories of my crowd defiance adventures are covered later in this chapter, I find it appropriate to first provide an account of the costs and benefits of crowd defiance, along with some do's and don'ts.

Simply put, one's integrity as a professional, a teacher, a scholar, a scientist, a practitioner, or a researcher demands that one venture forth aggressively in his or her professional enterprise with honesty and persistence. This is a general rule, applicable to situations in which one is not necessarily defying the crowd but is, rather, even in lockstep with the crowd. The essential point I wish to make here—and this deserves limitless emphasis—is that the key requirement is not defying the crowd; it is, rather, being honest, sticking to your guns, conveying and living by your thinking and your convictions, whether or not that thinking and those convictions resonate with the crowd or not. Isn't that the advice Shakespeare's Polonius gave his son, Laertes: "This above all: to thine own self be true. And it must follow, as the night the day, Thou canst not then be false to any man"?

So let's disabuse ourselves of the mistaken notion that honesty of convictions, being a gadfly, a whistle-blower, or whatever, is necessarily confined to defiance. Rather, these characteristics are the hallmark of honest people, people with integrity, people who respect themselves. You can utter your beliefs and convictions loud and clear even if the crowd is with you, and not only when the crowd is against you. Honesty, integrity, belief in your abilities to articulate your ideas and to rationally parse nature so as to make reasonable inferences and declarations, that's what is important, not that you're getting in somebody's face with your challenging or unpopular beliefs. Phrased a bit differently, you're not defying the crowd as a self-righteous sermonizer; rather, you are laying it on the line as you see it, whether or not your belief is in accord with mainstream thinking or at variance with it. When you have decided what your position on an issue is, you then move ahead, like a bull in a China shop, no matter the popularity of your position or its variance with the intellectual community you are addressing. You stick your chin out in the faces of foe and friend alike.

So the benefit of defying the crowd is that you are comfortable that you are behaving with integrity, with honesty. You're "doing your thing," which I suppose is a "cool" way of putting it. But the question arises, what are the costs of defying the crowd? The costs run the gamut from the unpleasantness of people disagreeing with you or walking to the other side of the street when they see you, to burning you at the stake. Realistically, of course, the costs are somewhere in between—not getting a promotion, not being hired, not getting a merit raise, not getting tenured, not having your article published. One must be willing to pay these prices, and one must have the self-confidence that sooner or later one will be vindicated, not vilified; rewarded, not punished; sought after, not avoided. Of course, honesty and scientific integrity demand that in the face of overwhelming evidence in some instances you must face up to the fact that you were wrong in the first place, that the basis for your defiance was flimsy, ill-founded.

Thinking back on my decades of crowd defiance, what would I have done differently? Frankly, not all that much, except that I would have been less confrontational, more civil, more polite, less offensively cocksure of myself. At the end of the day, however, I would not have changed one whit, one measly iota, of my persistence in pursuing what I thought or saw to be right.

The benefits of my defiance were twofold. First of all, the benefits arising from situations where my position prevailed, those benefits were enormous, simply enormous. Another benefit was looking at myself in the mirror and liking what I saw.

Advice I would give to those contemplating a life of defiance or episodes of occasional defiance: As I said above, be nice about it and, in addition, don't do it alone. Have an ally or two. The support of like-minded people comes in handy in many ways: It helps you share the burden of time and money and gives you greater credibility inasmuch as the fame and celebrity of others reinforces your ideas and enables skeptics to be more open-minded about the idea. Also, it is helpful to have someone to talk to after a long and arduous battle.

Another bit of advice is to drop it after encountering considerable and overwhelming opposition. Don't stick with your position "till death do us part." If the task is that formidable, you may be counseled to drop it and to start afresh with another crowd-defying scheme. You can't win 'em all. Life is full of tradeoffs. Drop a particular cause when it is intruding on your initiation of other causes.

Metaphors abound for sticking one's neck out, for defying the crowd and doing battle with the risk-aversive establishment. In his encomium to personal independence and civil disobedience, Henry David Thoreau (1854/1937) declared that "If a man does not keep pace with his companions, perhaps it is because he hears a different drummer. Let him step to the music which he hears, however measured or far away" (p. 290). James Madison, architect of the First Amendment (freedom of speech) of the Bill of Rights of the U.S. Constitution, reinforces and legitimizes confronting mainstream conformists, for defying them, for "getting in their face." Expressing yourself freely, outspokenly, is an honorable act of crowd defiance.

Douglas Martin's (2001) *New York Times* obituary of Frieda Pushnik reported how she "used being born without limbs to achieve a remunerative career by appearing in circus sideshows as the Armless and Legless Wonder" (p. 19). Thus armlessly and leglessly challenged, Pushnik defied mainstream people, those of us with arms and legs. She "ate it up and spat it out"!

Persistence in the Face of Failure

For many a year I have felt intuitively from a host of personal experiences that failure is a more powerful antecedent for modifying behavior so that it ultimately leads to success than success itself is efficacious in leading to continuous or expanded success. In other words, failure is a stronger precursor, a more likely guarantee, of reaching your goal than success itself is an agent of achieving the goal. (I suppose, come to think of it, that this is contrary to the Skinnerian notion that positive reinforcement is the magic wand for achieving a desired bit of behavior.) Equating failure with *bad* and success with *good*, you might say, then, that "bad is stronger than good," a proposition that I revisit later. First, I offer the following three personal examples, which illustrate how experiences of failure ultimately led to the achievement of success.

THE CASE OF TEMPLE UNIVERSITY

On my honorable discharge from the U.S. Army at the end of World War II, I entered (through the GI Bill of Rights) the undergraduate program at Temple University in Philadelphia in 1946, where I majored in psychology. Unaccustomed to objective, multiple-choice tests, I earned a disappointing grade of C on my first exam in the undergraduate psychology course. Here I was, a stalwart veteran of World War II, a Bronze Star Medal awardee to boot, devastated by such an inconsequential event as a C on an exam. I nearly wept. I was convinced that the multiple-choice format did me in, that in fact my knowledge of the material was not responsible for my mediocre grade, whereupon I foraged around to find out how better to take multiple-choice exams. Voila! It worked. On the second and subsequent exams in that course I received A's, crediting this improvement to lessons I learned on how to be test wise. I am convinced that had I received a B or an A on that very first exam, calling that a success, or something good, I wouldn't have been galvanized into learning how I could beat the system by becoming test savvy. And so that first failure stirred up a resolve to do something about it, to turn things around, which equipped me with knowledge that I used thenceforth in taking multiple-choice exams. Had I not been fired up by failure (the C grade), I wouldn't have been motivated to acquire test-taking smarts. So for me at least, this early failure was salutary, an episode in my early undergraduate years in which I am convinced that something bad (receiving a C) was stronger than would have been the success of something good (receiving a B or an A).

THE CASE OF THE AMERICAN BOARD OF EXAMINERS IN PROFESSIONAL PSYCHOLOGY (ABEPP)

Four or five years after I received my PhD at Ohio State University, I applied for what was then called an *industrial psychology* (and what is now known as *industrial/organizational psychology*) ABEPP. If one passed this examination, one was then entitled to call oneself a "Diplomate in Industrial Psychology." However, I failed the examination, and the feedback I received was that in the "practical field" phase of the examination, the diplomate who observed my field behavior said that I concentrated too much on objective indices of industrial behavior and gave short shrift to the practical dimensions characterizing success on the job as, say, a supervisor. Armed with this bit of intelligence, I revisited in earnest and in depth the environment in which employees, including supervisors, worked, giving me a fresh and more sophisticated orientation. Had I passed the exam the first time around, I would not have been as sensitive to the reasons why I had failed, and that insensitivity would certainly not have augured well as I continued on my journey as a career industrial psychologist. So, here again, thank goodness for failure, for something bad.

THE CASE OF THE PRESIDENCY OF THE AMERICAN PSYCHOLOGICAL ASSOCIATION

Here the situation is not as clear-cut as in the above Temple University and ABEPP narratives. In 1983, I ran for the presidency of the American Psychological Association (APA) and on the same ballot was the widely respected and universally known psychologist, Janet Taylor Spence. Janet won, and I came in second or third in a field of five nominees. So, in the throes of defeat I reorganized my campaign and developed a strategy—the details of which are not pertinent here—for better appealing to the electorate. That strategy, which was apparently successful since I won the next year's APA presidential race, helped me enormously in programs and initiatives I undertook during my term as president. So here is a third instance in which failure, something bad, helped me more markedly, I am convinced, than had something good (being elected when I first ran) graced my doorstep.

Bad Is Stronger Than Good

Earlier in this chapter I promised to elucidate further on the idea that bad is stronger than good. This extraordinarily and perhaps trailblazing seminal idea is articulated by Baumeister, Bratslavsky, Finkenauer, and Vohs (2001). In what I am convinced will become a heavily cited article, Baumeister et al. pointed out that bad events are more powerful than good events, that

> bad emotions, bad parents, and bad feedback have more impact than good ones, and bad information is processed more thoroughly than good . . . and taken together, [the] findings suggest that bad is stronger than good, as a general principle across a broad range of psychological phenomena. (p. 323)

The relevance of this principle, that bad trumps good in eliciting sought behavior, for this section of my chapter is that failure (something that is bad) can lead to success, where in the context of this chapter *success* is when one prevails having defied the crowd or the mainstream. The importance of this principle is that when one defies the crowd and swims upstream (opposing the mainstream, as it were), one will more often than not fail. After all, the mainstream does not welcome upstarts with open arms; rather, it seeks to put them in their place, and the lesson for upstarts is not to cry in their beer but, instead, to stay the course, endure the failure, and continue with their disagreeable (to the mainstream) agenda.

There is more than anecdotal evidence (Johnson, 2001) that "motivational speakers"—commanding thousands of dollars for lecturing at corporate seminars—are changing their tune from rah-rah rhetoric spinning success to enrapturing their audiences with talk about failure, with speech titles like "How I Learned From Big Mistakes," "My Darkest Hour," "Rebounds," "Mea Culpa," and "Rocky Balboa."

In his *Rotten Rejections: A Literary Companion*, Bernard (1990) chronicled the persistence in the face of failure by authors who would not take no for an answer and who, despite "rotten rejections," eventually prevailed and basked in the sunshine of literary success. Here are some examples of these publisher-defying heroes and heroines:

- *This Side of Paradise*, by F. Scott Fitzgerald, 1920: "It seems to us in short that this story does not culminate in anything" (p. 36).
- *The Diary of Anne Frank*, by Anne Frank, 1952: "The girl doesn't . . . have a special perception or feeling which would lift that book above the curiosity level" (p. 37).
- *Catch-22*, by Joseph Heller, 1961: "I haven't the foggiest idea about what the man is trying to say. . . . This constitutes a continual and unmitigated bore" (pp. 48–49).
- *Lady Chatterley's Lover*, by D. H. Lawrence, 1928: "For your own good do not publish this book" (p. 59).

- *The Spy Who Came in From the Cold*, John LeCarré, 1963; "You're welcome to LeCarré—he hasn't got any future" (p. 61).
- *Atlas Shrugged*, by Ayn Rand, 1957: "I regret to say that the book is unsaleable and unpublishable" (p. 79).
- *Man and Superman*, by George Bernard Shaw, 1905: "He will never be popular in the usual sense of the word, and perhaps scarcely remunerative" (p. 85).

The foregoing authors were not immobilized by failure, by having their books rejected. They were not intimidated by rejection, nor were they discouraged from continuing to believe in themselves and in the publication worthiness of their manuscripts. Their resolve and ultimate successes are a testimony to the following piece of advice:

> Experiment. Innovate responsibly. Take risks judiciously. Do not shrink from new ventures [or from crowd defiance] for fear of failure [or of rebuke]. No one is immune from adversity. The hallmark of a successful achieving person [aka a "crowd defier"] is his or her ability to snap back after misfortune and to benefit from and not be immobilized by failure [that is, not to be intimidated by the mainstream crowd]. (Perloff, 2001b, p. 4113)

There are times when even the most fearless rebels should be enjoined against defiance and carrying on like a bull in a china shop.

In *No Way: The Nature of the Impossible*, edited by P. J. Davis and D. Park (1987), compelling arguments are advanced for defying "the impossible" and "fighting city hall" or "banging your head against a stone wall":

- "To live at the boundary between the possible and the impossible, and to be aware of it, is to be truly alive" (p. xv).
- Time was when "people declared that a four-minute mile would never be run" (p. xvi).
- It was not supposed to be possible to climb Mt. Everest without carrying oxygen along, but Reinhold Messner did it (p. xvi).

Davis and Park, on the other hand,

> have come to see that a grasp of the world's meaning requires a sober view of its impossibilities. A sense of the impossible leads to coherence and sanity. . . . Some of the most important lessons of childhood are those that teach what not to expect of the world or of ourselves. . . . Thus, while respectfully dismissing the impossible, we seriously require that it be there, and from the tension of these opposing frames of mind arises a part of man's creative power. (p. 318)

Substantive Examples in Which Defiance Appears to Pay Off

The following personal experiences illustrate situations and issues that were pursued, successfully, through one degree or another of defiance.

PERFORMANCE EVALUATION

It is conventionally assumed that when a subordinate is evaluated by a supervisor, the subordinate should be forthright, but respectful, of course, in confronting the supervisor about a perceived error in attributing inadequate performance to the subordinate.

I have held that quarreling or disagreeing with the supervisor turns the supervisor off, as it were, and thus reinforces the supervisor's view of the contentious or questioning subordinate. When the subordinate listens intently to the supervisor, even when not necessarily agreeing with his or her assessments, the supervisor assumes a friendlier and more supportive posture. Thus, the supervisor is more inclined to work with this agreeable and perhaps even compliant subordinate, yielding opportunities to mentor and help the subordinate, the result of which may, in time, elevate the subordinate's performance, later evaluations, and rewards.

A Fortune-500 corporation in Pittsburgh sanctioned an experiment testing the hypothesis that subordinates who agree with, comply with, or reinforce their supervisors will, in the long run, perform better than quarreling evaluatees. The hypothesis was sustained, by and large, although the study has not yet been written up for publication (Schoenfeld, 1994).

PSYCHOLOGY AND OTHER DISCIPLINES

"Beyond Psychology: Literature and the Arts as Supplements for Understanding and Predicting Behavior" (Perloff, 2001a) opened up an entirely new and, in my judgment, improved and broadened realm for preparing job descriptions and for other research, conceptualizing, inquiring, and publishing in many other areas of psychology. I am thus proposing herein that psychologists partner with the aforementioned specialists in the arts and the humanities to enlighten the research and practice endeavors in which psychologists are engaged. In a word, behavior is entirely too varied and heterogeneous to confine behavioral inquiries to behavioral scientists alone. Poets, for example, see, hear, and smell things that psychologists are not especially prone to see, hear, and smell. It was a poet, William Blake, and not a psychologist with a PhD, who crafted the lines "To see a world in a grain of sand, and a heaven in a wild flower, hold infinity in the palm of your hand, and eternity in an hour" ("Auguries of Innocence," in Stevenson, 1988, p. 147).

Copies of an abstract of this article were sent to a score of eminent psychologists whose reactions, generally, mirrored that of Matarazzo: "This is brilliant! and also *refreshing* to read about a new and potentially more powerful paradigm" (personal correspondence, January 9, 2001).

Karl E. Scheibe, author of *The Drama of Everyday Life* (reviewed by Harré, 2000), argued for the use of "schemata through which the indeterminate world around us can be made to disclose some of its features" (Scheibe, cited in Harré, 2000, p. 1303). "To achieve this task for human life, Scheibe . . . describes and makes use of an image of the world as a dramatic performance" (p. 1303), called the *dramaturgical point of view*. Harré is not sanguine that Scheibe's defiant heresy will convince the crowd of mainstream psychologists whom, he fears, "are locked into their own little boxes. Like the apocryphal savants at Pisa who refused to look through Galileo's telescope, they will not read Scheibe's fascinating and subtle book. The loss is theirs" (pp. 1303–1304).

SELF-INTEREST

In my politically incorrect APA presidential address (Perloff, 1987), I sought to challenge mainstream psychologists who view with great disapproval the "greedy" and "materialistic" concept of self-interest. I reasoned that self-interest was getting a bum rap and deserved to be viewed more favorably as a psychological concept. Virtual vindication of my thesis appeared 11 years later insofar as my presidential address, originally published in the *American Psychologist*, was selected as one of the 50 articles published in that journal over the past 50 years that could be regarded as a classic in the evolution of psychology (Perloff, 1998).

CONVERSION THERAPY

In the mid-1990s, the APA's Board of Scientific Affairs (BSA) and other APA boards and committees were asked to comment on a resolution proposed by a group of gay and lesbian psychologists. The resolution declared that any psychotherapist member of APA who undertook a gay client seeking to convert to heterosexuality would be in violation of APA's ethical standards. The basis for this resolution was that the preponderance of studies showed that conversion therapy was generally unsuccessful and that to undertake on behalf of a client the goal of conversion was therefore unethical because of the certainty, as these gay and lesbian psychologists insisted, that such psychotherapy was doomed to failure; to undertake such an effort, they argued, would mislead the client into thinking that he or she might be successfully converted to a heterosexual orientation.

As a member of BSA I counseled BSA to oppose this resolution, for the following reasons:

1. It is accepted practice in psychotherapy to take seriously a client's wishes and not to decline to serve a client, out-of-hand, on the basis of political ideology.
2. To brand such psychotherapy unethical would in fact make it impossible for further research to be conducted in the area of conversion from a homosexual to a heterosexual orientation. Such a ban would clearly violate the scientific spirit.
3. Very often in psychotherapy a client's statement of his or her problem, expressed at the onset of therapy, turns out not to be the underlying problem identified by the psychotherapist. Thus, clients whose main issue was not actually one of sexual persuasion (though they described it as such) would have been deprived, under the proposed ban, of the opportunity to have a psychotherapist assist them in identifying and working on the underlying source of their psychological discomfort.

The BSA agreed with my reasoning; it decided to oppose the proposed resolution and asked me to represent BSA in that opposition.

> Ultimately, my opposition prevailed, and the proposed resolution was abandoned in its original form and reworded in such a way as to accommodate my objections. So here is a situation in which defying the crowd was successful.

THE RECOGNITION FUND OF THE AMERICAN PSYCHOLOGICAL FOUNDATION: HAILING THE "COMMON MAN"

For decades the American Psychological Foundation's (APF) only form of conferring awards to deserving psychologists was through its program of gold medal awards to those who had distinguished themselves in their respective endeavors or in the public interest. In the early 1990s I proposed that this program be augmented by, in effect, recognizing "the common man," that is, recognizing ordinary psychologists who were about to retire, for example, or honoring ordinary psychologists for good deeds but deeds not as stellar as the gold medal awards. Such recognitions would be manifest in terms of contributions to APF in the name of the psychologists so recognized. The Recognition Fund became an instant success, honoring hundreds of psychologists not for careers of great distinction but, rather, for more garden-variety deeds. The Recognition Fund is now a regular program within APF's array of awards, scholarships, and designated research funds.

Here is a case in which the mainstream was not defied per se, but a conventional practice was expanded, resulting in honoring scores and scores of men and women and in raising funds for APF to accomplish desirable research and scholarly objectives.

Another way of viewing the APF Recognition Fund is through a metaphor for the common man, celebrated in the following citations:

1. Aaron Copland's famed composition, "Fanfare for the Common Man" (1942), was designed patriotically to bolster American spirits during World War II.
2. E. Y. Harburg and Jay Gorney's tribute to common men thrust into poverty and helplessness by the Great Depression of the 1930s is their haunting song, "Brother, Can You Spare a Dime?" whose leading refrains are as follows:

   > Once I built a railroad,
   > Made it run,
   > Made it race against time.
   > Once I built a railroad,
   > Now it's done,
   > Brother, can you spare a dime?
   > Once I built a tower
   > To the sun,
   > Brick and rivet and lime.
   > Once I built a tower,
   > Now it's done,
   > Brother, can you spare a dime?[1] (cited in Gottlieb & Kimball, 2000, p. 259)

3. *Let Us Now Praise Famous Men* (C. J. Agree & W. Evans, 1941), the ground-breaking portrait of American poverty, was a title of irony, because the "famous men" were common men, forgotten men, penurious sharecroppers in Alabama in 1936, dealing with the plight of depression-era tenant farmers. (The Agee and Evans book title is from Ecclesiastics, chap. 44 of The Apocrypha: "Let us now praise famous men and our fathers that begat us.")
4. Andy Warhol's exaltation of the common man: "In the future everyone will be world-famous for fifteen minutes" (cited in Bartlett, 1992, p. 758).

---

[1]From "Brother Can You Spare a Dime?" by E. Y. Harburg and J. Gorney. Copyright 1932 (renewed) by Warner Brothers Inc. Reprinted with permission.

5. Walker (2000) characterized John Steinbeck's *Travels With Charley in Search of America* as a book "shot through with . . . *respect for the common man* [italics added]" (p. 205).

FALSE ACCUSATIONS

Two colleagues, one a political scientist and the other a psychologist, were victimized by accusations that, if sustained, would have resulted ultimately in disenfranchising them from their respective professions. In the case of the political scientist, I single-handedly championed his cause through a coherent, systematic, and step-by-step tedious strategy, showing the accusation to be ill grounded. The accusation was essentially withdrawn, thereby restoring the political scientist to a respected status in his profession. In the case of the psychologist, a handful of colleagues and I labored incessantly to show that the psychologist's behavior was misconstrued, eventually resulting in a restoration to the aggrieved psychologist of his rightful place of respect in his chosen field.

These two episodes illustrate how defiance or challenge to mainstream accusations can help to establish fairness and balance in situations that, if left undefied, could have produced irreparable harm in the lives of productive, contributing scholars and researchers.

Concluding Comments

Defying the crowd or mainstream thinking should be undertaken not to be defiant per se but, rather, to articulate in a principled manner one's beliefs and convictions about significant scientific and professional matters or issues. Thus, one's deep-felt convictions should be no less vigorously expressed when one is in lockstep with mainstream ideology than when one is alone or in the minority.

A frequent or an inescapable consequence of defiance is failure: failure to be heeded, failure to have one's propositions well regarded, failure to receive a grant, or failure to have an article or a book published. Failure, however, can be a powerful antecedent to success, an outcome of the declaration that bad is stronger than good. The examples I've provided in this chapter were intended to illustrate that failures might well be transformed into successes and that a by-product of defiance in many cases is its capacity to turn things around, to make a difference, to show that the popular or mainstream view is not necessarily the correct view.

But, most of all, the benefit of defiance is one of self-respect, that one stood up for one's beliefs, no matter how politically incorrect they might have appeared to the crowd or to mainstream players.

References

Agee, J., & Evans, W. (1941). *Let us now praise famous men*. New York: Houghton-Mifflin.

Bartlett, J. (1992). *Bartlett's familiar quotations* (16th ed.) (J. Kaplan, Ed.). New York: Little, Brown.

Baumeister, R. F., Bratslavsky, E., Finkenauer, C., & Vohs, K. D. (2001). Bad is stronger than good. *Review of General Psychology, 5*, 323–370.

Bernard, A. (Ed.). (1990). *Rotten rejections: A literary companion*. Wainscott, NY: Pushcart Press.

Copland, A. (1942). Fanfare for the common man. (Commissioned by the Cincinnati Symphony Orchestra and conducted by Eugene Goosens at the premiere in 1943, by Classical Compact Disc SBTC, 62401)

Davis, P., & Park, D. (Eds.). (1987). *No way: The nature of the impossible*. New York: W. H. Freeman.

Gottlieb, R., & Kimball, R. (Eds.). (2000). *Reading lyrics*. New York: Panther.

Harré, R. (2000, August 25). Acts of living. *Science, 289*, 1303–1304.

Johnson, R. (2001, January 16). For motivational speakers, nothing succeeds like failure. *Wall Street Journal*, p. B2.

Martin, D. (2001, January 7). Frieda Pushnik is dead at 77; turned her deformities into a career. *New York Times*, p. 19.

Perloff, R. (1987). Self-interest and personal responsibility redux. *American Psychologist, 42*, 3–11.

Perloff, R. (1998). Self-interest and personal responsibility redux. In J. M. Notterman (Ed.), *The evolution of American psychology: Fifty years of the* American Psychologist (pp. 657–676). Washington, DC: American Psychological Association.

Perloff, R. (2001a, July). *Beyond psychology: Literature and the arts as supplements for understanding and predicting behavior*. Paper presented at the meeting of the Interamerican Congress of Psychology, Santiago, Chile.

Perloff, R. (2001b). [Entry in *Who's who in America*.] New Providence, NJ: Marquis.

Schoenfeld, G. A. (1994). *Performance appraisal ratee training: A longitudinal field study experiment and call for a new paradigm*. Unpublished doctoral dissertation, University of Pittsburgh.

Sternberg, R. J. (1998). Costs and benefits of defying the crowd in science. *Intelligence, 26,* 209–215.

Stevenson, W. H. (Ed.). (1988). *William Blake: Selected poetry.* New York: Penguin Books.

Thoreau, H. D. (1937). *Walden and other writings of Henry David Thoreau.* New York: Modern Library. (Original work published 1854)

Walker, M. (2000). *America reborn: A twentieth century narrative in 26 lives.* New York: Knopf.

Determined not to follow the path he believed the majority of his peers to be on, Paul Rozin headed in different directions. Over the course of his 30-plus-year career, Rozin has studied a wide variety of subjects he felt the establishment had foolishly ignored, including the fascinating if oft-forgotten topic of food. His motivation to study, as he puts it, "robust phenomena that relate to real life," has often led to a lack of funding and numerous rejections by major journals, whose critiques of his work have often stated that the topic did not cover major conceptual issues in psychology—a comment Rozin thought ridiculous. In his ever-evolving attempts to reject fads and trends, he has succeeded in bringing much-needed attention to various areas that he hopes the next generation will continue to explore.

Paul Rozin

Fighting the Fads and Traveling in the Troughs: The Value (as Opposed to Growth) Approach to Inquiry

12

Traveling in the Troughs

Academic disciplines, and psychology in particular, are as subject to fads as the stock market and fashions. Such behavior seems to be a fundamental feature of humans as social organisms. I seem to be relatively immune to this tendency: I have always liked value over growth stocks, and I am unmoved by current clothing fashions. And so it goes with the opportunities for research in psychology. A landscape of research possibilities dominated by peaks of a high concentration of effort on a few "hot" topics necessarily leaves many troughs, and it is there that I travel.

I have experienced the fads of psychoanalysis and behaviorism and the current excitement about cognitive science, cognitive neuroscience, and to a lesser extent evolutionary and cultural psychology. Each of these movements had (has) much to recommend it, but was (is) simply oversold. Like technology stocks, each represents an important movement but less than it claimed. So my strategy for better and for worse has been to walk where few psychologists choose to tread. If one examines contemporary introductory psychology texts, one notes a striking disregard of the major activities of humans. Work, leisure, and food choice, which occupy the great majority of waking time, are barely mentioned. The material on eating is almost exclusively about how much is eaten, not the much richer topic of what is eaten and why. Religion is barely mentioned, nor is money. The 90-some percent of the world that is not White gets minimal attention. Some of the world's greatest problems, such as globalization, the decay of traditional values, and ethnopolitical conflict, receive minimal attention, although much psychology is involved in each case. Rather, the focus has been on fundamental processes such as perception, motivation, learning, and social cognition, which are considered to be relatively constant across cultures and domains of life. Insofar as these processes are domain independent, the strategy is likely to be adaptive. But there is now much evidence that domains such as language and eating have specific adaptations, sometimes called *dedicated modules*, that are shaped to their special needs.

The Trough Within the Trough: Studying the Food Hole

Psychology has obligingly provided me with many opportunities to work on important things that have been ignored. I have spent most of my effort on one ignored area, that being food, and in particular, food selection. The hole in our knowledge about food is illustrated by the lack of knowledge about the hole dedicated to eating, the mouth. This fascinating hole, sole route for ingestion, one of two routes for breathing, and the way that our thoughts, encompassed as speech, exit our body, is amazingly complex. Together with the tongue, teeth, and lips, the mouth is an exquisite exploratory organ, a food processor, a generator of speech, a sensory cornucopia for a wide variety of densely packed receptors. And yet, there is no systematic study of this aperture or, by the way, of any of the six other holes in the body. So the study of our holes is one of the holes in our field!

About 7 years ago, some students and I wrote an article on the holes in the body (called *apertures* in more polite discourse) and their psychological properties (Rozin, Nemeroff, Horowitz, Gordon, & Voet, 1995). Following on Sigmund Freud, the last psychologist to take apertures seriously, we wondered how people deal with these sites of ambivalence, where the inside of the body meets the outside world. Drawing on some empirical results, we noted, for example, that apertures are focal points of concern and that the breaching of an aperture is a matter deserving of attention. But this breaching has two separable aspects, which we called "intrusion sensitivity" and "contamination sensitivity." *Intrusion sensitivity* is about concerns for the breach of the aperture (e.g., the entry of something into the body through the aperture). *Contamination sensitivity* refers to concern about what is breaching the aperture rather than the breaching itself. Thus, the anus is very high on intrusion sensitivity (after all, it is an "out" hole), but it is not too particular about what goes in. The mouth on the other hand, is quite content with entries (fortunately for our nutritional survival), but it is very contamination sensitive; it cares deeply about what enters. Anyway, a number of points like this were made in this work, with evidence. The article was rejected by four psychology journals as not being relevant to major current issues in psychology. Finally, it saw print, with two very positive reviews, in David Funder's *Journal of Research in Personality*, which has been on a number of occasions a savior for me. I am grateful to Funder and his selected reviewers.

Opposing the Crowd in Studying the Regulation of Intake

Another recent example has to do with the regulation of food intake in humans. This is a very important topic, supported as a phenomenon by the stability of weight in nondieting human adults over months and years and by a large animal literature. The focus of this research has been almost entirely about the physiological events that trigger and terminate meals. More than 50 years of research on this topic has produced substantial progress, but our understanding is still very incomplete. The meal was selected as an obvious unit of regulation, even though data on animals and humans show that environmental influences can drastically change meal intake and meal patterns. For humans, it is surely true that the amount served and palatability of the food offered is more important for intake in any given meal than state of energy balance. Furthermore, for humans, it is clear that when and how much we eat are heavily influenced by cultural rules and our memory for our recent eating activities. To emphasize this, we recently showed that densely amnesic patients will eat three consecutive lunches, in the absence of the memory of having just eaten (Rozin, Dow, Moscovitch, & Rajaram, 1998). This study could have been done 50 or even 100 years ago; it wasn't done as a consequence of taking a reasonable hypothesis (and a preference for physiological and metabolic accounts of eating) to the point where almost no other alternatives were investigated.

The Plusses and Minuses of Traveling in the Troughs

One advantage to working in ignored areas is that there is relatively little literature to master, freeing one to read more widely. The marginal contribution to the problem at hand is high, working on a base of nothing or very little. And, at least to me, it is exciting to get a general lay of the land, to get a sense of what is going on.

But there are also problems with working in ignored areas. There is no ready-made community of scholars to exchange ideas with, publication is difficult (why work on a new topic when there are so many problems remaining with the old ones?), and it is very difficult to get grants (my record testifies to this). Work in new areas is exploratory, less likely to consist of elegantly controlled experiments, and more likely to be descriptive. That is not the type of research that psychology lionizes or that granting agencies support (Rozin, 2001).

My Style and Background

Writing this chapter has caused me to think for the first time about why I am the way I am, and at least I have enlightened myself about some commonalities in my academic trajectory. I have noticed a few patterns in my work: hopping from trough to trough, clearing the brush, getting an idea of how things work, and then moving along, experiencing the frustrations of publication and grant support with almost every new venture. Both of my parents were oddballs; my father was the only one of eight Russian-born siblings who very early in life staked out a career in the arts. He was a musician. My mother, one of seven siblings of Latvian descent, was the only one in her family with any dedicated interests in the arts; she was originally a dancer, and later, a painter and mask maker.

I was lucky enough to go to the University of Chicago under the Hutchins great book program and had to take 11 one-year courses, based on original source readings, covering the major domains of human knowledge. (Undergraduates today are distressed if they have to take more than 3 or 4 "general education" courses.) It was exhilarating. In keeping with my family's anomalous status, I entered Chicago in an unusual way, after only 2 years of high school. I couldn't find a major at Chicago, partly because I found lots of things interesting. I started as a physics major, switched to math, had a very brief flirtation with economics (one course convinced me not to go on), and then found biological psychology.

I went to graduate school in psychology at Harvard University, whose three leading lights were eminent psychologists whose work I had studied as an undergraduate: Edwin G. Boring, B. F. Skinner, and S. S. Stevens. In keeping with my anomalous streak, I decided to get a joint degree in biology and psychology (with part of the first 2 years of medical school thrown in) and ended up working with none of the great figures that attracted me there. My first research project, with fellow graduate student Jerry Hogan, under the general direction of Edwin Newman, was to see if an innate releaser (in this case, the display of a male Siamese fighting fish, *Betta splendens*), could serve as a reinforcer, thus bridging between two areas that weren't speaking to each other at the time: operant psychology and ethology. I ended up doing my dissertation with Jean Mayer, a professor of nutrition at the Harvard School of Public Health, having essentially completed an undergraduate biology degree while a graduate student. I loved biochemistry, zoology, and physiology and almost switched to biology. My PhD was jointly in biology and psychology.

My thesis settled into another trough. I was interested in the regulation of food intake, and at the time, a major theory was thermostatic: Intake was partly regulated by the temperature changes that occurred during eating, interacting with the temperature homeostatic system. I thought it would be interesting to see if the basic structure of regulation would be the same in an animal (in this case, the goldfish) that could not internally regulate its temperature. As it turned out, goldfish regulation looked pretty much like rat regulation. That got me interested in behavioral versus physiological temperature regulation, and I did an operant study showing that one could train a goldfish to press a lever to change the temperature in its tank (Rozin & Mayer, 1961). After this was learned, the fish maintained the temperature roughly constant (in the face of increasing temperature of their water if they did not respond). This showed that *poikilotherms* (cold-blooded animals), or at least this species, preferred a constant temperature; without internal means to maintain it, they could become effective homiotherms behaviorally.

Specific Hungers: A Puzzling and Ignored Phenomenon: The Description of Adaptive Specializations

I continued my research for 2 years as a postdoctoral fellow at the Harvard School of Public Health, with Mayer. I soon became interested in a different problem. Curt Richter had shown in the 1930s and 1940s that rats showed specific hungers: When deprived of a variety of nutrients, they would make selections to compensate for the deficiency. I was puzzled by this because I was convinced that this whole set of hungers was not innate; there were empirical indications of that, and it seemed unreasonable that rats would have systems dedicated to correcting some 40 possible nutritional deficiencies, most of which they would never experience in a lifetime. It seemed more likely that they had a general way of learning what was nutritive and what was harmful. But the problem was that the effects of foods occur hours after ingestion, and there were no learning principles that could be applied in that type of situation. I guessed that if I could figure this out, I would have to invoke something new in learning—I couldn't imagine what that might be, which made it all the more exciting.

It turns out I guessed correctly. This line of research, parallel with the work on poisoning by John Garcia and others, led to the isolation of a number of specific adaptations for learning about food: learning over long delays, the special link between chemical stimuli and gastrointestinal effects (which I called an *adaptive specialization* but which is now referred to as *belongingness* or *preparedness*, or more generally, *modularity*), the tendency to associate changes with novel events, and particular sampling strategies that allowed the rat to unconfound what would otherwise be multiple foods associated with a positive or negative event (Rozin & Kalat, 1971).

The beginnings of my work on specific hungers got me my first and only job, a faculty position at the University of Pennsylvania. I had two mentors for this early work. Mayer, whose broad knowledge of metabolism gave me a sense for how a richly complex system could work, left me alone to do my thing with appropriate encouragement. Richter became the exemplar for me. Richter, whom I have described as the "compleat psychobiologist" (Rozin, 1976a), and whom I consider the pre-eminent psychobiologist of the 20th century (Blass, 1976), was a "big-phenomenon" discoverer. In his long life, he uncovered an enormous array of important relationships and conducted pioneering work on biological rhythms, the establishment of specific hungers, and major insights into neural organization, domestication, and so on. Richter had a great nose for phenomena, and I wanted a nose like that.

My early work at Penn was primarily about specific hungers in animals, and in particular, the shaping of learning principles to adapt to particular types of ecological problems. Along with John Garcia, Sara Shettleworth, and Martin E. P. Seligman, and at about the same time, I wrote about adaptive specializations in learning with my student, James Kalat (Rozin & Kalat, 1971). Although the work I was doing was novel and challenging to learning theory, I met little resistance, unlike Garcia, who was doing similar work. I owe this in part to the vision of Eliot Stellar, editor at the time of the *Journal of Comparative and Physiological Psychology*, through whose good offices most of my work was published in a premier journal. My early success in this domain, and in getting grants, was never again to be duplicated.

Why Is Learning to Read So Hard? The Issue of Accessibility

I got sort of bored doing rat research, and I had a wonderful student, Kalat, who was going great guns on these problems, so I figured I would leave this area of research to him. I faced two choices, as I saw it. One was moving on to study a socially important human phenomenon (reading acquisition), which I could actually link to the adaptive learning ideas I had developed. The other was branching off in a totally different direction, much more biological, to try to understand how the incredibly complex nervous system was actually assembled in development. I was fascinated by research on the development of the eye by Roger Sperry and others and how the developing optic nerve managed to connect with the appropriate cells in the brain. I couldn't imagine how this could happen. So I went to The Wood's Hole Marine Biological Laboratory in my last year as an assistant professor and took a course in embryology. I loved it, but I also realized that the technical tools at hand, and the conceptual base for this type of research, did not make it as ready for attack as I had thought. I also realized that, as important as the problem was, the actual research wasn't as much fun to do as working with humans, watching them and talking to them. So I took a major turn in my life's research: from rat feeding to the acquisition of human reading.

This change was prompted by a feeling that I should relate my work to some kind of important real-world problem. My attention was captured at this time by an important real-world problem that was right at my doorstep. The children in the inner-city elementary schools around Penn were having great difficulty learning to read. But this seemed really odd to me, because they spoke English perfectly well and could learn to name objects in the world with ease. By any reasonable account, learning to speak is much harder than learning the mapping of 26 letters to sounds, which is then, of course, parasitic on the already learned speech. This linked to my rat work; it seemed to me that we were biologically adapted to learn language by the ear–mouth route, and work by scholars such as Eric Lenneberg already suggested this. On the other hand, learning to read the alphabet was a new event in our species, and it turns out it involved appreciating that the speech system segments the sound stream into phonemic units, units that have reality in the brain analysis of speech but are not directly accessible to consciousness (e.g., *bat* has three sounds to alphabetic readers, but one sound to anyone else).

This led to a line of research, much of it in collaboration with Lila Gleitman, on learning to read (e.g., Gleitman & Rozin, 1973; Rozin & Gleitman, 1977). We showed that much of the problem in reading has to do with phonemic segmentation. One study showed that children who did not learn to read the alphabet in over a year of elementary school could learn to read Chinese, which does not require phonemic segmentation, in a few hours. This study (Rozin, Poritsky, & Sotsky, 1971) was published in *Science*, and it is perhaps the most widely cited article I ever wrote, in China as well as in the United States. It was the last article I succeeded in getting published in *Science*. It formed part of the foundation for my idea of accessibility: that one aspect of learning, another novel type of learning, is gaining access in a new domain to a system already in the head in a more dedicated circuit (Rozin, 1976b).

Gleitman and I had a lot of trouble publishing our reading work, because it took a new approach. And the research was tiring, because it was done in classrooms and involved coordinating students, parents, teachers, principals, and school boards. It became tedious, and my eye was caught by another set of interesting phenomena, the now familiar fascinating patterns of defect that one sees after brain damage in humans. I had studied neurology at Harvard Medical School while in graduate school, and with this background I launched into studies of what we now call *cognitive neuroscience*, at a time when it had not yet become a discipline. I did a few interesting studies on amnesia and wrote a review article (Rozin, 1976c), but I experienced frustrations in getting access to patients. And I had a lot of difficulty in publishing my one empirical article on memory and amnesia (Diamond & Rozin, 1984), even though it has turned out to be a major source of the idea of priming of entities in the brain.

Back to Food, but This Time in Humans: Cuisine, Flavoring, and the Acquisition of Likes

At about this time, my mind was captured by another interesting phenomenon, one that came right out of my home. My wife at that time,

Elisabeth Rozin, was writing a cookbook (*The Flavor Principle Cookbook*, 1973), in which she noted that most of the world's cuisines have a characteristic set of flavorings that they put on all of their foods. I thought this interesting and odd and worthy of study. It brought me back to my original interests in food, now in a human frame, an interest that I have maintained to this day.

I was particularly attracted by an anomalous feature of human flavor preferences. In most cultures, a strong preference is developed for some innately unpalatable foods. Common examples are coffee, tobacco, very sour foods, or irritant spices, like chili pepper. I thought this odd and noted that we had no models to explain it. By this time, I was learning about myself, that I liked to study problems for which my knowledge of psychology and biology did not provide a reasonable model. When I had a model in mind, one that I thought was probably on the mark, I sort of lost interest in the problem. So I set out to do a study of one innately unpalatable substance, chili pepper, probably the most widely used spice in the world. I picked it, in part, because unlike some of the other innately unpalatable substances (e.g., coffee, tobacco, alcohol), it was not addictive and hence perhaps less complicated.

So I went to Mexico, where chili pepper comes from, to find out how it was that all these little Mexican kids came to like this unpleasant burn in their mouths (something that I had great difficulty accomplishing for myself). This led to a line of research on the acquisition of preferences, focusing on chili pepper. I'm happy with what I found (Rozin, 1990), although my main contribution was only to highlight an important problem in the study of preferences and to lay out some possible solutions. (One of them, "benign masochism," has particular appeal to me.) My attention was subsequently captured by a related big gap in my new area: human food selection. Well, the whole area is a big area of ignorance through inattention, but even in this area, there are troughs within troughs.

Getting a sense for how innately unpalatable substances come to be preferred is really a subcase of the general problem about how any object or entity becomes liked. And in the studies on chili pepper, I came to realize that we could not adequately account for preferences, even though they are a very salient part of life and a ground-rock base for the discipline of economics. Why do some people like lima beans while others do not? It seemed reasonable that parental influence (preferences) would be important, both because of shared genes and control of early environment. So I collected some data on this in 1986, and again more systematically in 1991, and found to my astonishment that parent–child correlations of preferences were extremely low, in the range of .15! The methodology used was valid, because in the same sample, we obtained correlations in the .3 to .6 range for parent–child resemblance in values. I called this the *family paradox*, and it is still a paradox. I couldn't publish this article in a mainline developmental journal, but it eventually appeared in *Appetite*, where unfortunately, it remained unread by all but food psychologists (Rozin, 1991).

Around this same time, in the 1980s, I became engaged by another puzzling feature of preferences. Some of our preferences are based on liking, whereas others are based on more instrumental motives, such as becoming healthier. I realized that we didn't really know how things came to be liked or disliked. I worked on this problem with my student, Marcia Pelchat, with our focus on taste aversion learning in humans and rats. Following on work by others, we noted and documented that nausea plays a special role in creating dislikes. A detailed survey of human participants indicated that nausea following ingestion of a food tended to produce a subsequent dislike for the food, whereas other negative events, like hives or respiratory distress, tended to produce an avoidance but not a dislike (Pelchat & Rozin, 1982). We were able to extend this finding to rats, using Grill and Norgren's measures of facial expression in rats (Pelchat, Grill, Rozin, & Jacobs, 1983).

Finding Flavor Between Taste and Smell

Some time during the same period, I was attracted to another gap, this one in the study of sensation. It is well known in sensation that almost all the work is on vision and hearing and that the chemical senses, of special importance to eating, are rather ignored. But even within the chemical senses, there is a gaping gap within the gap. With respect to food, the predominant sensation is flavor, and this is an integrated mouth sense, combining texture, taste, and odor into what is perceived as an indivisible whole. So the question is, how are mouth objects constructed? We are back to the ignored mouth, again. Flavor is perhaps the only case in which humans misattribute which sensory system is being stimulated, referring the principal component of flavor, olfaction, to the mouth. Workers in this field generally study either taste or smell, when in fact one of the most important things in the field is the combination of taste and smell. In 1982, I wrote an article calling attention to the problem of flavor and arguing that in the presence of oral stimulation, olfactory input was referred to the *mouth*. This referral is so complete that it is undetectable, such that an odor (e.g., fish or cheese) could be unpleasant to the nose but pleasant when that same odor stimulated the same olfactory mucosa through the mouth (Rozin, 1982). The problem remains.

Craving: Very Common but Rarely Studied

In the later 1980s, I received a rash of telephone calls from the press asking me what I knew about craving. Craving is of great popular interest, which stimulated these reporters. I told them that I knew almost nothing about craving, and neither did anyone else, so far as I knew. Then I thought that was strange and launched some research on chocolate craving, simply because this seemed to be the most common craving. The nicest outcome of this was Willa Michener's doctoral thesis, in which we demonstrated that whatever prompts chocolate craving is satisfied by the sensory experience of chocolate and not the pharmacological effects (which are many) of chocolate (Michener & Rozin, 1994). We sent this set of definitive results off to a major journal, and it was rejected on the grounds that it "did not address a fundamental conceptual issue in psychology." I guess not; we had just found something important and somewhat counterintuitive (judging by speculations prior to our article) about something that happens to more than 30% of Americans!

Disgust, the Ignored Emotion

Somewhat parallel, but lagging behind the work on chili pepper, another very robust phenomenon came to my attention. Rejection of foods on the grounds of disgust seemed to be the strongest food reaction. It was odd because many of the disgusting foods, like worms, eyeballs, and insects, were quite nutritive (high in micronutrients, protein, and fat). Meat-eating nonhuman animals did not seem put off by these creatures, and neither did human infants. This anomaly gave rise to perhaps my major line of research for the past 15 years (Rozin & Fallon, 1987; Rozin, Haidt, & McCauley, 1993). The work on disgust took two directions. On the one hand, there was the problem of establishing the relation between disgust as a food-related emotion (so clear in the face and in nausea, the physiological sign of disgust) and the fact that most of the things that people find disgusting are not foods: They are things like filth, death, body deformities, disliked other people, and a variety of moral violations. This broad domain of disgust led to research on the expansion of the disgust elicitors and meanings, whereas the expressions of disgust (facial, nausea, the feeling of offense) remained rather constant. This led to the ideas, developed with April Fallon, that a broader category of disgust meanings had to do with rejection of reminders of our animal nature, particularly death (Rozin & Fallon, 1987).

Later development of these ideas with Jon Haidt and Clark Mc-Cauley led to a full theory of the cultural evolution of disgust, from "get this out of my mouth" to "get this out of my soul," the disgust of moral violations (Rozin et al., 1993). The link to morality was completed in a sense with our claim that one of the world's basic moral systems, divinity (as described by Richard Shweder, 1991) seemed to have disgust as its emotional expression (Rozin, Lowery, Imada, & Haidt, 1999), in what we described as the CAD theory: the three emotions of **c**ontempt, **a**nger, and **d**isgust link respectively to each of Shweder's three moral systems: **c**ommunity, **a**utonomy, and **d**ivinity. This entire turn to disgust and morality was actually initiated by Haidt, who as a graduate student studied why and when people think that things like eating dog meat are immoral (Haidt, Koller, & Dias, 1993). The total account we have proposed relies on *preadaptation*: the use of something that evolved for one purpose (in this case, oral rejection) for other purposes, general offense. This becomes a major means of socialization; by making something disgusting, it becomes an internalized rejection.

It is curious that although disgust is listed as one of the five to seven "basic" emotions in almost all psychology texts, until recently (and unlike the other basic emotions) it wasn't even studied. This is particularly odd because (a) it is particularly easy to elicit disgust in ecologically valid and ethical ways in the laboratory, and (b) in the long and frustrating search for physiological signatures of each emotion, disgust was not considered even though it has the most distinct physiological sign (nausea). Maybe disgust was too disgusting to study.

From Disgust to Contagion and Magical Thinking

A second aspect of disgust that was very striking from the first work with Fallon (Rozin & Fallon, 1987) was the link to the magical principles of contagion and similarity. If something disgusting touches something else, it renders it inedible (contagion), and something that looks disgusting but is known to not be composed of what it looks like is still found offensive (similarity). Carol Nemeroff and I, picking up on the turn-of-the-century descriptions of these laws by three famous anthropologists (Edwin Tylor, James Frazer, and Marcel Mauss), showed how powerful these principles were in educated westerners and linked these findings to issues in emotion and decision making and in attitudes toward AIDS (Rozin, Millman, & Nemeroff, 1986; Rozin & Nemeroff, 1990).

Opening up to Culture and Social Structure

My first year at the Center for the Study of Behavioral Sciences at Stanford University really broadened my view. I had a lot of contact with Richard Shweder, who reinforced my nascent interest in other cultures, something that both my interest in cuisine and disgust had prepared me for. As a result of this contact, I sort of evolved into a cultural psychologist, and through Shweder's fieldwork connections in India, I spent a month living and poking around in a small city there. This experience really turned my head around. I realized how different psychology would be if it had started in India. Our predominance of free choice was largely replaced by tradition, and disgust was a powerful moral emotion; social structure, as manifested in the caste system, was a powerful force. I realized that although it was a great advance that social psychology was opening itself up to other cultures, this movement had its own blinders, being rather indifferent to historical changes or social structure. My colleague at Penn, Alan Fiske, and his brilliant book, *Structures of Social Life* (1991), gave me new direction. Among other things, I recently submitted an article for publication (Rozin, 2002) in which I argued that generational differences in the United States are substantial and that our grandparents were a lot more like Asian Indians than we are. In that same article, I noted that in our understandable emphasis on how cultures shape minds, we have neglected the great importance of the physical environments that cultures have created. My work in France suggests that many differences between American and French life, in food and related domains, have to do with the structure of the physical artifacts that culture creates. If snack food is constantly available, we snack; if smaller portions of food are served, we eat less; if it is hard or expensive to park or drive, we walk more.

Moralization

The concerns about morality and disgust led to a line of research on the process of moralization: how preferences turn into values. I was impressed with how smoking had become an essentially immoral act in the United States and thought I saw some of the same thing happening to meat eating in some vegetarians and to fat for many Americans. The link to disgust was clear; the immorality of smoking is associated with finding ashes, smoking, and the odor of tobacco disgusting (Rozin, 1997). Along the same lines, we showed that moral vegetarians tended to find meat disgusting, whereas health vegetarians did not (Rozin, Markwith, & Stoess, 1997).

New Interests

I have developed five newer interests in the last 5 years or so. Four of them derive from the study of food that I have discussed, and the other is brand new. One of the food lines has to do with the American obsession with diet and health. I became interested in why many upper-middle-class Americans think every bite of food is potentially carcinogenic, artery-clogging, and obesity producing. This led me to look at how food risks are presented to Americans by the medical research complex and the media and into the sociology of modern grant-driven medicine.

Second, I noted much less apparent concern with diet and health in France (although mad cow disease is changing that). I love food, and it seemed to me we had something to learn from the French, who are at least as healthy as Americans but much less ambivalent about food, even though they eat a diet that is higher in animal fat than Americans. Some recent research in collaboration with French food sociologist Claude Fischler (Rozin, Fischler, Imada, Sarubin, & Wrzesniewski, 1999) documented these differences in attitudes. (We had trouble publishing this article as well; it was rejected by a major medical and major psychological journal but was eventually published in *Appetite*.) We are continuing this research, now adding analysis of cookbooks and magazines, tallying types and sizes of food portions available in stores and restaurants, and noting people's behavior on the streets (e.g., snacking). One big thing is obvious: The French eat less, and this is at least in part because they are served less (Rozin, 1998, 1999).

This developing line of research is modeled on the superb, multi-method analysis by Nisbett and Cohen (1996) in *Culture of Honor*. We plan to do an analysis of this type on the differences between the French and Americans with respect to food and pleasure. Once again, as with the chocolate craving article, the crabbiness of editors and reviewers contrasted with the great interest in this work in people in general and in the press. I didn't try to get federal grant support for this work, because it runs counter to the current thrust on changing diet (primarily, reducing fat intake) to improve health that is dominant in the American medical establishment and the National Institutes of Health.

In both my work on food preferences and on disgust and contagion, I noticed a big asymmetry between positive and negative events. Negative events seemed to be more potent (negative potency) and to overwhelm positive events when the two combined (negativity dominance). This led me (later on in collaboration with Edward Royzman) to develop the general principle of negativity bias. This wasn't the first time this principle was enunciated, but our original contribution was to subsume a great many phenomena from diverse areas of psychology under this principle and to highlight the principle of negativity dominance. This is most clearly illustrated by contagion, where brief contact of a positive entity by a negative one ruins the positive one, whereas brief contact of something negative by a positive entity does nothing to improve the negative entity (Rozin & Royzman, 2001).

Another line of current research also derives from the pleasures of eating and builds on the pioneering work of Daniel Kahneman and his collaborators on the nature of pleasure (particularly the distinctions among experienced, anticipated, and remembered pleasure). We are now looking at how people anticipate, experience, and remember meals (and music, incidentally).

In the late 1990s, Martin Seligman, president of the American Psychological Association, and Peter Suedfeld, president of the Canadian Psychological Association, concluded that psychology had contributed rather little to what they saw as perhaps the greatest challenge to the success of our species: ethnopolitical conflict. They discovered another trough. They proposed a systematic approach to ethnopolitical conflict from the viewpoint of psychology, exchanging with and learning from the disciplines that have already made major efforts in this direction (history, sociology, anthropology, political science). It turned out (for complicated reasons not resulting from Seligman's own affiliation at Penn) that Penn seemed like the natural place to start it. (Criteria for selection of a place included being a distinguished private university and having a clinical program.) Seligman presented the possibility to my department, which had no one with direct interest in the area. With my cultural interests, I seemed "relevant," and I offered to get this going. I quickly allied with Clark McCauley, my colleague at Bryn Mawr, whose interests were more aligned with ethnopolitical conflict (working on stereotypes, terrorism, identification), and together we built what is now the thriving Solomon Asch Center for Study of Ethnopolitical Conflict. It now has its own space and five postdoctoral fellows, and it is developing important lines of research on identification and forgiveness, among other things. We hope our clinical folk will take a major interest in the problems of some 40 million refugees and internally displaced persons around the world. This is the first truly interdisciplinary venture I have been involved in, with substantial input from political science, anthropology, history, and sociology. It is exhilarating to be working on such an important problem, with so much to be found out. My own contribution is partly administrative, but I have developed some work on identification in collaboration with McCauley and on forgiveness.

Summing Up: Mentors, Students, Styles, and Options for Inquirers

This has been a rather long story of my adventures in psychology. If I had to summarize the style, it is working where no one else does, on robust phenomena that relate to real life. It is never method driven, and I prefer to take multiple perspectives, with interest in behavioral, physiological, and mental levels of function and in immediate causes, adaptive values, evolution, and development. I have dabbled at all levels when my curiosity was piqued, a combination of something relevant and puzzling, and some sense that the problem could be studied. (I never worked on dreams.)

Research can be intellectually interesting, it can be important, and it can be fun to do. I end up, I suppose, not having been the master of anything but having called the attention of psychologists to a number of important things and setting out the outlines of research on them. I have been fortunate to get in early on a number of things that later became fads: biological boundaries of learning and modularity, cognitive neuroscience, evolutionary psychology (Rozin & Schull, 1988), and cultural psychology, among others. As I said at the beginning, I like value stocks, and I sell them after they become popular (if they do).

It would be a gross exercise of the fundamental attribution error to think I had done what I did without help. I got a great, broad undergraduate education and was not impeded when I combined psychology, biology, and some medical school for my graduate degree. I had the good fortune to happen on Richter as a model for my work (Blass, 1976). I was fortunate to join a wonderful department at Penn, which encouraged breadth and historical perspective, gave me great stimulation, and didn't care (and still doesn't) that I'm not good at getting grants. And, later in my academic life, I had the wonderful opportunity of getting to know Solomon Asch and learning from him about the importance of context, of the broad view, of a balanced view of human nature. Asch (1952/1987) saw the good things in the various fads of psychology and learned from them. I have tried to imitate him and have particular pleasure that our new center for studying ethnopolitical conflict bears his name. Asch was an optimist about the human condition, and our center bears out this trait.

I have also had wonderful students. Some, like Bennett Galef, James McClelland, Morris Moscovitch, and Jonathan Schull, I hardly collaborated with but just had the pleasure to watch and help them grow. Others, including Norman Adler, Jim Kalat, Jon Haidt, Carol Nemeroff, April Fallon, Marci Pelchat, and Adam Cohen, have been more like collaborators. I have learned from all of them. All through my career, I have been blessed with large numbers of excellent undergraduate research students; I have probably made more contributions in collaboration with them than with graduate students.

If you are going to explore new terrain, you have to be willing to be an outsider and willing to find yourself on the wrong track. I've never thought I could explain more than 20% of the variance and feel lucky if I can do that. It is and has been great fun; my main complaint about the trouble I have had publishing my work is that I have had to waste a lot of time rewriting and resubmitting articles, often without any improvement in them. But I must say that I'm pleased that I made the contribution I did with minimal grant support. And along the way, I have received some valuable financial support, from foundations like Whitehall, Mellon, MacArthur, and my own university, and from two wonderful years at the Center for Advanced Study in the Behavioral Sciences at Stanford. I guess my current view on one good way to do science is summarized in my recent article on what's wrong with social psychology (Rozin, 2001), dedicated to Solomon Asch. I have no problem with the current methodologies favored in social psychology (the elegant laboratory experiment) or the current focal topics (such as attribution theory and stereotypes); I just think we are overinvesting in them. It seems as though it is always the same story.

I believe the same faddishness we see in the selection of problems appears in the selection of methodologies. Breakthrough methodologies appropriately produce a burst of interest and applications. But it is my sense that they are often the subject of overinvestment. One general problem I see is that psychology is anxious to adopt the trappings of science, to establish itself among the natural sciences. Psychologists do not adequately consider whether the problem of interest is ready for precise, laboratory study, that is, whether its validity, generality, and contextual support is well enough understood to justify experimentation. Experimentation is a great tool, but usually only after one knows the lay of the land. Psychologists would be surprised to realize how much of modern biology is not "experimental" (in the sense of running controls) but rather descriptive, and how much is motivated by curiosity rather than explicit models (see Rozin, 2001, for documentation of these points). In short, I have taken very much to heart Asch's (1952) point:

> In their anxiety to be scientific, students of psychology have often imitated the latest forms of sciences with a long history, while ignoring the steps these sciences took when they were young. They have, for example, striven to emulate the quantitative exactness of natural sciences without asking whether their own subject matter is always ripe for such treatment, failing to realize that one does not advance time by moving the hands of the clock. Because physicists cannot speak with stars or electric currents, psychologists have often been hesitant to speak to their human subjects. (pp. xiv–xv)

I have retrospectively discovered two themes that seem to organize much of what I have done. One is the problem of internalization. Much of my work has had to do with the origin of preferences. My work on chili pepper, food preferences, and acquisition of liking for foods, in general, and the family paradox falls in this domain. But so does the work on disgust, because the acquisition of disgust leads to a strong dislike and constitutes a major mechanism in socialization. The acquisition of moral value (moralization) changes the preference structure and often invokes, in negative cases, the emotion of disgust. And the general problem that arises from all of this, related to positive psychology, is the extent to which we like what we would like to like, and we like what we value. In this regard, a remarkable undergraduate thesis under my direction by Amy Wrzesniewski (Wrzesniewski, McCauley, Rozin, & Schwartz, 1997) addressed the question of when and how work, our major waking activity, comes to be internalized and valued, that is, how callings develop. Callings can develop for some people in any occupation; this is, as I now see it, a natural extension of my long-standing interest in preference and value, an interest that has led to a first draft of a book on this subject with Clark McCauley and Barry Schwartz.

The second general theme has to do with the process of change. Early in my career (Rozin, 1976b), I suggested the notion of accessibility to describe the situation in which an evolved adaptation or module, limited to particular inputs and outputs, gets coopted in development and spreads to wider and wider domains. The Piagetian concept of *decalage* captures this fact, and it was best illustrated in my research by the linkage of the phonological segmentation "module" to the process of reading in alphabetic systems. Much later on, in work on disgust, I came to the view that preadaptation, the parallel mechanism in biological evolution to access in development, was a major aspect of cultural evolution. This is our basic model of the cultural evolution of disgust, from a food rejection system to a carrier of a wide range of social values.

So I now see the basic process of preadaptation (using something evolved for one purpose for another purpose) as a substantial force in biological and cultural evolution and in development.

So even my travels in troughs has led to some kind of synthesis. And it is even getting easier to publish things, now that I am in my 60s. Overall, it has been and continues to be an engaging venture, and I would do it over rather than move with the pack. I appreciate that I have never had to really worry that someone else was doing what I was doing and might publish before me. It has been easy for me to talk openly about my ideas and studies, even before I start on them. No one is interested in rushing into the problems I work on. I couldn't function in modern molecular biology.

I have no particular advice to offer young scholars. A lot depends on temperament. Some people do physics instead of psychology because they can't tolerate the complexity of psychological phenomena and favor formalization. Others find psychology too scientific. Within psychology, some like to drill consistently and deeply at one point in the landscape, often taking a lifetime elegant path to a detailed and enlightening account of some phenomena. A minority of others, like me, prefer to skip along the landscape, stopping in this trough or that. Many of the psychologists I admire most, Robert Rescorla, for example, have brilliantly explored a domain that they laid out broadly in graduate school. Others, more my style, like Daniel Kahneman and Richard Nisbett, have moved from problem to problem throughout their careers. There isn't a right answer or a right solution for everyone. It depends on tolerance for ambiguity, devotion to elegance, desire to be in a competitive environment, and the types of rewards one hopes for in one's work. I feel I have found out more on my path than I would have had I followed the fads, and the price I paid in publication problems and not getting grants was easily worth it.

References

Asch, S. E. (1987). *Social psychology.* New York: Oxford University Press. (Original work published 1952)

Blass, E. (Ed.). (1976). *The psychobiology of Curt Richter.* Baltimore: York.

Diamond, R. J., & Rozin, P. (1984). Activation of existing memories in anterograde amnesia. *Journal of Abnormal Psychology, 93,* 98–105.

Fiske, A. (1991). *Structures of social life.* New York: Free Press.

Gleitman, L. R., & Rozin, P. (1973). Teaching reading by use of a syllabary. *Reading Research Quarterly, 8,* 447–483.

Haidt, J., Koller, S., & Dias, M. (1993). Affect, culture, and morality, or is it wrong to eat your dog? *Journal of Personality and Social Psychology, 65*, 613–628.

Michener, W. A., & Rozin, P. (1994). Pharmacological vs. sensory factors in the satiation of chocolate craving. *Physiology & Behavior, 56*, 419–422.

Nisbett, R. E., & Cohen, D. (1996). *Culture of honor. The psychology of violence in the South*. Boulder, CO: Westview Press.

Pelchat, M. L., Grill, H. J., Rozin, P., & Jacobs, J. (1983). Quality of acquired response to taste depends on type of associated discomfort. *Journal of Comparative Psychology, 97*, 140–153.

Pelchat, M. L., & Rozin, P. (1982). The special role of nausea in the acquisition of food dislikes by humans. *Appetite, 3*, 341–351.

Rozin, E. (1973). *The flavor principle cookbook*. New York: Hawthorn.

Rozin, P. (1976a). Curt Richter: The compleat psychobiologist. In E. Blass (Ed.), *The psychobiology of Curt Richter* (pp. *xv–xxviii*). Baltimore: York.

Rozin, P. (1976b). The evolution of intelligence and access to the cognitive unconscious. In J. A. Sprague & A. N. Epstein (Eds.), *Progress in psychobiology and physiological psychology* (Vol. 6, pp. 245–280). New York: Academic Press.

Rozin, P. (1976c). The psychobiological approach to human memory. In M. R. Rosenzweig & E. L. Bennett (Eds.), *Neural mechanisms of learning and memory* (pp. 3–46). Cambridge, MA: MIT Press.

Rozin, P. (1982). "Taste–smell confusions" and the duality of the olfactory sense. *Perception and Psychophysics, 31*, 397–401.

Rozin, P. (1990). Getting to like the burn of chili pepper: Biological, psychological and cultural perspectives. In B. G. Green, J. R. Mason, & M. R. Kare (Eds.), *Chemical senses: Vol. 2. Irritation* (pp. 231–269). New York: Marcel Dekker.

Rozin, P. (1991). Family resemblance in food and other domains: The family paradox and the role of parental congruence. *Appetite, 16*, 93–102.

Rozin, P. (1997). Moralization. In A. Brandt & P. Rozin (Eds.), *Morality and health* (pp. 379–401). New York: Routledge.

Rozin, P. (1998). *Towards a psychology of food choice* [Danone Chair Monograph]. Brussels, Belgium: Institut Danone.

Rozin, P. (1999). Food is fundamental, fun, frightening, and far-reaching. *Social Research, 66*, 9–30.

Rozin, P. (2001). Social psychology and science: Some lessons from Solomon Asch. *Personality and Social Psychology Review, 5*, 2–14.

Rozin, P. (2002). *Five potential principles for relating cultural differences to individual differences*. Manuscript submitted for publication.

Rozin, P., Dow, S., Moscovitch, M., & Rajaram, S. (1998). The role of memory for recent eating experiences in onset and cessation of meals. Evidence from the amnesic syndrome. *Psychological Science, 9,* 392–396.

Rozin, P., & Fallon, A. E. (1987). A perspective on disgust. *Psychological Review, 94,* 23–41.

Rozin, P., Fischler, C., Imada, S., Sarubin, A., & Wrzesniewski, A. (1999). Attitudes to food and the role of food in life: Comparisons of Flemish Belgium, France, Japan and the United States. *Appetite, 33,* 163–180.

Rozin, P., & Gleitman, L. R. (1977). The structure and acquisition of reading. II. The reading process and the acquisition of the alphabetic principle. In A. S. Reber & D. Scarborough (Eds.), *Toward a psychology of reading* (pp. 55–141). Potomac, MD: Erlbaum.

Rozin, P., Haidt, J., & McCauley, C. R. (1993). Disgust. In M. Lewis & J. Haviland (Eds.), *Handbook of emotions* (pp. 575–594). New York: Guilford Press.

Rozin, P., & Kalat, J. W. (1971). Specific hungers and poison avoidance as adaptive specializations of learning. *Psychological Review, 78,* 459–486.

Rozin, P., Lowery, L., Imada, S., & Haidt, J. (1999). The CAD triad hypothesis: A mapping between three moral emotions (contempt, anger, disgust) and three moral codes (community, autonomy, divinity). *Journal of Personality and Social Psychology, 76,* 574–586.

Rozin, P., Markwith, M., & Stoess, C. (1997). Moralization: Becoming a vegetarian, the conversion of preferences into values and the recruitment of disgust. *Psychological Science, 8,* 67–73.

Rozin, P., & Mayer, J. (1961). Thermal reinforcement and thermoregulatory behavior in the goldfish, *Carassius auratus. Science, 134,* 942–943.

Rozin, P., Millman, L., & Nemeroff, C. (1986). Operation of the laws of sympathetic magic in disgust and other domains. *Journal of Personality and Social Psychology, 50,* 703–712.

Rozin, P., & Nemeroff, C. J. (1990). The laws of sympathetic magic: A psychological analysis of similarity and contagion. In J. Stigler, G. Herdt, & R. A. Shweder (Eds.), *Cultural psychology: Essays on comparative human development* (pp. 205–232). Cambridge, England: Cambridge University Press.

Rozin, P., Nemeroff, C., Horowitz, M., Gordon, B., & Voet, W. (1995). The borders of the self: Contamination sensitivity and potency of the mouth, other apertures and body parts. *Journal of Research in Personality, 29,* 318–340.

Rozin; P., Poritsky, S., & Sotsky, R. (1971). American children with reading problems can easily learn to read English represented by Chinese characters. *Science, 171,* 1264–1267.

Rozin, P., & Royzman, E. (2001). Negativity bias, negativity dominance, and contagion. *Personality and Social Psychology Review, 5,* 296–320.

Rozin, P., & Schull, J. (1988). The adaptive–evolutionary point of view in experimental psychology. In R. C. Atkinson, R. J. Herrnstein, G. Lindzey, & R. D. Luce (Eds.), *Handbook of experimental psychology* (pp. 503–546). New York: Wiley-Interscience.

Shweder, R. A. (1991). *Thinking through cultures.* Cambridge, MA: Harvard University Press.

Wrzesniewski, A., McCauley, C. R., Rozin, P., & Schwartz, B. (1997). Jobs, careers, and callings: A tripartite categorization of people's relations to their work. *Journal of Research in Personality, 31,* 21–33.

After stints studying physics, mathematics, and philosophy, Roger Shepard, renowned mathematical psychologist, finally discovered psychology in a course titled "Sensation and Perception." As a young child, Shepard was enamored of mathematics and physics, passions that he pursued, in one way or another, for many years. These arenas, however, failed "to provide any window on the inner phenomena of perception, illusion, mental imagery, and dreams—phenomena that seemed crucial in [his] own creative thinking and that were coming to fascinate [him] just as much as the external phenomena of physics." Although the establishment may not have embraced the coupling of mathematics and physics with psychology as fully as did he, Shepard has been able, using novel mathematical and physical models in the course of the past 50 years, to prove the symbiotic nature of the disciplines.

Roger N. Shepard

A Funny Thing Happened on the Way to the Formulation: How I Came to Frame Mental Laws in Abstract Spaces

13

> The object of all science, whether natural science or psychology, is to coördinate our experiences and to bring them into a logical system.
>
> —Einstein, *The Meaning of Relativity*

The "formulation" of my title is my formulation of proposed "universal" psychological laws of generalization and mental transformation in terms of distances, subregions, and shortest paths in abstract psychological space. The extent to which I may have "defied the crowd" on my way to proposing such laws (let alone, defied the crowd and "won") is best left to the judgment of others. Now well into my 70s, I am nevertheless

I gratefully acknowledge the National Science Foundation's (NSF) support of my research on mental representations and psychological laws for the 35 years following my move to academia in 1966 (most recently through NSF Award 9021648). The opinions and conclusions expressed in this article are my own, however, and do not necessarily represent those of the NSF. I also thank the editor, Robert Sternberg, an anonymous reviewer, and the very gracious Gregory Kimble for their excellent suggestions for improving the manuscript.

tempted to share with those still early in their careers why I regret that I had not, in several instances, been more defiant.

People differ in their inclinations to persist in trying to answer "why" questions (Shepard, 2001). Such differences, more than any elder's musings, may determine who is content to carry on the "normal science" business of using currently favored methods to test currently favored theories and who goes on to forge the "paradigm shifting" conceptions that reshape the very way in which we think about the world, our science, and ourselves.

My own early fascination with the physical, mechanical, and geometrical—more than with the social, cultural, or political—may be too atypical to justify many other psychologists taking my experiences as any guide. Yet, this particular constellation of interests may have contributed to my aversion to others telling me what to believe or what to do. I don't think I ever intended to be defiant, but I was strongly motivated by my curiosity and had a tendency to become so engrossed in my own project or enquiry that I would lose all sense of time and let everything else go. In any case (and I make this admission hesitantly with the awareness that it is probably the last thing any parent, teacher, or department head would want me to say), my own most creative work seems almost always to have been done when I was supposed to be doing something else—whether straightening my room, finishing my schoolwork, or attending to some administrative task.

Childhood and Early School Years

As a child, I had relatively little social contact with other children, except my 2-year-younger sister. From the time I was 4, we spent the three summer months on a lake at 7,500-foot altitude in the Sierra Nevada mountains, where my parents built a cabin that was without plumbing or electricity and that we accessed by canoe or a difficult trail. Whether up at the lake or back in Palo Alto, California, where my father was a member of Stanford University's engineering faculty, I often entertained myself by solitary exploring, imagining, drawing, or building things.

When I started school, I was socially immature. Despite being sent back from first grade to repeat kindergarten, my erratic application to school subjects continued to concern teachers and school counselors all the way up through my freshman year at Stanford University. The first day of second grade, I overheard my first-grade teacher inform the second-grade teacher that this was an excellent class except for two "impossible boys." To my total incomprehension and chagrin, one of the two names she pronounced was my own. In sixth grade, emboldened by my own observations from our recent drive across the country en route to my father's sabbatical at the Massachusetts Institute of Technology, I ventured to correct my Boston-area public school teacher on a point of U.S. geography. Whereupon this large and intimidating woman venomously intoned, "Alright, if you're so smart, you teach the class," then strode to the back of the room and squeezed her enormous bulk into an empty student desk chair, while the whole class sat in rigid silence for what seemed an eternity. For my first freshman English assignment, I turned in an essay titled "Dream Autobiography," which I had in fact reworked from a paper that had earned me an A+ in my senior year of high school. But when returned, my revised effort bore a huge red F and the admonition, "Mr. Shepard: If you have any intention of passing this course, turn in no more such nonsense as fills this paper."

Apart from school (and, typically, instead of my assigned work), however, I was, throughout my youth, pursuing my own self-initiated projects. During my preschool and elementary school years, I loved to tinker with old discarded clockworks, telephones, radios, electric motors, and appliance and car parts that I found in a vacant lot junk pile or in the attic of my grandparents' barn, and I eventually built a small robot from such scavenged parts. I was also drawing futuristic cars, boats, and space vehicles and repeatedly re-reading Lewis Carrol's *Alice's Adventures in Wonderland* and *Through the Looking Glass*.

During my junior high and high school years, I was drawing up plans for perpetual motion machines, designing and building trick wooden boxes to make objects appear or disappear, and, later, constructing models of regular polyhedra and three-dimensional projections of four-dimensional hypercubes, as well as a full-sized electrically controlled robot and devices for the electrical transmission of handwriting and for the detection of movement by reflected sound waves. In the public library, I found and devoured the writings of Arthur Eddington, James Jeans, J. B. S. Haldane, and Eric Temple Bell on relativity, cosmology, and mathematics. (When a teacher in one class asked what each of the students wanted to be as an adult, my unhesitating reply was "an astrophysicist.") I soon began searching the Stanford University library stacks for information about electronics, computing machines, and four-dimensional geometry. At the same time, I was reading the fantasies of Jules Verne, H. G. Wells, W. H. Hudson, Edgar Allen Poe, and H. P. Lovecraft and the poetry of Poe, William Blake, and Edith Sitwell, and I was listening, over and over, to recordings of Bach's organ fugues and attempting my own contrapuntal keyboard improvisations. Apart from my best high school friend (a future professor of chemistry), with whom I shared an interest in science fiction and fantasy, no one I knew was doing these things.

Stanford Undergraduate Years

At the end of my second quarter at Stanford, my grade point average had fallen to within one point of my being permanently dismissed. I was required to take a leave of absence for two quarters, followed by a period of probation. During my leave, I obtained employment at the Stanford Research Institute (now SRI International), working my way up to lab assistant to Dr. Elizabeth Roboz (later to become Albert Einstein's daughter-in-law). But it was some other scientists there who, taking a special interest in me, persuaded me that I would be unlikely to gain an opportunity for creative work in science unless I completed my education. So I returned to Stanford. But I also resumed my independent geometrical explorations. These now focused on the local connection statistics of homogeneous topological networks that rendered them the discrete analogues of continuous spaces that were either two- or three-dimensional and that had a global curvature that was zero (like the plane), positive (like the surface of a sphere), or negative (like a saddle-shape).

Although strongly attracted by the elegant four-dimensional non-Euclowskian and curved-space (Riemanian) geometries of special and general relativity, I feared that in failing to obtain a broad grounding in mathematics, I had already precluded a career in math or theoretical physics. Moreover, those disciplines did not appear to provide any window on the inner phenomena of perception, illusion, mental imagery, and dreams—phenomena that seemed crucial in my own creative thinking and that were coming to fascinate me just as much as the external phenomena of physics (see Shepard, 1978, pp. 167–183; Shepard, 1990, pp. 13–40).

I now learned that Stanford stipulated, for graduation, the satisfaction of what was to me a very irksome distribution requirement—completion of at least one course in either philosophy or sociology. Choosing what I regarded as the lesser of two evils, I reluctantly enrolled in "Introduction to Modern Philosophy," offered by an assistant professor, Alfred Glathe. Other students in this class were soon going to the chair of the philosophy department to complain that the lectures were incomprehensible. Yet that course had the most profound and lasting impact on me of any course I ever took. It awakened in me the realization that science must be built on what is given in the mind—not, as I had previously taken for granted, on an external material world (whose very existence, after all, is only inferred from what is given in the mind). I proceeded to take every course I could that was given by Glathe as well as by other philosophers—including Patrick Suppes and Donald Davidson. I now wanted to devote my life to philosophy, but I was dissuaded by Glathe, who was unhappy with his own life in the field. (Not long after I graduated, I was greatly saddened to learn that Glathe, having failed to secure tenure, took a personnel job in San Francisco and, soon after that, his own life.)

With my senior year approaching, I urgently sought a field in which the mental phenomena I now found so intriguing might somehow be understood through mathematics or even, I especially hoped, through geometry—which Einstein (1923b) had characterized as "the most ancient branch of physics" (p. 28) and Harvard mathematician W. F. Osgood (cited in Taylor, 1984) had characterized as its "noblest branch" (p. 607). The one field that seemed to claim a scientific approach to the mind was psychology, a field I had so far avoided as being hardly more scientific than sociology. Recalling how badly I had misjudged philosophy, however, I now registered for "Psych 1." But, as this class progressed, I found little that appeared susceptible to the kinds of theories that I so admired in physics and, certainly, nothing that looked geometrical. Growing desperate, I obtained permission to register, as the only undergraduate, in the graduate-level course "Sensation and Perception." Although offered by the same professor, Donald Taylor, who had taught the disappointing "Psych 1," this course turned out to be closer to my interests in perceptual experience and appeared to me more susceptible to a mathematical approach.

Late in this course, I finally found what I had been seeking. At the end of one class, Taylor casually mentioned a recent and as yet unpublished Stanford doctoral dissertation. In it, Fred Attneave, using stimuli that varied on perceptually distinct dimensions (such as size, shape, and color), had found evidence that both subjective judgments of the similarities among the stimuli and objective frequencies of their actual confusions during paired-associates learning were inconsistent with a Euclidean representation (see Attneave, 1950). Attneave's data implied that the "psychological distance" between stimuli did not equal the square root of the sum of the squares of separations on component dimensions, as required by the Pythagorean theorem for Euclidean right triangles. Instead, his data implied a non-Euclidean metric in which the psychological distance approximated the simple sum of those component separations. New vistas immediately opened before me, and I resolved to apply for graduate study in psychology.

Yale Graduate School Years

Yale offered me a research assistantship, which I accepted partly on the recommendation of Taylor (who would much later move to Yale himself). On arriving there in the fall of 1951, I found my assistantship was not at all what I had imagined. I was to condition rats to begin running in a wheel within 5.8 seconds of the onset of a light, to avoid an electric shock so intense that it caused the rats to jump, squeal, and, often, to urinate or defecate. I was to record the latency at which each rat began running following each onset of the light. After 60 trials, when most rats had learned to run quickly enough to avoid the shock, I was to disconnect the shock and to record how the latency of running increased over a series of 30 ensuing "extinction" trials.

I was then to drop them, one by one, into a large can and, as their final reward, to turn on the gas through an inserted hose until the muffled sounds of frantic scrambling and squeaking had finally ceased. I was then to dump the jumble of small limp bodies unceremoniously into a lidded garbage drum. Having no doubt that these fellow creatures had inner experiences much like my own—certainly including those of pain and suffering—this troubled me deeply.

The experiment had been designed to test a prediction of the stimulus–response learning theory of Yale's renowned Clark L. Hull, then a bent, thick-spectacled, reclusive presence in his basement labs and, as it turned out, in the final year of his life. According to Hull's theory (see Hull, 1943, 1952), the latency of the conditioned running response should gradually increase when, with the absence of the punishing shock, the accumulated "habit strength" of the response drained away, like fluid from a leaking drum. Despite my aversion to almost everything about the experiment (including the smell of rat urine and feces, which pervaded the lower level of the department), I couldn't help but notice that any one rat's latencies did not increase in the absence of shock. Instead, each rat continued responding to the light with undiminished alacrity until, on some seemingly unpredictable trial, it simply stopped running. (Of course, because different rats stopped at different times, the median latency for the group of rats as a whole did steadily increase.)

To look for any trend in the latencies prior to the variable stopping times, I took it upon myself to replot the mean latencies on shock-free trials relative to the most recent trial on which a rat had received a shock, regardless of when this occurred in the series of trials. This was justified because as long as a rat was responding within the 5.8 seconds and receiving no shock, it could not know whether the trial was a conditioning or an extinction trial. Although the variability of the means increased with the number of trials since last shock (because sample sizes decreased), there was no sign of a systematic increase in latency itself (see Panel A of Figure 13.1).

When a rat that had thus been responding with short latencies (averaging only 1.92 seconds) finally did delay its response, it did so discontinuously, refraining from running at all until the shock at 5.8 seconds caused it immediately to resume running to terminate the shock. Thus, the resumption of running following a shock and the cessation of running that brought on the next shock were equally discontinuous. I was able to show this on a single plot by linearly stretching or shrinking each intershock interval so that it fit between the same plotted shock-trial endpoints. Within each of seven equally spaced time slots between these endpoints, I then plotted the mean of the latencies of all the responses within that time slot (yielding a so-called "Vincentized" plot). Now, with reasonable sample sizes (from 19 to 71), the mean latencies were all very stable and absolutely flat throughout the shock-free interval (see Panel B of Figure 13.1).

It didn't look to me as if habit strengths were gradually decreasing in the absence of the shock. Rather, it looked as if the rats in their unhappy situation were doing just what I would have done (although, I might hope, without the urination and defecation). It was as if the rats had formed the hypothesis that the shock consistently follows the onset of the light unless they prevent it by quickly running in the wheel. So each time the light came on, they ran like hell to avoid the punishing shock. But after some time without shock, finding the running itself aversively exhausting, each rat would risk a test of its hypothesis about the connection between the light and the shock by refraining from running. If the shock occurred, reconfirming the hypothesis, the rat would resume running. But if the shock did not follow, the rat would then and there conclude that the connection between light and shock was broken and would discontinue running. I also plotted median latencies for shock-free trials just during extinction—but backwards in time, beginning with the last trial on which each rat responded. The median response latencies were again flat, manifesting no systematic increase until each rat failed to respond (within the 15-second period during which the light remained on).

Although intrigued by this suggestion of a cognitive process of hypothesis testing in the lowly rat, I was reluctant to approach either of the two most senior professors of animal learning, Neal Miller or Hull himself. Hull's longtime secretary, Ruth Hays, allowed those of us in Miller's learning seminar to read the manuscript for Hull's soon-to-be-published final book, *A Behavior System* (Hull, 1952). But she insisted that no problem concerning the book or the theory be brought to Hull's attention lest *that* shock precipitate in the frail Hull a final cardiac arrest.

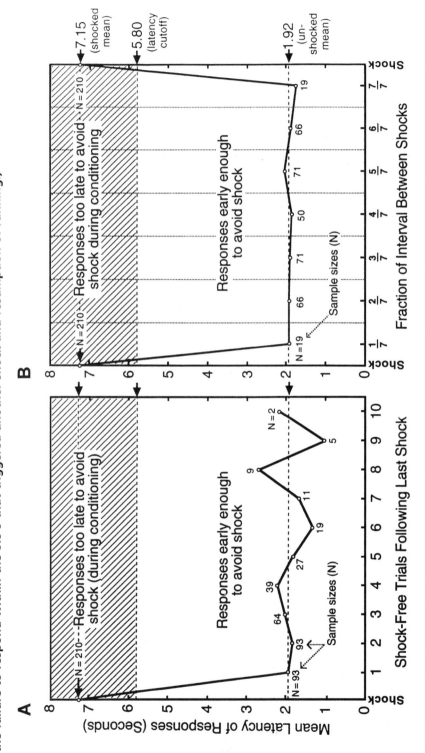

FIGURE 13.1

A: Rats' mean latencies of wheel running following onset of the conditioned stimulus on successive trials following the last shock. The graph shows responses with latencies of less than 5.8 s, the period within which the rats had to respond to avoid another shock. (Note, sample sizes are small for shock-free sequences of over six trials.) B: Mean latencies within successive sevenths of the shock-free intervals between successive shocks. (No increase in latency of conditioned response is evident until the failure to respond within the 5.8 s that triggered another shock and resumption of running.)

So, I took my plots, in turn, to the two assistant professors whose understanding (and appreciation!) of Hullian theory far exceeded my own. These were, first, the quite approachable and friendly Gregory Kimble, who had designed the experiment and, then, the rather more aloof and formal Frank Logan, who was working on a probabilistic version of Hullian theory. Nearly 20 years earlier, I later learned, Isadore Krechevsky had already published evidence for "hypotheses" in rats, albeit during discrimination learning (Krechevsky, 1932a, 1932b). Yet, Kimble and Logan (who later went on to their separate, distinguished careers at Duke and the University of New Mexico, respectively) both informed me that my plotted results made no sense. They suggested that my unconventional outcome-contingent ways of averaging the data were suspect. Insufficiently secure to defy even a "crowd" of two, I filed my plots away and never ventured to publish them (until now, exactly 50 years later). From that day on I did, however, decline to undertake any further experiments on subjects that are unable to provide informed consent.

A decade later such discontinuities in learning performance were being confirmed—and by means of similar outcome-contingent averaging of data—by Bower and Trabasso (1963, 1964); Levine (1966); Levine, Miller, and Steinmeyer (1967); Restle (1962); and, in a somewhat different way, by myself (Shepard, 1963, 1966a). These experiments were, however, on humans rather than on rats, and most of these were based on the new, mathematically elegant one-element stimulus-sampling and hypothesis models. This striking new evidence both benefited from and contributed to the then gathering shift from the more "thoughtless" or "hydraulic" explanations of external behavior to theories of the internal processing of information.

Meanwhile, I had asked Carl Hovland to be my dissertation advisor. Although Hovland had done his own doctoral research under Hull, he was the one senior member of Yale's experimental psychology faculty who seemed open to theoretical ideas that differed from the stimulus–response behaviorist approach prevailing at Yale. Indeed, anticipating the soon-to-flourish cognitive revolution, Hovland was beginning to explore an information–theoretic approach to human concept learning (later published in Hovland, 1952. For further reminiscences about Hovland and his contributions, see Shepard, 1998, 2000).

While still at Yale, I received particular inspiration from two young visiting colloquium speakers. One was William Estes, whose elegant stimulus sampling theory of learning (Estes, 1950) came as a breath of fresh air. In addition to laying the groundwork for the already mentioned one-element models of discontinuous learning, Estes showed how empirically testable functional relations could be derived, mathematically, from hypothetical, but simple and well-motivated elementary processes. This was a notable departure from Hull's practice of postulating such functional relations after empirically fitting curves of theoretically unmotivated functional form to animal data. Yet, when I confessed to Estes, after his colloquium, that I, too, aspired to develop mathematical models for psychological phenomena, he counseled me that from his own experience, psychologists were not ready for mathematically formulated theories. In fact, Estes's own dissertation advisor, B. F. Skinner, had this comment on Hull's theory building: "A science of behavior," because its problems are not of the same sort, "cannot be closely patterned after geometry or Newtonian mechanics" (Skinner, 1938, p. 437). Later, when Skinner and I were both at Harvard, Skinner liked to refer to mathematical models as "paper dolls." Nevertheless, I am grateful that neither Estes nor I heeded Estes's own advice against proposing mathematical formulations. (For more on Estes's path-breaking defiance, see Shepard, 1992.)

The other inspirational colloquium speaker was George Miller. He presented his information-theoretic analyses of the extensive data that he and Patricia Nicely had collected on the rates at which listeners confused 16 consonant phonemes with each other under 17 conditions of noise and filtering (Miller & Nicely, 1955). The challenge of trying to discover the dimensions of perceptual processing implied by this extraordinarily rich set of data strengthened my resolve—originally stimulated by the dissertation of Attneave (1950)—to find a way of extracting spatial representations of stimuli from similarity, confusion, and generalization data. Moreover, when I and then my Bell Labs associates later succeeded in developing quite general computer methods of doing this by multidimensional scaling, tree-fitting, and clustering, Miller and Nicely's results proved to serve as the single most useful set of test data (Shepard, 1972, 1988).

I was now convinced that the problem of generalization was the most fundamental problem confronting learning theory. Because we never encounter exactly the same total situation twice, no theory of learning can be complete without a law governing how what is learned in one situation generalizes to another. Hull, recognizing the need for a law of generalization, had earlier persuaded Hovland to determine the functional form of the generalization function for his 1936 doctoral dissertation. Hovland (1937) tried this by measuring humans' generalized galvanic skin responses (GSRs) to tones differing in frequency from a training tone associated with (mild) electric shock. The averaged GSR strengths fell off with difference in frequency of tone in an apparently concave-upward manner suggestive of an exponential decay function. Accordingly, Hull then added an exponential-decay generalization function as "Postulate 5" in his *Principles of Behavior* (Hull, 1943). But GSR data are notoriously variable, and Spence (1937) argued that Hovland's data were in fact too noisy to determine whether the generalization function was concave or convex—let alone specifically exponential.

I saw a still more fundamental problem. Even if reliable measures of generalization could be found, generalization functions could not in general be monotonic, let alone invariant, when plotted on a physical dimension. There is greater generalization between tones separated in frequency by an octave than between tones separated by somewhat less than an octave. There is greater generalization between spectral hues of the shortest and longest visible wavelengths (violet and red) than between either of these and a hue of an intermediate wavelength (green). And there is greater generalization between the vertical and horizontal orientations of a rectangle than between these and the rectangle's 45 oblique orientation (see Shepard, 1965, 1987).

In my 1955 doctoral dissertation, with the supportive encouragement and helpful suggestions of two Yale assistant professors, Robert Abelson and Burton Rosner, I developed a method for recovering a spatial representation of stimuli from generalization data, without reference to any physical dimensions. I required only that the generalization function yield approximate satisfaction of the three axioms for distances (most critically, the "triangle inequality," which holds that the sum of any two distances between any three points cannot be less than the remaining, third distance between those points). I applied this method to humans' generalization errors during paired-associates learning (which proved to be much more stable than GSR data). This enabled me to obtain the first reliable evidence for the exponential form of the generalization function (Shepard, 1955, 1957, 1958a, 1958b).

Although I passed my oral examination on the dissertation, I subsequently learned that one of my Yale examiners, Fred Sheffield, had expressed the view that "this sort of thing should not be encouraged." I had previously heard Sheffield opine that psychology was advanced not by constructing mathematical theories but by designing experiments such that the final report could be written in advance of collecting the data, leaving only spaces to fill in the appropriate statistics and associated *p* values. I could only wonder how Einstein would ever have arrived at the theory of relativity by following such advice.

Bell Laboratories Years

After three postdoctoral associate years (two with George Miller at Harvard), I joined the technical staff of the Bell Telephone Laboratories in 1958. Inspired, in part, by a summer workshop with Allen Newell and

Herbert Simon on their new computer-simulation approach to cognitive processes, I had formed the idea of using the Bell Labs's computer facilities to simulate the evolutionary formation of perceptual–cognitive mechanisms. Then I had my first lunch with John R. Pierce, the executive director of the large division that included my department. I had only just mentioned the emerging field of artificial intelligence when Pierce (an eminent engineer well known for his sharp mind and outspokenness) rocked back in his chair and exclaimed, "Ah yes, AI. There's no holding it up; it keeps hitting new lows!" Because this was my first real job and I now had a family to support, I decided this was not the time to be defiant.

I proceeded to use Bell Labs' computer facilities to work, instead, to find better ways (at least better than the crude hand-computation one developed in my dissertation) to extract spatial representations from matrices of similarity ratings or frequencies of confusion or generalization. This led to the development of the first of the methods now known as "nonmetric" multidimensional scaling (Shepard, 1962a, 1962b). Without requiring any assumption about the metric properties of the data, these methods yielded metric spatial representations (Shepard, 1966b). Moreover, they provided for solutions in non-Euclidean as well as in Euclidean spaces (Kruskal, 1964a, 1964b; Shepard, 1980, 1991). Because such methods have proved widely useful in the behavioral, social, and cognitive sciences as well as in my own subsequent research on perception, cognition, and imagery, I do not greatly regret my lack of defiance in this instance.

I did begin to feel a little guilty, though, because the basic research I was doing at Bell Labs, although rewarding for me, seemed unlikely to lead to anything that would earn money for the Bell System. I then had an inspiration for an experiment of potential practical value. My research assistant and I had people look up and dial 7-digit telephone numbers in either of two ways. One was the usual way; the other was reversed so that the less familiar 4-digit line number appeared to the left and was to be dialed before the generally more familiar and memorable 3-digit local central office code. We found that reversing the order in this way cut both the lookup-plus-dialing time and the frequency of dialing the wrong number approximately in half (Shepard & Sheenan, 1965). In addition to aiding telephone users, such a change could have saved the Bell System vast amounts of money. Moreover, such a change was just then becoming implementable as computer-controlled switching was replacing the old sequential stepping switches. But when I circulated a draft of our report to the applied and engineering divisions, the feedback I uniformly received was to go back, as one respondent put it, to my "ivory tower." The system, they said, was too big to make such a change, especially one that would in any way affect subscribers.

I returned to my basic research and, from then on, accepted my pay-checks without qualm.

Stanford Faculty Years

It was during my ensuing academic tenures—for 2 years at Harvard and the following 30, back at Stanford—that my research finally began to converge toward the general theoretical "formulation" referred to in my title. The guiding idea was that adaptations to the most pervasive and enduring of the biologically relevant features of the world should be favored as organisms evolve more highly developed perceptual–motor and cognitive capabilities, wherever such organisms may arise in the universe. But the most pervasive and enduring features tend to be quite abstract. For example, space (on a biologically relevant scale) is three-dimensional and Euclidean, and the objects that live and move in this space are of discrete basic kinds with corresponding biologically relevant consequences. If so, I reasoned, we might aspire to a psychology that can, like physics, boast universal laws (Shepard, 1987, 1994, 2001). But what specific psychological laws would mesh with such abstract, universal features of the world?

Beginning with what seemed to me the most fundamental of psychological laws, that of generalization, I applied multidimensional scaling to generalization data from many experiments on both human and animal learning and using a great variety of visual and auditory stimuli. In every case, generalization approximated an exponential decay function of distance in the recovered psychological space. But to claim that this is a universal law, I needed to show why such a law would be optimum in any world in which objects belong to distinct kinds.

I argued that if a particular object has been found to have a significant consequence, the probability that a newly encountered object would have that same consequence should be given by a summation over all hypotheses about which objects might have that consequence. Such a subset would be represented in the abstract representational space of objects by a suitable (e.g., connected) "consequential" region. Intuitively, it seemed clear that points corresponding to more similar objects and, hence, lying closer together in the representational space will jointly fall within more of the small, potentially consequential regions than will the more widely separated points corresponding to more dissimilar objects. Quantitatively, I found that summation (more generally, Bayesian integration with minimum-knowledge priors) does indeed robustly yield the empirically confirmed exponential decay function (Shepard, 1987). In addition, such summation automatically explains why the metric of the representational space approximates the Minkowski r-metric, and especially the Euclidean case ($r = 2$), when the objects differ along perceptually "integral" dimensions, and the "city block" case ($r = 1$), as implicated by Attneave (1950), when the objects differ along perceptually "separable" dimensions (see Shepard, 1987, 1991).

In contrast to my gradually evolving thinking about generalization, my work on mental transformation had an abrupt beginning. As I was drifting toward wakefulness on the morning of November 16, 1968, I experienced a spontaneous hypnopompic image of three-dimensional objects majestically turning in space. Even before rising from bed, I had mentally worked out the design of the first experiment (Shepard & Metzler, 1971) in what was to become a continuing series—first on "mental rotation" and then on "apparent motion" (Shepard, 1984; Shepard & Cooper, 1982). The ensuing work established that in identifying objects in different orientations as being of the same shape, people pass through a series of intermediate mental representations of the object in successively more rotated orientations. This led me to propose another universal law: Transformation time increases linearly with the length of the path traversed in the abstract representational space of possible positions of an object. Moreover, this law appeared to hold both for decision time, as in the cognitively effortful task of mental rotation, and for the minimum stimulus-to-stimulus onset time yielding perceived rigidity, as in the perceptually automatic experience of visual apparent motion.

But, again, to claim that the proposed law might be a mental universal required an argument as to why the "analogue" process giving rise to this law might be optimal in the world. I reasoned that it was advantageous to an individual to identify two stimuli as the same external object as quickly as possible. In general, I argued, this could only be accomplished by simulating a rigid transformation from the one to the other over the simplest and most direct path according to the kinematic geometry of the three-dimensional Euclidean space in which we have evolved.

The abstract space of possible positions is not three-dimensional and Euclidean, however. It is six-dimensional, because there are three degrees of freedom of location and three degrees of freedom of orientation. It is also curved, because rotation through a full circle brings the object back to its original orientation. Moreover, if the object possesses some symmetry, this space becomes more convoluted, because rotation through some smaller angle (such as 180°, in the case of a rectangle) leaves the final appearance of the object unchanged. The quantitative development required highly abstract mathematical concepts seldom used in psychological science (such as those of group theory and of geodesic paths in curved manifolds—see Carlton & Shepard, 1990a,

1990b; Foster, 1975). Yet, application of multidimensional scaling (as extended by my former Bell Labs associates Carroll & Chang, 1970) to human chronometric data, which Farrell and I obtained for objects of specified symmetries in various orientations, yielded exactly the paths predicted for the stimuli we devised (viz., geodesic paths lying in the curved surface of a torus in four-dimensional space; Shepard, 1994; Shepard & Farrell, 1985).

Admittedly, these proposed universal laws of generalization and mental transformation are framed with respect to highly abstract representational spaces and are tested by highly purified and constrained laboratory experiments. As such, they are far removed from our everyday experiences and common understandings of life's concrete, highly complex situations. But this is not unlike the case of physics, where the "hypotheses with which it starts become steadily more abstract and remote from experience" (Einstein, 1949a, p. 91) and take their purest form under highly simplified and controlled conditions. As Einstein eloquently put it, the scientist (like the artist) erects a "simplified and lucid image of the world," lifting into it "the center of gravity of his emotional life" (Holton, 1973, p. 377).

Personal Defiance and Psychological Science

HOW HAVE I BEEN MOST DEFIANT?

That I chose to study such subjective phenomena as perceptual similarity and mental imagery might seem most defiant of the behaviorism that prevailed at mid-century. The behaviorists shunned such phenomena as irremediably subjective and qualitative. Yet, I found ways to render these phenomena both objective and quantitative.

In the case of similarity, I did this in two ways. First I developed data-analytic methods of multidimensional scaling capable of yielding reliable and quantitative psychological representations of stimuli independent of any knowledge of their physical dimensions (Shepard, 1962b, 1980). Second, I showed that the obtained representations were the same whether the data were subjective judgments of similarity or objective frequencies of confusion or generalization during learning. (Indeed, others subsequently used these methods to obtain similar representations for the perceptual spaces of nonverbal animals; e.g., Blough, 1985.)

In the case of imagery, my students and I also did this in two ways. First we probed internally generated or transformed mental images with externally presented stimuli and measured the time to make a response that was objectively classifiable as correct or incorrect (Podgorny & Shepard, 1978; Shepard & Cooper, 1982; Shepard & Metzler, 1971). Second, we showed that multidimensional scaling of similarities yielded the same, interpretable spatial representations, whether the things to be compared were physically presented or only imagined (Shepard & Chipman, 1970; Shepard & Cooper, 1992; Shepard, Kilpatric, & Cunningham, 1975).

But what might be less palatable to the mid-20th century behaviorists—and even to many present day psychologists (as acknowledged in Shepard, 2001)—are the following claims:

- We can best arrive at general psychological laws not by collecting data about the observable behaviors or the physical brains of any particular animals on this planet but, rather, by thinking deeply about the general nature of the problems any cognitive agents face in the world.
- Learning in the individual cannot alone explain the emergence of any behavioral capacities, because neither the principles of learning nor the innate metric of similarity that initially underlies generalization are learned; they must have arisen through natural selection.
- Laws that arise as adaptations to those features of the world that hold throughout all environments conducive to the evolution of intelligent life tend to be universal laws.
- The laws applying to the widest ranges of phenomena, are also (just as in physics) highly abstract ones based on mathematical structures (such as those of group theory and non-Euclidean geometry) and, hence, very remote from our everyday "folk-psychological" understandings.

WHAT PREDISPOSES ONE TOWARD SCIENTIFIC CREATIVITY AND DEFIANCE?

The processes of mental transformation to which my students and I gained a degree of objective and quantitative access seem not unlike the creative processes that Einstein described as "visualizing . . . effects, consequences, possibilities" by means of "images which can be 'voluntarily' reproduced and combined" (quoted in Hadamard, 1945, p. 142; Wertheimer, 1945, p. 184). Indeed, accounts of other creative scientists, mathematicians, and inventors similarly emphasize the power of spatial visualization. With a sense of *déjà vu*, I have read that during childhood, many (including Isaac Newton, James Clerk Maxwell, Hermann von Helmholtz, Ernst Mach, and Einstein) were relatively isolated from peers, owing to various circumstances as well as to their own preference for the less social pursuits of observing nature, solving puzzles, or building or tinkering with mechanisms (Shepard, 1978, pp. 134–159, especially p. 155). Given a young peer group's well-known intolerance for deviant beliefs and values, it is perhaps not surprising that such a group may discourage the development of novel interests and ways of thinking. Paradoxically, although even we scientists naturally hope our own offspring will be popular with their peers, the cognitive uniformity required may reduce the chance of such a child becoming another Newton, Darwin, or Einstein.

Throughout, I have particularly quoted Einstein for two reasons. First, he is widely regarded as the greatest scientist of the 20th century (if not, indeed, of all time). Second, his creative work—which used thought experiments to arrive at revolutionary geometrical conceptualizations (in terms of non-Euclidean spaces and geodesic paths)—inspired much of my own thinking. Perhaps significantly, Einstein also was notably defiant. One teacher told him he would never amount to anything, adding, "Your very presence destroys my respect in class." At the age of 16, Einstein renounced his German nationality, later characterizing the German professors in 1901 as "a pompous group, all of them," and writing that "The stupor of authority is the greatest enemy of the truth" (cited in Loewenberg, 1988, pp. 510–511).

The relative contributions to scientific creativity of genetic predisposition and individual experience are difficult to assess. I believe there is a powerful synergy between the two. People crave to exercise those capabilities they already possess, whether physical or cognitive. After developing skill in ice skating, I experienced an aching desire to exercise that skill. Then, when the only accessible ice rink was converted to an aircraft factory during World War II, the ache mounted until I gloriously skated away the nights in my nocturnal dreams. Given the plasticity of the brain, mental exercise of such capabilities must further develop the relevant neural circuits. At the same time, there is some evidence for a trade-off between innate predispositions toward social intelligence and abstract physical–mathematical intelligence (e.g., Holden, 2000).

I suspect that in addition to a degree of social reserve, I inherited some innate aptitude for spatial cognition and manipulation from my engineer father (who, in his early youth, built a prize-winning erector-set derrick, a motorized wagon, and a crystal radio receiver) and an aptitude for visualization from my artist mother. This may partly account for my own penchant, as a child, to immerse myself in solitary imagining, drawing, manipulating, and investigating physical objects and, perhaps, thereby to sharpen my spatial imagery skills. What may be unusual is that one with my particular geometrical and mechanical inclinations should end up in psychology. I like to think the rather different (if circuitous) path along which I have stumbled into this field has led me to a correspondingly different vision of what a science of psychology might be.

PSYCHOLOGY: POTENTIALLY A SCIENCE SECOND TO NONE?

However important psychologists may judge their own work to be within the field of psychology, they may harbor doubts about the status of their research and of psychological science in general vis-à-vis the more established and esteemed physical and biological sciences. My former Stanford mathematical psychologist colleague, Richard Atkinson, when director of the National Science Foundation, complained that whereas delegations of physicists, chemists, and biologists were constantly visiting the foundation offices in Washington to boast of the latest advances in their fields, psychologists rarely showed their faces. Nor have we succeeded in giving the general public an understanding or appreciation of psychology as a science. (To compare the periodicals *Psychology Today* and *Physics Today*—or just their covers!—is enough to make a scientifically oriented psychologist wince.) When a lay person asks what I do, any mention of "psychology" and "mathematical laws" in the same sentence elicits expressions of incredulity or incomprehension. Even cognitive psychologists may regard the particular laws I have proposed for generalization and mental transformation as too esoteric and abstract to have any significance for psychological science or human destiny.

Yet, as Einstein (1923a) noted, even physics is "a creation of the human mind" (p. 2), and the laws of physics cannot be derived, by such a mind, from observation but require "free inventions of the human intellect" (Northrop, 1949, p. 392). Certainly, as remarked by Weinberg (1992), "Einstein did not develop general relativity by poring over astronomical data" (p. 104). If, however, we take "freely invented" to invoke a process that is merely random or capricious, how would such a process ever have led to general relativity or to quantum mechanics? In my 1994 William James Lectures at Harvard ("Mind and World"), I argued that the processes of generalization and imagined spatial transformation may underlie the thought experiments through which Archimedes, Copernicus, Galileo, Newton, Maxwell, and Einstein made their revolutionary discoveries. Thus, "In a certain sense," as Einstein wrote, "pure thought can grasp reality, as the ancients dreamed" (Einstein, 1949b, p. 398). If the laws of physics are discovered and comprehended in minds governed by mental laws that partake of the elegance and universality of the laws of physics and geometry, are not the prospects for the science of psychology as inspiring as those for any science?

Concluding Observations

No doubt defiance of the establishment can entail personal costs as well as benefits. Probably everyone encounters, as I did, at least a few teachers, supervisors, reviewers, or editors who are to various degrees intolerant, dogmatic, or defensive. One may have to choose one's strategic balance between defiance, submission, and total escape from the field. I may have been lucky. Despite my share of detractors, there usually were some who encouraged my self-confidence and unconventional explorations. Even when I lacked the will to be defiant, I usually found another problem or another approach that proved to be satisfying. Although I regret the time wasted in finding my way, what should have been done is always clearer in retrospect.

To anyone who would work toward a psychological science of grandeur, I would say this: Don't be easily discouraged by establishment advisors, journal editors, or grant reviewers. Although rejection is certainly no guarantee that your ideas are any good, immediate acceptance raises the question of whether your ideas are truly revolutionary.

References

Attneave, F. (1950). Dimensions of similarity. *American Journal of Psychology, 63,* 516–556.

Blough, D. (1985). Discrimination of letters and random dot patterns by pigeons and humans. *Journal of Experimental Psychology: Animal Behavior Processes, 11,* 261–280.

Bower, G. H., & Trabasso, T. (1963). Reversals prior to solution in concept identification. *Journal of Experimental Psychology, 66,* 409–418.

Bower, G. H., & Trabasso, T. (1964). Concept identification. In R. C. Atkinson (Ed.), *Studies in mathematical psychology* (pp. 32–96). Stanford, CA: Stanford University Press.

Carlton, E., & Shepard, R. N. (1990a). Psychologically simple motions as geodesic paths: I. Asymmetric objects. *Journal of Mathematical Psychology, 34,* 127–188.

Carlton, E., & Shepard, R. N. (1990b). Psychologically simple motions as geodesic paths: II. Symmetric objects. *Journal of Mathematical Psychology, 34,* 189–228.

Carroll, J. D., & Chang, J.-J. (1970). Analysis of individual differences in multidimensional scaling via an *N*-way generalization of "Ekart–Young" decomposition. *Psychometrika, 35,* 283–319.

Einstein, A. (1923a). *The meaning of relativity*. Princeton, NJ: Princeton University Press.

Einstein, A. (1923b). *Sidelights of relativity*. New York: E. P. Dutton.

Einstein, A. (1949a). The problem of space, ether, and the field of physics. In P. A. Schilpp (Ed.), *Albert Einstein: Philosopher–scientist*. Evanston, IL: Library of Living Philosophers.

Einstein, A. (1949b). The world as I see it. In P. A. Schilpp (Ed.), *Albert Einstein: Philosopher–scientist*. Evanston, IL: Library of Living Philosophers.

Estes, W. K. (1950). Toward a statistical theory of learning. *Psychological Review, 57*, 94–107.

Foster, D. H. (1975). Visual apparent motion and some preferred paths in the rotation group SO(3). *Biological Cybernetics, 18*, 81–89.

Hadamard, J. (1945). *The psychology of invention in the mathematical field*. Princeton, NJ: Princeton University Press.

Holden, C. (2000, February 25). Math and asociality [Random samples]. *Science, 287*, 1395.

Holton, G. (1973). *Thematic origins of scientific thought: Kepler to Einstein*. Cambridge, MA: Harvard University Press.

Hovland, C. I. (1937). The generalization of conditioned responses. I. The sensory generalization of conditioned responses with varying frequencies of tone. *Journal of General Psychology, 17*, 125–148.

Hovland, C. I. (1952). A "communication analysis" of concept learning. *Psychological Review, 59*, 347–350.

Hull, C. L. (1943). *Principles of behavior*. New York: Appleton-Century-Crofts.

Hull, C. L. (1952). *A behavior system*. New Haven, CT: Yale University Press.

Krechevsky, I. (1932a). "Hypotheses" in rats. *Psychological Review, 39*, 516–532.

Krechevsky, I. (1932b). "Hypotheses" versus "chance" in the presolution period in sensory discrimination-learning. *University of California Publications in Psychology, 6*, 27–44.

Kruskal, J. B. (1964a). Multidimensional scaling by optimizing goodness of fit to a nonmetric hypothesis. *Psychometrika, 29*, 1–27.

Kruskal, J. B. (1964b). Nonmetric multidimensional scaling: A numerical method. *Psychometrika, 29*, 115–129.

Levine, M. (1966). Hypothesis behavior by humans during discrimination learning. *Journal of Experimental Psychology, 71*, 331–338.

Levine, M., Miller, P., & Steinmeyer, C. H. (1967). The none-to-all theorem of human discrimination learning. *Journal of Experimental Psychology, 73*, 568–573.

Loewenberg, P. (1988). Einstein in his youth. *Science, 239*, 510–512.

Miller, G. A., & Nicely, P. E. (1955). An analysis of perceptual confusions among some English consonants. *Journal of the Acoustical Society of America, 27*, 338–352.

Northrop, F. S. C. (1949). Einstein's conception of science. In P. A. Schilpp (Ed.), *Albert Einstein: Philosopher-scientist*. Evanston, IL: Library of Living Philosophers.

Podgorny, P., & Shepard, R. N. (1978). Functional representations common to visual perception and imagination. *Journal of Experimental Psychology: Human Perception and Performance, 4*, 21–35.

Restle, F. (1962). The selection of strategies in cue learning. *Psychological Review, 69*, 329–343.

Shepard, R. N. (1955). *Stimulus and response generalization during paired-associates learning*. Unpublished doctoral dissertation, Yale University, New Haven, CT.

Shepard, R. N. (1957). Stimulus and response generalization: A stochastic model relating generalization to distance in psychological space. *Psychometrika, 22*, 325–345.

Shepard, R. N. (1958a). Stimulus and response generalization: Deduction of the generalization gradient from a trace model. *Psychological Review, 65*, 242–256.

Shepard, R. N. (1958b). Stimulus and response generalization: Tests of a model relating generalization to distance in psychological space. *Journal of Experimental Psychology, 55*, 509–523.

Shepard, R. N. (1962a). The analysis of proximities: Multidimensional scaling with an unknown distance function. Part I. *Psychometrika, 27*, 125–140.

Shepard, R. N. (1962b). The analysis of proximities: Multidimensional scaling with an unknown distance function. Part II. *Psychometrika, 27*, 219–246.

Shepard, R. N. (1963). Comments on Professor Underwood's paper "Stimulus selection in verbal learning." In C. N. Cofer & B. S. Musgrave (Eds.), *Verbal behavior and learning: Problems and processes* (pp. 48–70). New York: McGraw-Hill.

Shepard, R. N. (1965). Approximation to uniform gradients of generalization by monotone transformations of scale. In D. I. Mostofsky (Ed.), *Stimulus generalization* (pp. 94–110). Stanford, CA: Stanford University Press.

Shepard, R. N. (1966a). Learning and recall as organization and search. *Journal of Verbal Learning and Verbal Behavior, 5*, 201–204.

Shepard, R. N. (1966b). Metric structures in ordinal data. *Journal of Mathematical Psychology, 3*, 287–315.

Shepard, R. N. (1972). Psychological representation of speech sounds. In E. E. David & P. B. Denes (Eds.), *Human communication: A unified view* (pp. 67–113). New York: McGraw-Hill.

Shepard, R. N. (1978). Externalization of mental images and the act of creation. In B. S. Randhawa & W. E. Coffman (Eds.), *Visual learning, thinking, and communication* (pp. 139–189). New York: Academic Press.

Shepard, R. N. (1980, October 24). Multidimensional scaling, tree-fitting, and clustering. *Science, 210,* 390–398.

Shepard, R. N. (1984). Ecological constraints on internal representation: Resonant kinematics of perceiving, imagining, thinking, and dreaming. *Psychological Review, 91,* 417–447.

Shepard, R. N. (1987, September 11). Toward a universal law of generalization for psychological science. *Science, 237,* 1317–1323.

Shepard, R. N. (1988). George Miller's data and the development of methods for representing cognitive structures. In W. Hirsh (Ed.), *The making of cognitive science: Essays in honor of George A. Miller* (pp. 45–70). Cambridge, England: Cambridge University Press.

Shepard, R. N. (1990). *Mind sights.* New York: W. H. Freeman.

Shepard, R. N. (1991). Integrality versus separability of stimulus dimensions: From an early convergence of evidence to a proposed theoretical basis. In G. R. Lockhead & J. R. Pomerantz (Eds.), *Perception of structure: Essays in honor of Wendell R. Garner* (pp. 53–71). Washington, DC: American Psychological Association.

Shepard, R. N. (1992). The advent and continuing influence of mathematical learning theory: Commentary on Estes and Burke (1955). *Journal of Experimental Psychology: General, 121,* 419–421.

Shepard, R. N. (1994). Perceptual–cognitive universals as reflections of the world. *Psychonomic Bulletin & Review, 1,* 2–28.

Shepard, R. N. (1998). Carl Iver Hovland, June 12, 1912–April 16, 1961. *Biographical memoirs* (Vol. 73, pp. 230–260). Washington, DC: National Academy Press.

Shepard, R. N. (2000). Carl Iver Hovland: Statesman of psychology, sterling human being. In G. A. Kimble & M. Wetheimer (Eds.), *Portraits of pioneers in psychology* (Vol. 4, pp. 284–301). Washington, DC: American Psychological Association.

Shepard, R. N. (2001). On the possibility of universal mental laws: A reply to my critics. *Behavioral and Brain Sciences, 24,* 712–748.

Shepard, R. N., & Chipman, S. (1970). Second-order isomorphism of internal representations: Shapes of states. *Cognitive Psychology, 1,* 1–17.

Shepard, R. N., & Cooper, L. A. (1982). *Mental images and their transformations.* Cambridge, MA: MIT Press/Bradford Books.

Shepard, R. N., & Cooper, L. A. (1992). Representation of colors in the blind, color blind, and normally sighted. *Psychological Science, 3,* 97–104.

Shepard, R. N., & Farrell, J. E. (1985). Representation of the orientations of shapes. *Acta Psychologica, 59,* 104–121.

Shepard, R. N., Kilpatric, D. W., & Cunningham, J. P. (1975). The internal representation of numbers. *Cognitive Psychology, 7,* 82–138.

Shepard, R. N., & Metzler, J. (1971, February 19). Mental rotation of three-dimensional objects. *Science, 171,* 701–703.

Shepard, R. N., & Sheenan, M. M. (1965). Immediate recall of numbers containing a familiar prefix or postfix. *Perceptual and Motor Skills, 21,* 263–273.

Skinner, B. F. (1938). *The behavior of organisms: An experimental analysis.* New York: Appleton-Century.

Spence, K. W. (1937). The differential response in animals to stimuli varying within a single dimension. *Psychological Review, 44,* 430–444.

Taylor, A. E. (1984). A life in mathematics remembered. *American Mathematical Monthly, 91,* 605–618.

Weinberg, S. (1992). *Dreams of a final theory.* New York: Pantheon.

Wertheimer, M. (1945). *Productive thinking.* New York: Harper.

It's a good thing Dean Keith Simonton studies creativity, because he's been blessed with plenty of it. Simonton has spent a lifetime (and a profitable one at that, he notes) studying genius, creativity, leadership, and talent, and he did so by refusing to bow to an establishment that was bent on placing him in a box. In his chapter, Simonton publishes the results of an ongoing longitudinal case study of one DKS, the study's lone participant. In what promises to be a major breakthrough in anti-naysayer research, results thus far have shown fairly conclusively that defying the establishment can be highly rewarding, both intellectually and financially. Simonton acknowledges the study's flaws ($N = 1$) but thinks the data may have profound effects in persuading psychologists of the next generation to move outside of traditional circles.

Dean Keith Simonton

It's Absolutely Impossible? A Longitudinal Study of One Psychologist's Response to Conventional Naysayers

14

"I t can't be done!" "You won't be able to do it!" "Your plans are pure fantasy!" "Why don't you try something more reasonable?" "Shouldn't you be more realistic?" "Don't you think your luck has run out?"

How many ambitions have been squelched by such cynical exclamations and rhetorical questions? How often has a great idea been nipped in the bud? Sometimes these comments are motivated by envy and thus reflect the personal ego needs of the speaker. But more often such remarks come from well-meaning people who only seek to give you the best possible advice. They are merely warning you that your ideas or plans go against conventional wisdom or that they do not conform to what is normally expected. The discouraging comment is being altruistically dispensed to save you grief, to help you avoid bitter disappointment. Yet in terms of adverse consequences, the motives behind the admonitions probably matter very little. Whether the person who utters these warnings is pusillanimous or magnanimous, the net effect is the same. Recipients of such free advice feel the pressure to abandon their dreams or inspirations. And often they do so. That abandonment is not only their loss, but society's, too. The world will then have to wait a bit longer before someone else with the same idea has whatever it takes to run the gauntlet of naysayers.

Fortunately, I have conducted an extremely ambitious longitudinal study that specifically addresses this issue. The study is not ambitious in terms of sample size. On the contrary, it is merely a single-case ($N = 1$) investigation. Nor is the investigation ambitious in terms of its duration. After all, this longitudinal inquiry has been going on only for a few decades (albeit future waves of data collection are still planned). Rather, what makes the study ambitious is that to pursue his highly distinctive vision, the single participant was obliged to put his whole professional career at stake. Nowadays, in fact, it is questionable whether the study would pass muster with the Human Subjects Committee. The ethical ambiguities are not ameliorated by the fact that this high-risk investigation tested but one simple hypothesis: Unlike crime, defying the crowd can indeed pay.[1]

Method

SAMPLE

The lone research participant was Dean Keith Simonton (henceforth referred to as DKS).[2] This participant was recruited for the investigation during his senior year in college. This is a little later than the norm for most psychological studies, which most often sample sophomores enrolled in introductory psychology courses. Also contrary to standard protocol, DKS was not randomly chosen from the general population of students. Instead, he was chosen because he met three rigorous criteria.[3]

Criterion 1: A Previous History of Defying the Crowd

This stipulation was imposed to ensure that I would be likely to see additional episodes of such behavior during the course of the partici-

---

[1] I realize that this hypothesis may seem outdated given Sternberg and Lubart's (1995) book *Defying the Crowd: Cultivating Creativity in a Culture of Conformity*, not even considering this book that you are currently reading. Nonetheless, none of these books then existed, although I suspect that Sternberg probably had some of the same ideas in incipient form about the same time that this longitudinal study was initiated.

[2] The use of such initials is common practice in single-case studies, most often to maintain the anonymity of the participant. The usage here has a different basis, however. Because the participant and investigator happen to be both intimate friends and close relatives, referring to the former as DKS permits the latter to display more scientific disinterest. The practice also avoids the negative impression provoked by excessive use of the first-person pronoun (unhappily capitalized in English).

[3] More truthfully, I used a "convenience sample," DKS being the only person available. But that minor departure from the specified procedures has no impact on the validity of the reported findings.

pant's career development. DKS had demonstrated many instances of refusing to conform to the expectations of others. In junior high school, for instance, DKS received a discouraging reaction when he told a school counselor of his desire to sign up for college-preparatory courses. DKS was informed that this would be foolish, given his excellent performance in shop classes and his socioeconomic background. (He came from a working-class home, his father having dropped out of high school.) DKS insisted anyway. He thought he could do it, his counselor's misgivings notwithstanding. He persisted because he wanted to become a teacher some day. This episode is typical of many others that occurred throughout his schooling.

Criterion 2: Unusual or Unconventional Interests

This criterion was chosen to guarantee that the participant in the single-case study would not have an easy time "fitting in." Obviously, if someone has no interests other than those that fit neatly with some mainstream topic in the discipline, conformity pressures are minimal, and there is no need whatsoever to rebel against the norms. In the case of DKS, he was simultaneously interested in both the sciences and the humanities. In fact, when he applied to college, he wavered between chemistry and history as majors. From his elementary school days, he had been an amateur chemist and naturalist, with some dabbling in physics and astronomy, too. Yet he also performed in drama productions in both high school and college, played rhythm guitar in rock groups, wrote poetry (albeit very bad stuff, in my opinion), and created artworks in various media (e.g., one of his pastels was chosen to decorate the principal's office at his high school). He was also an avid reader, using his hard-earned money from a job at a car wash to purchase the anthology *Great Books of the Western World* (Hutchins, 1952), a collection he still owns and reads. Trying to incorporate all of these interests and abilities into a coherent career path was not going to be easy, yet DKS really wanted to do so. The greater the integration, the more enjoyable his career was likely to be.

Criterion 3: Demonstrated Scientific Potential

Clearly, it does no good to defy the crowd to pursue unusual interests if someone has no potential of making some scientific contribution to the discipline. If someone lacks the talent or commitment to do science, then all will be wasted effort. DKS satisfied this criterion reasonably well. For at least a decade prior to his recruitment as the research participant, he had shown a high degree of promise as a future behavioral scientist. In junior high school, for example, DKS was chosen to participate in a special summer program designed by the Los Angeles City School District to cultivate young scientific talent. By the time he graduated from high school he had received special awards in both the natural and the social sciences. As a consequence of these accomplishments, he obtained a financial "free ride" in both college and graduate school, in the latter case supported by a Fellowship from the National Science Foundation.

TESTS AND MEASURES

Having chosen DKS as the participant in this single-case longitudinal investigation, the next step was to expose him to various kinds of in-vivo assessments. In one way or another these would test his commitment to his own peculiar mission as a scientist or psychologist. The details about these trials are described in the Results section, yet I should point out that a preliminary test was run to make sure that DKS was the appropriate research participant. He had applied to various graduate programs in social psychology and waited eagerly for the outcome.

Eventually, two distinguished social psychologists telephoned DKS just 2 days apart. Each psychologist represented a prestigious university (Harvard and Stanford). Both told him that he was admitted and that they were enthusiastic about his accepting their admission offer. But when DKS made it very explicit that he wished to study the social psychology of creativity, the representative of one institution backtracked and strongly suggested that maybe there was not such a good fit after all. That institution was Stanford. The representative of the other institution made no judgment other than saying that students often change their interests during the course of their graduate study. That institution was Harvard. So, DKS chose Harvard over Stanford largely because he at least had a reasonable prospect of pursuing his major interest.[4] Of course, this outcome is not too surprising. At the time he was making this decision, Stanford's psychology department was quite mainstream, and its faculty had few interdisciplinary interests. In contrast, the social psychology program at Harvard was still housed in the highly interdisciplinary Department of Social Relations, a unit that included sociologists and cultural anthropologists along with personality, developmental, and social psychologists. Harvard would therefore be more likely to support DKS's unconventional ideas.

---

[4]Years later, DKS learned the wisdom of his decision. Some psychologists who had earned their doctorates at Stanford University in the 1970s told him that it would have been extremely unlikely that he would have been able to do the research that was the eventual basis for his Harvard doctoral dissertation. Both the methodology and the subject matter would have departed too drastically from the mainstream.

Results

The data collected during this longitudinal study can be presented in two sections. The first deals with the period of graduate training and the second with the period of career development.

GRADUATE TRAINING

When DKS began the Harvard graduate program in 1970, he found himself quickly disappointed. One problem was that the Department of Social Relations was in the process of falling apart. Sociology had just left, and cultural anthropology was soon to follow. By the time DKS finished graduate school, in fact, the psychologists from the various subdisciplines had merged to form the Department of Psychology and Social Relations. The interdisciplinary environment he had anticipated had vanished. Accordingly, if he was going to obtain a broad understanding of the phenomena that interested him, he was going to have to do it alone. However, this was not going to be easy, because the social psychology program was heavy on course requirements and light on the mentoring of individual research (unless it happened to be part of a faculty member's research program). Many of the required courses and seminars seemed totally peripheral, even irrelevant, at least as far as DKS was concerned. As a consequence, he put in minimal effort, just enough to get passing grades. Moreover, his comportment in class was often less than ideal. Feeling like an outsider looking on a discipline whose methodological and theoretical commitments he could not always accept, he often found himself challenging his professors during discussion. Once he interrupted a professor's presentation so frequently with critical remarks that the seminar was terminated early, the professor refusing to continue. Admittedly, this interruption was not a solo operation. This was the heyday of the Vietnam War, when it was commonplace not to "trust anyone over 30" and to "question authority." But DKS was widely considered the worst of the bunch, a genuine "rebel without a cause."

Not surprisingly, more than once a faculty member advised DKS that he might be better off withdrawing from the graduate program. If DKS couldn't make his ideas conform to those of the faculty, what was the point of him staying anyway? Furthermore, DKS was repeatedly told that his research ideas were not going to go anywhere. Creativity was a dead subject in general and had no place in social psychology anyway. Creativity may not even be a psychological phenomenon, at least not in science, as proven by the occurrence of multiples (i.e., where two or more scientists independently make the same discovery). Besides all this, the social psychology of creativity could not be studied using mainstream methodologies, namely, laboratory experiments. DKS was explicitly warned that his research would not possibly get accepted in the most prestigious journals of his discipline and that it certainly would never make it into the American Psychological Association's *Journal of Personality and Social Psychology* (*JPSP*). By the early 1970s, *JPSP* seldom published research on creativity, and the few articles that did appear on that subject invariably used conventional methods. If DKS did not publish in *JPSP*, he could not expect to have a successful academic career as a psychologist.

Everything was going to come to a head at the end of the second year in graduate school. Then DKS would have to pass the Doctoral General Exams. If he failed to do so, he was out of the program, with an "exit" MA at best. Because all students in the same class had to take the same exams at the same time, they formed a study group to prepare for the big event. Surprisingly, given his academic performance to date, DKS declined to participate. By studying the recommended reading on his own, he would have more control over his precious time, permitting him to continue the pursuit of his outside interests. One nice feature about the exams was that the essays were all typed and numbered so that they could be graded anonymously by a faculty committee. That meant that if DKS bit his lip and conformed to the norms for but a single day, he could avoid revealing his identity and thus be assured that his knowledge would be assessed without preconceptions created by his aberrant academic performance. It worked beautifully. Not only did DKS pass, he also "passed with distinction," receiving the highest score in his class!

That occurred in 1972, and afterward the picture brightened considerably. The faculty realized that whatever faults DKS may have had, ignorance of the field was not one of them. In addition, certain external events began to leave him more intellectual breathing space. For instance, McGuire (1973), a former editor of *JPSP*, had published an article in which he argued for more theoretical and methodological openness in the field. In particular, he argued for a "new paradigm . . . deriving hypotheses from a systems theory of social and cognitive structures that takes into account multiple and bidirectional causality among social variables," one in which "hypotheses testing will be done in multivariate correlational designs with naturally fluctuating variables" (p. 446). As Elms (1975) was to point out 2 years later, social psychology was undergoing a "crisis of confidence" with respect to its paradigmatic commitments. This growing disintegration of the disciplinary consensus was coupled with the addition of David Kenny to the graduate program. Having just received his PhD under Donald Campbell, Kenny was both methodologically sophisticated and substantively flexible. He was thus willing to take on DKS as his first graduate student.

All this gave DKS the wiggle room he needed. In 1973 he wrote his required special topic paper, "Time-Series and Longitudinal Analyses of Archival Data: A Suggestion for the Social Psychology of Innovation." With typical interdisciplinary flair, this paper combined cultural anthropology (cross-cultural research methodology), economics (econometric models), history (cliometrics), sociology (theories of sociocultural change), psychoanalysis (psychohistory), and psychology (psychometrics and research on creativity and genius). This paper led immediately to his thesis proposal. Although the oral defense did not go all that well (for narrative, see Simonton, 1990)—skepticism about the feasibility and value of the project was rampant—the proposal eventually passed. He finished the dissertation a year later, on August 5, 1974. Titled "The Social Psychology of Creativity: An Archival Data Analysis," it represented the first example of the research program that DKS wished to pursue for the rest of his career. He was compelled to hurry, though, for he had to load up a truck to move all of his belongings to where he was going to assume the responsibilities of his first academic job. Classes were to begin soon thereafter, and his career had begun.

CAREER DEVELOPMENT

The position was in the psychology department at the University of Arkansas. This was not his first choice. He had hoped to get a position closer to California and would have liked to be affiliated with an institution with a research reputation more like that of Harvard, Stanford, Yale, or Michigan. But he had to be realistic. The job market for new faculty was in the doldrums in those days, and things would likely not be better for a fresh PhD with such unconventional research interests. To be sure, DKS also had been invited for interviews at Cornell University, Wellesley College, and the University of California at Davis, but these visits did not produce job offers. Although DKS did receive subsequent interview inquiries from Yale and Johns Hopkins, these came after he had already accepted the position at Arkansas. Besides, the faculty in his new department made it very clear that he would not have to compromise his research program, so long as something was published somewhere. He certainly did not have to publish all (or even any) of his research in *JPSP*.

This latitude turned out to be especially critical, because DKS discovered something a bit disconcerting during the course of his job interview at Arkansas. It was revealed that the author of one "letter of recommendation" had observed that DKS had some very interesting ideas but that these ideas would certainly not be publishable in any prestigious journal, including *JPSP*. With a letter of support like that, DKS could not possibly expect to win a position at a major research university. It began to look like the worst-case scenario was actually the best-case scenario. If the author of this letter was correct, there was no way DKS could hope for more. Furthermore, even if the letter's author was wrong in his prediction, the best option for DKS was to use Arkansas as a springboard for his career advancement.

Happily, the adverse prediction was disproved shortly after he began his teaching duties in Arkansas. DKS had converted three chapters from his dissertation into journal articles, and all three were accepted for publication, two of them in high-impact journals. Indeed, one of these journals was none other than *JPSP*, which on December 16, 1974, decided to publish an article titled "Sociocultural Context of Individual Creativity: A Transhistorical Time-Series Analysis" (Simonton, 1975). Within a short time, other publications accumulated on the DKS curriculum vita, so that in less than 2 years when he ventured into the job market a second time, he had nearly a dozen articles published or in press. He ended up much closer to home, in the psychology department at the Davis campus of the University of California, the same department that declined to offer him a position when he was in his final year at Harvard.

The longitudinal study did not end here. Instead, DKS was exposed to various naturalistic interventions to see if he would ever compromise his research. For example, when he was subjected to a midcareer evaluation to determine his prospects for eventual promotion to a tenured associate professorship, some of his colleagues insisted that he needed to publish investigations using more conventional methods (viz., laboratory experiments). This DKS refused to do, seeing it as an imposition on his academic freedom as well as his scientific integrity (albeit since getting tenure he has published studies using more mainstream techniques; e.g., Simonton, 1985, 1986a). Furthermore, DKS would often have to endure the most brutal evaluations on the part of manuscript referees. One reviewer even proclaimed that one of DKS's manuscripts was the worst one ever read in his or her entire career! Needless to say, DKS has probably accumulated more rejection letters than most psychologists of his cohort. Yet he did not allow these rejections to stop him. He simply revised the manuscript and resubmitted it to another journal. Some of his best articles went through two or more editorial cycles before finding a home. This was not necessarily a bad thing; the article almost always got much better as a direct result. One manuscript was improved so much by the rounds of submission and rejection that he ended up submitting the revision to a journal better than the three others that had refused publication. It was accepted! The lesson here is clear: Perseverance works—at least when coupled with a willingness to accommodate constructive criticisms.

Even when the initial evaluations all went extremely well, DKS sometimes encountered strangely negative editorial comments. In 1979 two referees determined that a manuscript submitted to *JPSP* for publication was acceptable without *any* revision, a truly rare event in anyone's career. Yet the editor could not resist saying in his acceptance letter that "it is possible that your well may be running dry; the present paper begins to show signs of strain." Because DKS had to include this letter with the materials he submitted when he was going up for tenure, he asked the editor, as politely as possible, to write a revised letter with that comment omitted. This request was necessary because during his tenure appraisal some members of his department also feared he was going to "run dry." After all, when DKS used up all the information available in the histories, biographies, encyclopedias, dictionaries, and anthologies, what else was he going to do with his time? Evidently, the entire record and repository of human civilization couldn't possibly contain as much information as was available from college sophomores in laboratory experiments!

These fears were clearly unjustified. Since those premonitions were expressed, DKS has added more than 200 publications to his CV. It is significant that this output was accomplished without any grant support. It is not that he never tried. Shortly after he was promoted to associate professor in 1980, he made a serious effort to send grant proposals to every funding agency he could think of, both public and private. Each one was shot down. DKS soon learned that it required only one evaluator to dislike one's ideas for funding to be denied, no matter how worthy the proposal was in the minds of the other evaluators. Furthermore, funding was quite obviously confined to research projects that departed less drastically from the mainstream. The most common criticism was that the proposed research could not possibly be carried out, or, if it could, the results would not be worth publishing in any respected journal. These remarks would later evoke many ironic smiles when the research described in these rejected proposals was later accepted for publication in top-tier psychology journals. Nevertheless, DKS had learned his lesson. If he wanted to make substantial contributions to his field, writing grant proposals would not get him where he wanted to go.

As part of this longitudinal study, I kept a detailed record of everything DKS published. In 1982 there appeared an uncharacteristic dip in his output—only one publication, and that only a brief comment in the *American Psychologist*. That was the price he paid for wasting time writing grant proposals that, at best, were "approved but not funded." The count for 1982 contrasts greatly with his normal annual output ($p < .001$). Between 1975 and 2000, he averaged about 8 publications per year, and twice he could claim 18 publications in a single year. These publications include 8 books and more than 3 dozen publications in top journals, including the American Psychological Association's own *American Psy-*

chologist, Psychological Review, Psychological Bulletin, Psychological Methods, Developmental Psychology, Psychology of Aging, and, most astonishingly, *JPSP*! In fact, DKS has now published more articles in the leading journals than the Harvard professor who predicted that he would not publish any!

These publications have earned DKS a considerable amount of professional recognition.[5] More pertinent to this study's initial hypothesis, however, is that DKS also earns an excellent income. He has progressed steadily through the academic ranks, often obtaining accelerated advancements and promotions, so that he now stands at the top of the regular pay scale in University of California's professorial series. This yields an annual salary nearly twice as high as the median income for full professors with appointments in the psychology departments of U.S. research universities. Better yet, prize and award monies, consulting fees, honoraria, and royalties amply supplement this regular salary. Ergo, it is decidedly proven that "defying the crowd pays," QED.

Interestingly, when I permitted DKS to read a first draft of this report, he immediately protested the foregoing conclusion. It sounded too mercenary, as if he does what he does to make money. Although he recognizes the need to earn a living, his primary motivation comes from neither the financial rewards nor the professional awards. Rather, he immensely loves what he does. DKS has devoted his life and career to the scientific study of exceptional creators and leaders, geniuses and talents, masterpieces and historic events—what he has called *significant samples* (Simonton, 1999). Hence, his research "subjects" or "participants" have recognizable names or identities: (a) individuals like Confucius, Isaac Newton, Napoleon Bonaparte, and Marian Anderson; (b) products like *Hamlet, Citizen Kane*, the *Origin of Species*, and Symphony No. 5 in C Minor; and (c) events like the Golden Age of Greece, the multiple discovery of Mendelian genetics, the defeat of Robert E. Lee at Gettysburg, and King George III's 1788 lapse into insanity. These personalities, accomplishments, and occurrences span almost all civilizations and historical periods and encompass virtually every domain of achievement, from composers to presidents and from patents to motion pictures. All of his subjects are intrinsically fascinating, so much so that they invariably earn entries in encyclopedias and biographical diction-

---

[5]Complete documentation of his awards and honors, both national and international, and for both research and teaching, is provided at DKS's home page at http://psychology.ucdavis.edu/Simonton. Admittedly, the fact that DKS was asked to write this chapter could itself be considered tentative evidence that he had "made it" as a psychologist. Yet I find this evidence overly contingent on the opinion of this book's editor, whose judgment may be off base in the current case (however correct with respect to the remaining contributors to this collection).

aries. Certainly these cases are far more interesting than those most typical of psychological research. In addition, DKS uses his significant samples to test what he considers to be extremely important hypotheses about the psychology of genius, creativity, leadership, and talent. These tests have yielded a large inventory of fascinating findings (Simonton, 1984, 1994a).

Admittedly, all of these tests require that vast stores of qualitative information be first converted into quantitative measurements, compiled in computer databases, and subjected to elaborate statistical analyses (Simonton, in press). But even here, DKS managed to make enjoyable what might otherwise be considered a tedious process. This playful opportunism was apparent in his inquiries concerning the 154 sonnets penned by William Shakespeare (e.g., Simonton, 1989). The computerized content analysis could not proceed without first placing the sonnets in machine-readable form. So the very first thing he did each morning after turning on his home computer was to key in a single sonnet. He thus accomplished 1/154th of the requisite task, while at the same time having a "poem of the day" to contemplate and appreciate. Even the statistical analyses usually turned into a welcome phase of excitement and exploration. Besides satisfying the long-standing curiosity about which of his hypotheses would survive empirical test, DKS often took great pleasure in looking at the residual errors of his prediction equations (e.g., Simonton, 1986b). Which cases had scores that fell right on the regression line and which departed from the norm, providing intriguing outliers that refused to conform to our psychological theories? The departures helped DKS better understand the genuine uniqueness of so many celebrities of civilization and history—another special asset of his decision to study famous personalities.

In addition, DKS reiterated the fact that his original rationale for entering the academic world was to become a teacher. One of the wonders of his research program is how well it contributes to his teaching. He now teaches a popular psychology course on Genius, Creativity, and Leadership and has recruited nearly 300 undergraduates to participate in his research. Just as significant, his extensive inquiries into the psychology of science have inspired his approach to teaching the capstone course on the history of psychology. DKS examines the major figures in the annals of our discipline from the standpoint of what psychologists have so far learned about the cognitive, developmental, dispositional, and social factors that contribute to success as an outstanding scientist (Simonton, 2002). Students taking the course have a term paper assignment in which they analyze a particular notable psychologist in terms of this psychological research (Simonton, 1994b). Students thereby learn how psychology can enhance our comprehension of those who have most contributed to psychology's emergence as a scientific discipline. Along the way, students also learn what it takes to make their own contributions to the field.

In a nutshell, DKS claims that the pleasures he gets from research and teaching are far more critical than the checks he receives. Defying the crowd certainly pays, but the biggest portion of that payment is intellectual, emotional, and aesthetic rather than material. He asked me to include this clarification, and I have complied.

Discussion

Without doubt, this longitudinal study has many limitations.[6] One patent shortcoming is that it is only a single-case inquiry. DKS may not necessarily be representative of all maverick psychologists. Another weakness is that it was a correlational rather than experimental study. It would have been advantageous to impose the various tests as active manipulations rather than just let things happen randomly (albeit the ethics of deliberately imposing such career obstacles would be questionable). Finally, it might be argued that it is premature to report these results now. According to his own empirical and theoretical research, DKS still has some good years ahead of him, and so his reputation (and earnings) will probably continue to grow (Simonton, 1991, 1992, 1997).

Yet putting these limitations aside, the career of DKS demonstrates the validity of the study's hypothesis for at least one psychologist who has attained more than the usual success. Hence, I decided to ask DKS four questions that might be of interest to future psychologists trying to decide whether they should defy the crowd, either in graduate school or as assistant professors. I will merely present his responses without comment. They pretty much speak for themselves.

1. WHAT, IF ANYTHING, WOULD YOU DO DIFFERENTLY NOW?

I guess I would have been both more diplomatic and more assertive when encountering obstacles to my chosen path.

---

[6]I must admit that the most serious liability of this longitudinal investigation is that it is actually a retrospective study. Thus, data reliability is contingent entirely on the accuracy of the participant's "autobiographical memory"—this when we have ample empirical evidence that such memories cannot be completely trusted. Even so, DKS informed me that these data reflect his best recollections. I can only hope that the episodes he recalled are replicated by future studies using a truly longitudinal design but with different research participants.

Particularly when I was at Harvard, I would often "come on too strong," sometimes even "flying off the handle." This only polarized people, and sometimes alienated those who might otherwise have taken my side. If I could go back in a time machine and rewrite the true biography, I would lower the pitch and decibel level of my voice, firmly saying without adrenaline accompaniment something like, "I appreciate why you find that important for me to know (or do), and I really wish I could do so, but at present it doesn't seem to have as much importance as some other things I must know (or do). Even so, I'll try to come back to your suggestion in the future." Whether I could pull this off without sounding insincere or ingratiating is another question altogether. Nonetheless, I must admit that after about a decade into my career, I formally apologized to the Harvard professor who received the biggest dose of my ire.

2. WHAT WERE THE COSTS TO YOU PROFESSIONALLY OF DEFYING THE ESTABLISHMENT?

My feelings here are mixed. On the one hand, being a "lone wolf" has definite negative consequences. Many psychologists still don't feel that I'm doing psychology, and some still confuse what I do with psychohistory and psychobiography. So, if I had only "joined the pack," I might have ended up at one of the top 10 research universities. I probably would also have been far more successful in my quest for extramural funding. These two consequences likely would have enabled me to attract more high-quality graduate students and therefore to acquire more intellectual successors than I do today. During the course of my career I've seen many young talents who had an intense interest in my research and yet who declined University of California at Davis's admission offer because they were offered more money to go to a more prestigious university—to do what they did not find particularly to their liking. It would be nice to have had the cash and the name to motivate these talents to "keep the faith." On the other hand, I'm doing as well as most ambitious psychologists could reasonably expect—and especially well for someone who wasn't supposed to be "college material" or who had no chance of publishing in first-tier psychological journals. I don't think I'm being complacent when I say that I have attained some degree of success. And, besides, I can live with myself, knowing I did my best to do what I do best.

3. WHAT WERE THE COSTS TO YOU PERSONALLY OF DEFYING THE ESTABLISHMENT?

At the personal level, too, the benefits far outnumber the costs. Naturally, my first 2 years in graduate school were extremely stressful, and going up for tenure when you're a nonconformist is not a relaxing experience, particularly when your university must solicit letters from extramural experts who will evaluate your work. At times, my health and my personal relationships suffered. Yet, it is clear that I'm a far happier person "doing my own thing." If I had gone along with what everyone expected me to do, I probably would have had a midlife crisis motivated by a deep realization that I had sold myself short. Despite my Buddhist predilections, I'm not a believer in reincarnation, and accordingly I believe that if you can't be true to yourself in this life, there is no second chance.

4. WHAT ADVICE WOULD YOU GIVE OTHER SCIENTISTS WHO CONSIDER FOLLOWING A SIMILAR PATH?

Given the potential obstacles and frustrations, the decision should not be taken lightly. So, by all means, be honest with yourself, almost brutally so. After all, this consideration requires the most objective self-appraisal. Yet if you know deep down that you have the ability and knowledge necessary to give your ideas the careful attention they deserve; if you know at your very core that your vision would enable you to realize most fully your potential as a human being, psychologist, and scientist; if you know that you have the persistence and patience to put up with all of those who tell you *it* can't be done or *you* can't do it; if you are willing to be a lone wolf and give up the security of belonging to the pack . . . if you can fulfill all these conditions, then I have one and only one recommendation: *Do it!* You owe it not just to yourself, but to psychology as a discipline.

After I informed DKS that the poststudy interview and debriefing session had been completed, he spontaneously volunteered one last comment. He said, "I hope that graduate students and younger colleagues with great creative ideas will benefit from the results of your longitudinal study." So do I.

References

Elms, A. C. (1975). The crisis of confidence in social psychology. *American Psychologist, 30,* 967–976.

Hutchins, R. M. (Ed.). (1952). *Great books of the Western world* (54 vols.). Chicago: Encyclopaedia Britannica.

McGuire, W. J. (1973). The yin and yang of progress in social psychology: Seven koan. *Journal of Personality and Social Psychology, 26,* 446–456.

Simonton, D. K. (1973). *Time-series and longitudinal analyses of archival data: A suggestion for the social psychology of innovation.* Unpublished special topic paper, Harvard University, Cambridge, MA.

Simonton, D. K. (1974). *The social psychology of creativity: An archival data analysis.* Unpublished doctoral dissertation, Harvard University, Cambridge, MA.

Simonton, D. K. (1975). Sociocultural context of individual creativity: A transhistorical time-series analysis. *Journal of Personality and Social Psychology, 32,* 1119–1133.

Simonton, D. K. (1984). *Genius, creativity, and leadership: Historiometric inquiries.* Cambridge, MA: Harvard University Press.

Simonton, D. K. (1985). Intelligence and personal influence in groups: Four nonlinear models. *Psychological Review, 92,* 532–547.

Simonton, D. K. (1986a). Dispositional attributions of (presidential) leadership: An experimental simulation of historiometric results. *Journal of Experimental Social Psychology, 22,* 389–418.

Simonton, D. K. (1986b). Presidential personality: Biographical use of the Gough Adjective Check List. *Journal of Personality and Social Psychology, 51,* 149–160.

Simonton, D. K. (1989). Shakespeare's sonnets: A case of and for single-case historiometry. *Journal of Personality, 57,* 695–721.

Simonton, D. K. (1990). History, chemistry, psychology, and genius: An intellectual autobiography of historiometry. In M. Runco & R. Albert (Eds.), *Theories of creativity* (pp. 92–115). Newbury Park, CA: Sage.

Simonton, D. K. (1991). Career landmarks in science: Individual differences and interdisciplinary contrasts. *Developmental Psychology, 27,* 119–130.

Simonton, D. K. (1992). Leaders of American psychology, 1879–1967: Career development, creative output, and professional achievement. *Journal of Personality and Social Psychology, 62,* 5–17.

Simonton, D. K. (1994a). *Greatness: Who makes history and why.* New York: Guilford Press.

Simonton, D. K. (1994b). Scientific eminence, the history of psychology, and term paper topics: A metascience approach. *Teaching of Psychology, 21,* 169–171.

Simonton, D. K. (1997). Creative productivity: A predictive and explanatory model of career trajectories and landmarks. *Psychological Review, 104,* 66–89.

Simonton, D. K. (1999). Significant samples: The psychological study of eminent individuals. *Psychological Methods, 4,* 425–451.

Simonton, D. K. (2002). *Great psychologists and their times: Scientific insights into psychology's history*. Washington, DC: American Psychological Association.

Simonton, D. K. (in press). Qualitative and quantitative analyses of historical data. *Annual Review of Psychology, 54*.

Sternberg, R. J., & Lubart, T. I. (1995). *Defying the crowd: Cultivating creativity in a culture of conformity*. New York: Free Press.

Robert Sternberg is a crowd defier who has lived to tell the tale. In the sometimes-cutthroat world of intelligence theory, his has often been (and continues to be) a loud voice of dissent. His theory of successful intelligence (which traces its roots to his own childhood fears of intelligence measures) managed to thoroughly alienate the old guard of intelligence, just as subsequent theories have made waves in their respective topics of study. Sternberg continues to enjoy what he calls "being on the fringe" as director of the Yale Center for the Psychology of Abilities, Competencies, and Expertise.

Robert J. Sternberg

It All Started With Those Darn IQ Tests: Half a Career Spent Defying the Crowd

15

The Prehistory

If it weren't for the darn IQ tests, my whole life might have been different. As a child, I was very test anxious (and probably everything else anxious, too). The school psychologist would enter the elementary school classroom, and I immediately knew why she was there—to give us a group IQ test. Immediately, I would tighten up like a drum. She would hand out the test booklets, but all I could focus on was my test anxiety. She would say "Begin," and I would watch other students answer the problems. I would look at the problems, but I hardly could read them, so tense was I in their presence! Then the other children would start turning pages, and I was still on the first or second problem. It was over—another failure.

I eventually cured myself of the test anxiety when, as a sixth grader, I was sent back to a fifth-grade classroom to retake the fifth-grade intelligence test. The school officials apparently did not think me bright enough to be able to cope with the sixth-grade test. At that point, I was in the final grade of elementary school, and like all other sixth graders,

Preparation of this chapter was supported in part by National Science Foundation Grant REC-9979843 and by Javits Act Program Grant No. R206R000001 as administered by the Office of Educational Research and Improvement, U.S. Department of Education. Grantees undertaking such projects are encouraged to express freely their professional judgment. This article, therefore, does not necessarily represent the position or policies of the Office of Educational Research and Improvement or the U.S. Department of Education, and no official endorsement should be inferred.

I viewed myself as eminently superior to the younger kids, who I perceived as little more than infants. Certainly I could compete with fifth graders! So I took the test without anxiety, and the test anxiety disappeared and never returned.

What did not disappear, however, was a life-long interest in the nature, measurement, and development of intelligence. This interest was rather strange for a young child, and it was not a whole lot less strange among the cognitive psychologists with whom I was trained in graduate school and with whom I would later associate as a professor. The interest started early: Even in elementary school, every year I would write a workbook with exercises that I thought would help children in the grade I was in to develop their intelligence. But I was interested not only in developing intelligence—I wanted to test it.

In seventh grade, at age 13, I wanted to understand intelligence, and implicitly, why I had done so poorly on the tests. Test anxiety was a concept with which I was not yet familiar; but stupidity was something I was quite familiar with, and I wondered whether I was afflicted with it. So when we were asked to come up with ideas for science projects, I generated an idea that almost certainly had not been tried by others in Mr. Adams's seventh-grade science class. I proposed to do a project on the development of mental testing. As part of the project, I invented my own test, the Sternberg Test of Mental Abilities which, like my workbooks (and my childhood comic books), is long since lost. In visiting, for the first time, the adult section of the Maplewood, New Jersey, town library, I discovered the book *Measuring Intelligence* (Terman & Merrill, 1937), which contained the verbal materials for the Stanford-Binet Intelligence Scales (2nd ed.). I thought it would be a good idea to get some practice in administering the tests to some classmates.

The first classmate to whom I gave the test was a girl in whom I was romantically interested. I was rather shy and thought that perhaps giving her the IQ test would help break the ice. I was wrong. She did very well on the test, but the romantic relationship never got started. The second classmate to whom I gave the test was one I had known from the Cub Scouts. Another disaster. He told his mother, who told the junior high school guidance counselor, who told a school psychologist. I was called away from a social studies class one day, balled out for 40 minutes, and informed by the psychologist that if I ever brought the book into school again, he personally would burn it. He suggested that if I had to study intelligence, I study it instead in rats. I don't think he was offering himself as a subject.

At this point, I learned a lesson about defying the crowd, a lesson I relearn on a regular basis: Defying the crowd has costs, sometimes steep ones. It almost always is easier to follow the crowd and join in the fads (Sternberg, 1997a). Fortunately, my science teacher stood up for me, and the consequences were not as serious as they might have been: no suspensions, no expulsions. I decided at that point that I had to do what I had to do. For me, it was a calling. Today, I view it as a mission. I continued to study intelligence, but underground. I did not come out from the underground until several years later.

In 10th grade, I was suspicious that the Biological Science Curriculum Study (BSCS) biology program we were using was not really teaching us much biology. So, with the support of my biology teacher, Mrs. Stewart, I designed an experiment to test how scores of the students in BSCS biology would compare with those of comparable students in the standard biology course, both for the BSCS exams and the standard exams. True to my prediction, the two groups did equally well on the BSCS test, but the students in the standard course outperformed the BSCS students on the standard exam.

The summer after 10th grade, I went to a summer program in marine biology, and the program directors were not thrilled when I proposed to study human intelligence, but they caved in. So I studied the effects of distractions on mental test performance and discovered that neither a car headlight shining in one's eyes nor a metronome disrupted mental test performance, but a Beatles record playing "She's Got the Devil in Her Heart" improved mental test performance.

A year later, my physics teacher, Mr. Genzer, was wonderfully supportive when I did a strange physics project, the development of a physics aptitude test. I was trying, in part, to figure out why I was doing so poorly in physics. The test correlated about .65 with physics grades and was actually used by the high school for several years as a screening device for admission to the advanced physics class.

So if I ask myself why I can defy the crowd and live with it, I attribute much of it to the wonderful support I had both from my parents and from early teachers, like Mr. Adams, Mrs. Stewart, and Mr. Genzer. They provided an atmosphere where one could go one's own way and be rewarded for it. Yet I knew from my seventh-grade experience that there were costs, and this is a lesson I keep relearning.

Ancient History

I went to college and discovered that not much was going on in intelligence research at Yale University. The one professor interested in the field was perturbed. He had spent his time using calculators to predict students' Yale grade point averages (GPAs) from variables in their admissions folders, such as scholastic aptitude test (SAT) scores and high school GPAs. But Yale had introduced computerization, and so the calculations he had lovingly done over months now took a matter of seconds. He took to checking the computer calculations by hand, but fortunately for all, retired soon thereafter.

I pursued my interests by doing research on undergraduate admissions—resulting in two published articles—and by studying thinking with Professor Alexander Wearing. The admissions office had mixed feelings about my research. They had these long admissions meetings where they spent several weeks, meeting for many hours per day, deciding who should be admitted. I showed that, for about three-quarters of the cases, an algorithm could predict what they were doing with roughly 98% accuracy (Sternberg, 1972). In another study, I showed that the admissions office interview was a poor predictor of admissions outcomes (Sternberg, 1973). But I recommended that the office keep the interview, because students liked it and thought they did much better than they did with respect to the evaluation they received.

After my junior year, Professor Wearing took a position in Australia, and I became a student of Endel Tulving. Tulving was a wonderful mentor whose trademark, at that point, was defying the crowd. If people believed one thing, he would show them that the opposite was true. So if they believed, for example, that repetition always improved recall, he would show them that it could actually result in worse recall (Tulving, 1966). If they believed that recognition memory was always better than recall memory, he would show that recall memory could be better than recognition memory (Tulving & Thomson, 1973). Tulving was a wonderful role model: a scientist who had defied the crowd and won!

A year later, I went to Stanford University to study under Gordon Bower. For my first-year project, I continued with work I had started on negative transfer in part–whole and whole–part free recall, and I did a series of studies providing an explanation of the phenomenon that was different from Tulving's (Sternberg & Bower, 1974). One might have expected Tulving to protest. Quite the contrary. He was totally supportive, teaching me another lesson. The true scientist is out to discover the truth, wherever it may be found. And sometimes, one discovers that the truth is not where one has been looking.

Tulving and I continued to collaborate during my relatively brief time at Stanford. The collaboration was facilitated by his spending a year at the Center for Advanced Study in the Behavioral Sciences, which was nearby. We wrote an article on the measurement of subjective organization, which advocated a type of measure that was rather unpopular at that time. We submitted the article to the *Psychological Bulletin*, and it was rejected. I needed to cite the article in another article I was writing, and I asked Tulving how I should cite it. He stared me straight in the eye and replied something like, "Well, cite it as 'Rejected by *Psychological Bulletin*, of course.'" At the time, I thought this a most bizarre answer. We were going to brag about getting our article rejected? I later realized the message he was sending me (or, at least, I thought he was sending me): If you defy the crowd, you will get rejections. They are not a badge of shame, but rather, a badge of honor. If you never get anything rejected, the one thing you know about yourself is that you never took the risk of defying the crowd. Eventually, *Psychological Bulletin* accepted the article (Sternberg & Tulving, 1977). When, years later, I became editor of this same journal, I wrote an editorial encouraging people to be unconventional in their submissions. And by encouraging such submissions, and providing for others the same kind of encouragement that I myself had gotten from my mentors, the journal did indeed receive and publish articles that defied the crowd.

My heart was in intelligence research, not in memory research, however, and so I was casting about for ideas about how to study intelligence. I got some ideas the summer after my first year of graduate study, and so was born the componential analysis (Sternberg, 1977a, 1977b, 1983) of human intelligence. To his great credit, my advisor, Bower, was wholly supportive of my working in a field totally outside his area and outside the area of anyone else in the department. He even supported my research from his grant. But I also discovered that the general climate of the psychology department was not highly favorable for the kind of research I was doing. It just didn't fit. I decided to take some courses in education, an idea that also did not receive much support from the psychology department. But I went my own way and thereby met Lee Cronbach, another great influence on my life. Later, as editor of *Psychological Bulletin*, I was to discover that of the 10 most frequently cited articles in the history of the journal, Cronbach had authored or coauthored 4 of them (Sternberg, 1992). Here was a man who went his own way! He helped invent the field of psychometrics as we now know it.

Early History

Stanford was a wonderful place, but in some respects, I felt that the atmosphere was not right for me. I had the impression, at least at the time, that Stanford was into trends, whereas I tended to buck, or at least ignore, trends. Because I was finishing up, I applied during my third year there for some jobs, and Yale University hired me. Yale was full of idiosyncratic people who seemed to go their own offbeat ways. It was full of trend busters! It seemed right for me. And so I packed up and went back to Yale, pained, however, that my mentor Tulving had left.

Yale proved to be the right place for me. Offbeat people such as myself were valued. But as soon as I left the campus, I found that the sledding got tougher, and sometimes the sled seemed to overturn.

In my first year, I received a colloquium invitation from a major testing organization. I was thrilled. This was going to be my chance to really change things. After all, who more needed to hear what I had to say about intelligence than the old fuddy-duddies at testing organizations, who had been producing essentially the same tests for close to a century? I went to the colloquium full of enthusiasm.

The talk bombed. I was stunned. How could my wonderfully fresh and creative ideas about intelligence go over so poorly? Maybe they weren't so fresh or even so wonderful! Over time, I came to realize the nature of at least part of the problem. The testing organization had a very substantial vested interest in its existing products. What I was proposing was essentially that those products were nowhere near as good as they thought they were. This was not the message that such an organization wanted to hear. What did I expect—that people 20 or 30 years my senior would come up to this 25-year-old and thank him for saving them from wasting the rest of their careers as they had wasted them up to that point? Those who defy the crowd should not expect accolades from the crowd.

There is an even more difficult problem: The fact that one defies the crowd does not mean that one's ideas are good. There are plenty of crowd-defying ideas that are crowd-defiant simply because so few people would be foolish enough to believe them. For example, few people today believe that little green people live on Mars. Believing in such creatures would be crowd defying, but, in all likelihood, foolish as well. Wendell Garner once told me of a comment made to him by Michael Posner. The comment was that the easiest papers to get accepted by journals, and the easiest proposals to get funded by granting agencies, were those that were middling in quality. They made a contribution but offended no one. The hardest pieces to get accepted were those that were awful, because they were awful, and those that were wonderful, because they often went against the way things were being done at the time.

I have learned this lesson from both directions. Some of what I considered my best articles had to be revised many times before being accepted. But perhaps more revealing was an incident with another article. I wrote an article on the development of linear syllogistic reasoning (Sternberg, 1980a), which is the kind of reasoning used in problems such as "John is taller than Mary; Mary is taller than Susan; who is tallest?" After submitting the article, I came to realize it was really quite trivial. The article basically took a theory of linear-syllogistic reasoning I had proposed (Sternberg, 1980b) and applied it developmentally. There was nothing new in the article. I thought about withdrawing it and then decided I would just let it get rejected and die a quiet death. To my astonishment, I got back three glowing reviews. It was at that point I learned that, in the short run, the research that is most valued is often that which threatens no one. It makes a small contribution and claims to be nothing more than a small contribution.

I've found Posner's wisdom to be very useful to me over the years. The problem, of course, is that one can never be sure if one's rejected article or grant proposal is an unappreciated gem or a rightly rejected dud. I often use a "three-time" heuristic. I submit an article or proposal to up to three places. Each time it is turned down, I try to improve it. If, after three tries, it is still rejected, I put it in a file drawer (or, today, on the hard drive of my computer) and let it incubate. I cannot be sure if the idea is a good one or a bad one; what I can be sure of is that I have not persuaded others of the value of my idea. And part of the creative process is persuading others that one's ideas have value (Sternberg & Lubart, 1995, 1996).

I have not always succeeded in persuading other people of the value of my ideas, and sometimes, for good reason. During my first year at Yale, I became convinced that Garner's (1974) viewpoint regarding structure inhering in the stimulus rather than in the interaction between person and stimulus was wrong. So I did some research to knock down his theory. I felt truly defiant: I was defying the views of a senior member of my department! I submitted the article to a journal, and it was rejected. I presented the research as a talk, and it was destroyed.

One day, Garner called me into his office. Of course, he had been one of the reviewers of the article, and a fair one. He told me that there was a lesson to be learned from this experience. The lesson was that one is judged by posterity for the positive contributions one makes, not for the negative contributions. I have tried to learn that lesson and to make contributions that seek to build rather than destroy. It is easy to be defiant and knock down someone else's work. What is hard is to come up with a better idea.

In my third year, John Anderson left to go to Carnegie–Mellon, and a senior slot opened. I applied for it but didn't get it. The department offered the position to Bill Estes. I consoled myself by telling myself he was more than twice my age. But he turned down Yale to go to Harvard, so the slot remained open, and I was again considered for the tenured position.

I started hearing rumblings that Yale was getting letters back from referees stating, implicitly or explicitly, that it was not at all clear that they should hire me for the slot. Intelligence, these referees thought, was a rather junky field, and with a limited number of senior slots, Yale might do better to select someone in a better field. This information depressed me, and I began to question whether defying the crowd and working in the field of intelligence—which indeed did not have a very good reputation—was such a great idea, after all. I talked to Garner, my informal senior faculty mentor, and told him that perhaps I had made a mistake. I said that, when all was said and done, I could have done exactly the same work I had been doing, but labeled it as work in thinking or problem solving. Either of these fields had higher prestige, and perhaps if I had labeled my work thus, my employment prospects would not now be in jeopardy. Garner gave me what I consider to be some of the best advice I have received in my entire career. It went something like this:

> You're afraid that your intelligence research may cost you your job, and you're asking me what to do about it? You're right. Your intelligence research may cost you your job. You want my advice, so I'll give you my advice. You should go on doing exactly what you have been doing. When you came here, your mission was to make a difference to the field of intelligence. And that's what you have to do, even if it does cost you your job.

Tulving and Bower gave me similar advice. I took it, and I'm still at Yale. I should say, though, that studying intelligence and related phenomena has not been cost-free.

One day, Yale was hosting a very well-known cognitive psychologist from an esteemed institution. He came to chat with me in my office, and I mentioned some cognitive research I was doing. He commented to me something like, "You know, Bob, you're not really a cognitive psychologist anymore." At the time, I was stunned. I took pride in being a cognitive psychologist, and here I was being told by an eminence that I was anything but. I have come to realize that he was not alone: Despite Cronbach's (1957) plea for a unification of the two disciplines of scientific psychology and despite my own efforts at unification (e.g., Sternberg, 1978), the two disciplines have never become truly unified. Their practitioners often have eyed one another with suspicion. And those who choose a path that bridges them may end up being viewed with suspicion by practitioners in both camps!

Modern History

As the years went by, the character of my research began to change. Less and less of it was in the laboratory, more and more of it out in the everyday world. I was looking less and less like the standard cognitive psychologist, or psychologist of any particular kind at all. I was not entirely alone, however.

Dick Neisser wrote what I consider to be two classic books in his career. The first, *Cognitive Psychology* (Neisser, 1967), largely established Neisser's career and also was instrumental in establishing the field of cognitive psychology. It provided a theoretical framework for much laboratory-based cognitive psychology. It was well received and has been widely cited. The second book, *Cognition and Reality* (Neisser, 1976), argued for the importance of studying cognition in context. It has never had anywhere near the influence of the earlier book, and research resulting from it has even generated some broadside attacks (e.g., Banaji & Crowder, 1989).

I liked the first book and loved the second. People who study intelligence in its everyday manifestations find that it seems to behave according to different rules in everyday life than those that obtain when people solve rather structured and formal problems of the kinds found on intelligence tests (Sternberg et al., 2000). My ventures into psychology in the everyday world have met with the approbation of some and the disapproval of others. Those in the traditional intelligence fraternity have reacted in various ways to the work I have done throughout my career, some ignoring it and others attacking it in various ways. I can happily say that only one of the many attacks I have seen has been vicious and personal, and that attack is not yet published and may not be, at least in the form it was originally written.

In my intelligence and other research, I have tried to take a balanced approach (Sternberg, 1985, 1990, 1997b). I tend to believe that truth often lies in the middle ground. My style tends to be integrative—seeking, for example, a rapprochement among psychometric, cognitive, and contextualist approaches to intelligence. But sometimes one finds oneself under pressure to choose sides. The message one receives is that either you are for the "Blue Team," or you are against it. Of course, you get the same message from the "Red Team." It often takes some strength to seek and stay on a middle course.

In the early years, the work we did in my research group, balanced though it may have been, was largely ignored by testing organizations. For a while, I worked with one such organization, but when the leadership changed, I was quickly dismissed. The head of one such organization used to walk out when I gave talks. More recently, leadership changes have resulted in our working with some of the same organizations that used to shun us. It is a challenge to work with such organizations, because our views on what needs to be measured do not always correspond to theirs. But we have found that, with open-minded leadership, one can go rather far. For example, right now we are involved in a 16-site project to develop instruments that might eventually be used to supplement the SAT for use in college admission. Our idea is to create research projects that have the maximum possible impact—scientifically, educationally, and societally.

Our expanded work in the everyday world is in large part a matter of mission—we, in my group, are trying to change the world, and we think the way to change the world is by working in and being a part of it. But there is another factor that has led us in this direction, one whose influence I underestimated when I was younger. As time went on, I have written many grant proposals. Some have been accepted, others rejected. But the accepted ones tended to be ones that were school or community based, and the rejected ones tended to be ones that were laboratory based. So I found, as have so many others, that my work was shaped not only by what I wanted to do, but also by what I was able to do with the funds at hand.

Not all our work has been funded, of course. In the early 1980s, my personal life was not going well. And just as my failures on intelligence tests had led me to the study of intelligence, my personal failures led me to the study of love. Love research was, at least at the time, one of the few areas in psychology that enjoyed even less prestige than did intelligence research, a distinction not easily attained. But I had some ideas first about how the structures (not the content) of psychometric theories of intelligence could be applied to the study of love (Sternberg & Grajek, 1984). So I started studying love.

I naively thought that people would commend me for broadening out in my theory and research. Not so fast. I found the reaction to be often more negative than positive. Some said that I had gone soft in the head; others that I had run out of ideas about intelligence; others that I wanted to be another Dr. Ruth. Instead of accolades, I was getting flack. I was therefore particularly pleased when a theory article (Sternberg, 1986) was published in the *Psychological Review,* perhaps the first theory of love published in that journal. But acceptances were mixed with rejections, and I continued to muddle through, much the way I had in the work I had done on intelligence. My articles on love as a story encountered rougher sailing, although eventually I found homes for them (Sternberg, 1995, 1996; Sternberg, Hojjat, & Barnes, 2001) and eventually simply decided to write a book on the subject (Sternberg, 1998b)—a book, incidentally, which, wonderful though it was, did not sell very well.

Oddly enough, it was not just the cognitive people who questioned my entrance into the love field. Some of the people in that field viewed me as some kind of interloper. I was an intelligence researcher. Who did I think I was studying love, a topic foreign to the bulk of my research? To this day, I have never been invited to speak at any conference on love, despite having published a fair amount of work in the field. Of course, there are multiple interpretations of my failure to have been invited to speak!

In recent years, the interests of my research group have diverged even more than in the past. We still study intelligence, creativity, love, and related topics, but I think I am most excited by three aspects of our research.

The first aspect is research in other cultures (e.g., Sternberg & Grigorenko, 1997, 1999). We have come to believe that psychologists cannot understand phenomena in their own culture unless they understand how, and whether, these phenomena apply in other cultures. Many of the things we take for granted, we stop taking for granted when we look at people in diverse foreign lands.

The second aspect is research in the schools (e.g., Grigorenko, Jarvin, & Sternberg, in press; Sternberg, Torff, & Grigorenko, 1998). What we find is that by using teaching methods based on my theory of intelligence (Sternberg, 1997b), we can make a difference in students' school performance: Students can achieve at higher levels when they are taught in a way that enables them to capitalize on strengths and to compensate for or correct weaknesses.

The third aspect is our research on wisdom (e.g., Sternberg, 1998a, 2001). There are many people who are intelligent, but they are not wise. According to the balance theory, people are wise when they apply their (successful) intelligence to a common good, seeking to balance their interests with the interests of other people and institutions.

One of the wonderful things about research in psychology is that one can apply what one studies to one's own life, or at least, try to learn from it. Studying wisdom has been a special opportunity to try to become more balanced in my thought and affect. I suppose that I have achieved greater balance even in my personal life. In recent years, I have taken up the cello after a hiatus of 30 years during which I stupidly defined myself as an "ex-cellist," have continued to exercise every day, and have started the study of a third foreign language. I am amazed by the opportunities that are out there, if only one finds (or, even better, creates) them.

Although one can try to be wise in one's life, the wise course of action often is not altogether clear. For example, recently, a new problem cropped up in my life. Although early in my career I found the psychology department at Yale to be a hospitable environment, I began to question that a couple of years ago. I increasingly felt isolated. This was not the "fault" of my colleagues. Rather, it seemed more and more that my own thinking and values were departing from others'. The composition of the department had changed, and I worried whether its ways of thinking and mine were parting company. I thought about leaving but ultimately found another solution.

In 2000, we opened the Yale Center for the Psychology of Abilities, Competencies, and Expertise. The center is housed in its own building —an old house in which two U.S. Presidents, Theodore Roosevelt and William Howard Taft, slept. Since we moved there, it has been close to paradise for us. We have established our own team-oriented culture and our own set of values regarding the importance of scientific, educational, and societal impact. We believe that teams, when well managed, produce work that is more than the sum of the parts (Sternberg & Grigorenko, 2000). At the same time, we remain part of the Department of Psychology. Our building is at the northern edge of campus, and when I selected the site, I found our moving to the edge of campus to be symbolic of the way we think. We hope we always stay at this edge.

My undergraduate advisor, Tulving, once said to me that I would be surprised at the amount of time it takes to have an impact—to make a difference. He was right. I'm 51, and I often feel frustrated with the lack of impact I've had. I'm hoping my career is only half done. Maybe in the second half I'll accomplish some of what I have failed to accomplish in the first.

If I do, it will be not because I follow the crowd, but rather, because I head where I need to go, regardless of where others go. I do not believe that all creative work is crowd defying (Sternberg, 1999a, 1999b). And certainly not all my work has been crowd defying. Early in my career, I did some work on metaphor (e.g., Sternberg & Nigro, 1983; Tourangeau & Sternberg, 1981), which at the time was a hot area. I enjoyed the work but did not enjoy the crowding. The field had too many people competing too furiously. I have always been susceptible to claustrophobia, and I felt claustrophobic. So for me, I do my best when the tune I play is the one I write. Each of us must create his or her path, and I am constantly trying to create my own.

References

Banaji, M. R., & Crowder, R. C. (1989). The bankruptcy of everyday memory. *American Psychologist, 44,* 1185–1193.

Cronbach, L. J. (1957). The two disciplines of scientific psychology. *American Psychologist, 12,* 671–684.

Garner, W. R. (1974). *The processing of information and structure.* Potomac, MD: Erlbaum.

Grigorenko, E. L., Jarvin, L., & Sternberg, R. J. (in press). School-based tests of the triarchic theory of intelligence: Three settings, three samples, three syllabi. *Contemporary Educational Psychology.*

Neisser, U. (1967). *Cognitive psychology.* New York: Appleton-Century-Crofts.

Neisser, U. (1976). *Cognition and reality.* San Francisco: W. H. Freeman.

Sternberg, R J. (1972). A decision rule to facilitate the undergraduate admissions process. *College and University, 48,* 48–53.

Sternberg, R. J. (1973). Cost-benefit analysis of the Yale admissions office interview. *College and University, 48,* 154–164.

Sternberg, R. J. (1977a). Component processes in analogical reasoning. *Psychological Review, 84,* 353–378.

Sternberg, R. J. (1977b). *Intelligence, information processing, and analogical reasoning: The componential analysis of human abilities.* Hillsdale, NJ: Erlbaum.

Sternberg, R. J. (1978). Intelligence research at the interface between differential and cognitive psychology. *Intelligence, 2,* 195–222.

Sternberg, R. J. (1980a). The development of linear syllogistic reasoning. *Journal of Experimental Child Psychology, 29,* 340–356.

Sternberg, R. J. (1980b). Representation and process in linear syllogistic reasoning. *Journal of Experimental Psychology: General, 109,* 119–159.

Sternberg, R. J. (1983). Components of human intelligence. *Cognition, 15,* 1–48.

Sternberg, R. J. (1985). Human intelligence: The model is the message. *Science, 230,* 1111–1118.

Sternberg, R. J. (1986). A triangular theory of love. *Psychological Review, 93,* 119–135.

Sternberg, R. J. (1990). *Metaphors of mind.* New York: Cambridge University Press.

Sternberg, R. J. (1992). *Psychological Bulletin's* top 10 "Hit Parade." *Psychological Bulletin, 112,* 387–388.

Sternberg, R. J. (1995). Love as a story. *Journal of Social and Personal Relationships, 12,* 541–546.

Sternberg, R. J. (1996). Love stories. *Personal Relationships, 3,* 1359–1379.

Sternberg, R. J. (1997a). Fads in psychology: What we can do. *APA Monitor, 28*(7), 19.

Sternberg, R. J. (1997b). *Successful intelligence.* New York: Plume.

Sternberg, R. J. (1998a). A balance theory of wisdom. *Review of General Psychology, 2,* 347–365.

Sternberg, R. J. (1998b). *Love is a story.* New York: Oxford University Press.

Sternberg, R. J. (1999a). The creativity paradox: Why everyone and no one seems to appreciate creative work. *APA Monitor, 30*(10), 17.

Sternberg, R. J. (1999b). A propulsion theory of types of creative contributions. *Review of General Psychology, 3,* 83–100.

Sternberg, R. J. (2001). Why schools should teach for wisdom: The balance theory of wisdom in educational settings. *Educational Psychologist, 36,* 227–245.

Sternberg, R. J., & Bower, G. H. (1974). Transfer in part–whole and whole–part free recall: A comparative evaluation of theories. *Journal of Verbal Learning and Verbal Behavior, 13,* 1–26.

Sternberg, R. J., Forsythe, G. B., Hedlund, J., Horvath, J., Snook, S., Williams, W. M., et al. (2000). *Practical intelligence in everyday life.* New York: Cambridge University Press.

Sternberg, R. J., & Grajek, S. (1984). The nature of love. *Journal of Personality and Social Psychology, 47,* 312–329.

Sternberg, R. J., & Grigorenko, E. L. (1997). The cognitive costs of physical and mental ill health: Applying the psychology of the developed world to the problems of the developing world. *Eye on Psi Chi, 2*(1), 20–27.

Sternberg, R. J., & Grigorenko, E. L. (1999). A smelly 113 degrees in the shade, or why we do field research. *APS Observer, 12*(1), 10–11, 20–21.

Sternberg, R. J., & Grigorenko, E. L. (2000). The myth of the lone ranger in psychological research. *APS Observer, 13,* 11, 27.

Sternberg, R. J., Hojjat, M., & Barnes, M. L. (2001). Empirical tests of aspects of a theory of love as a story. *European Journal of Personality, 15,* 1–20.

Sternberg, R. J., & Lubart, T. I. (1995). *Defying the crowd: Cultivating creativity in a culture of conformity.* New York: Free Press.

Sternberg, R. J., & Lubart, T. I. (1996). Investing in creativity. *American Psychologist, 51,* 677–688.

Sternberg, R. J., & Nigro, G. (1983). Interaction and analogy in the comprehension and appreciation of metaphors. *Quarterly Journal of Experimental Psychology, 35A,* 17–38.

Sternberg, R. J., Torff, B., & Grigorenko, E. L. (1998). Teaching triarchically improves school performance. *Journal of Educational Psychology, 90,* 374–385.

Sternberg, R. J., & Tulving, E. (1977). The measurement of subjective organization in free recall. *Psychological Bulletin, 84,* 539–556.

Terman, L. M., & Merrill, M. (1937). *Measuring intelligence.* Boston: Houghton-Mifflin.

Tourangeau, R., & Sternberg, R. J. (1981). Aptness in metaphor. *Cognitive Psychology, 13,* 27–55.

Tulving, E. (1966). Subjective organization and effects of repetition in multi-trial free-recall learning. *Journal of Verbal Learning and Verbal Behavior, 5,* 193–197.

Tulving, E., & Thomson, D. M. (1973). Encoding specificity and retrieval processes in episodic memory. *Psychological Review, 80,* 352–373.

Edward Zigler is probably best known for his work in helping to create the nation's first, and most successful, school-readiness program, Head Start. Zigler, a basic researcher himself, paddled against the establishment current in an effort to bridge the gap between basic and applied researchers, by heading to Washington to aid policymakers—many of whom knew little to nothing about the science behind their policies. Although heavily criticized by the pro-basic-research establishment for attempting to "sully" the science by mixing it with application, Zigler forged ahead and has been a vital part of the successful movement to boost the quality of life for poor children in America. In addition, his extensive work in the field of mental retardation has led to a revolution in the standard beliefs and practices in that field.

Edward Zigler

What Would Draw a Basic Scientist Into Head Start (and Why Would He Never Leave)?

16

When the call came from Washington, DC, I thought it must be for another Zigler. The famed pediatrician Dr. Robert Cooke was on the line, inviting me to join a committee that would design a school readiness program for children who lived in poverty. The effort was part of President Lyndon Johnson's War on Poverty, a campaign I had read about in the newspapers but that seemed far afield from the work I was doing in my research laboratory and classroom. Yet I accepted instantly, more out of a sense of patriotic duty than a belief that I could actually do something to break the cycle of poverty. It was not that long ago that I had served my country in the Korean War, and I was not of the emerging generation that would become known for draft protests and peace rallies. I guess I felt that I was being drafted again, and I had no choice but to serve.

This admission is probably not what the reader expects to see in a book about people who "battled the establishment." But, by accepting Dr. Cooke's invitation, I was unknowingly joining another battle that had nothing to do with our nation's war against economic inequality. The antagonists were basic and applied researchers, and their argument was about whether science belonged in the laboratory or in the field. Before I get to that dispute, I must confess that it was probably my somewhat antiestablishment thinking that caught Dr. Cooke's attention in the first place. I will tell that piece of the story now, partly to follow a logical chronology and partly to prove that I really have a devotion to psychological science despite what my seniors may have once said.

A "New" (in the 1950s) Approach to Mental Retardation

As a graduate student at the University of Texas in Austin, I was looking forward to serving an internship and becoming a clinical psychologist. However, not unlike graduate training today, I was required to take classes in theory, research methodology, and statistics and to apply these lessons by conducting empirical work. My field was child development, which was a specialty in its own right (unlike the study of mental retardation, which was a division of abnormal psychology). My advisor, Harold Stevenson, and I were churning out and testing hypotheses following what was then standard protocol: taking findings from animal studies (mostly rats) to see if they applied to children's behavior. One of our experiments was based on discoveries by Crespi (1944) and Zeaman (1949) that rats ran a maze faster when the reward was larger or tastier than when it was less desirable. But try as we might, the preschool children in our studies were not varying their learning speed to variations in the magnitude of the reinforcement provided. (The concept of intrinsic or mastery motivation, now the obvious reason for their lack of response, was still in the early stages of development and was not available as an explanatory edifice.) We tinkered with this and that variable until we had tested all the children in all the nursery schools in the city. Having exhausted my subject pool, I got the idea of introducing myself to the administrators of the Austin State School, a residential institution for individuals with mental retardation. I reasoned that IQ was irrelevant to my hypothesis and that I could continue the study by testing retarded individuals with mental ages comparable to those of the nursery school children.

What I learned in that institution was to change my career path and, eventually, the field of mental retardation (which did become a specialty in its own right). The retarded participants in my study behaved exactly the same as the nursery school children: They approached the learning task in the same way, and they were equally unresponsive to my experimental manipulations. But they were quite responsive to me and to the personal attention and positive interactions available in the testing situation.

To make a long story short, these observations led to my developmental approach to mental retardation (a pioneering effort in what would become the field of developmental psychopathology). I theorized that cognitive development in individuals with cultural–familial retardation proceeds in the same fashion as in nonretarded children, but at a slower rate and peaking at a lower level. Thus, when groups of retarded and nonretarded individuals are matched for mental age, their performance on cognitive tasks should be similar. Often, however, the retarded children appear to function at levels below what would be expected of their mental age. My studies began to uncover personality factors arising from their socialization histories that attenuated their performance. Prominent were frequent failure and a lack of positive social interactions. These led to traits such as fear of failure, learned helplessness, outerdirectedness, and tendencies to seek or avoid relating to others. (This work is detailed in Burack, Hodapp, & Zigler, 1998, and Zigler & Bennett-Gates, 1999.) I did not think these responses were unique to individuals with cultural–familial retardation but could appear in nonretarded people who also experienced repeated failure and social deprivation. Indeed, my subsequent research revealed that children of average intelligence who lived in impoverished families or in institutions (both circumstances common to cultural-familial groups) displayed similar motivational hindrances.

This work was perceived as verging on heretical in the area of mental retardation. At the time, the prevailing view was that retarded individuals had defective cognitive structures and that their intellectual functioning was therefore inherently different from that of individuals of average intelligence. I was saying that their experiences, not their cognitive structures, were different and caused motivational obstacles to optimal performance. The defect theorists (all respected, established scholars including the icon, Kurt Lewin) and I (an unknown newcomer) had heated debates in the literature and in lecture halls.

Dr. Cooke happened to be in the audience during one of these debates. He heard me argue that retarded children are so often confronted with tasks they cannot master that failure comes to dominate their self-images and to undermine the efforts they are willing to make in the future. Later, when he was asked by Sargent Shriver (President Johnson's chief strategist in the antipoverty war) to assemble a group of experts to design a program for the children of the poor, he thought about the detrimental behavioral effects I attributed to failure among retarded children. He believed that children living in poverty also experienced an inordinate amount of failure that eroded their ability to learn even before they started school. Dr. Cooke thought that, like the retarded children in some of my studies, poor children would have better chances of success in school if they could be given more success experiences. Hence, he thought I had something to contribute to his committee.

A Scientist Goes to Washington

When the Planning Committee of what would become Project Head Start convened in 1964, we started with a virtually blank slate. With the exception of a few small, experimental projects, there was little experience at the time to suggest how to meet the needs of economically disadvantaged preschoolers. The 14 committee members had backgrounds in medicine, mental health, social work, child development, and early childhood education, and each felt that his or her discipline should be part of the intervention. I was the youngest (a booming 34), and probably most demanding, person on the committee. I also came to the meetings with a different perspective than most of the others, save the one other developmental psychologist on the committee, the great Urie Bronfenbrenner. Whereas the majority worked in applied fields, I was trained in empirical methodology, hypothesis testing, and theory building. Thus I injected into our deliberations an often unwelcome dose of scientific skepticism and demands that our plans be knowledge based or at least piloted and carefully studied.

There was no real consensus among committee members about the basic question of how many children we should put into the program in its first summer of operation. Shriver went outside of the committee to ask the famous child psychologist, Jerome Bruner, how many children we should recruit for the opening class. Bruner recommended 2,500. That sounded fine to me, because I was then conducting studies with samples in the 30 to 90 range.

But Head Start was not meant to be a small, pilot project. For one thing, President Johnson demanded that Shriver fire a major volley in the war by starting out in a grand manner. For another, Shriver himself was thinking nationally and was not interested in a minor experimental effort. So the first number he gave the committee was 25,000 children, but even this magnification of Bruner's recommendation quickly grew to 125,000. Meanwhile, applications for Head Start grants kept pouring in from around the nation. The program's popularity was surprising in that there was not yet a single classroom in existence. When Head Start opened in the summer of 1965, just a few months after we finished our planning, more than half a million children attended.

I was troubled by this development. How could we subject all these children and their families to this hasty, unproven, indefinite program?

I came to terms with what we insiders dubbed "Project Rush Rush" because I was sure it would do no harm. The children would get immunized, have their teeth and eyes checked, and eat nutritious meals. Their families would receive some services and be invited to participate in parent education classes and in their children's early schooling. Some of this might do some good, but I didn't have particularly high hopes. Head Start was only a summer program; children attended for just 6 or 8 weeks before they started elementary school in the fall. No one on the planning committee believed we could break the cycle of poverty in such a short period of time. About all we were sure of was that even a small dose of preschool education, health care, and good nutrition was better than none. Even I didn't need hard data to agree with that.

It also occurred to me that when we were asked to plan a program, the result was expected to be an operational program. This was my first realization that policymakers and academic psychologists inhabit different worlds. Academics devise ways to test ideas using small groups, repeating the process as they refine both the ways and the ideas. Policymakers are action oriented. They mount real programs to serve real people and then go on to the next item on the social action agenda. It took me years to get used to that. Over time I came to accept that there will be occasions when psychologists do not think they have sufficient knowledge about a social issue to justify a policy recommendation, but they still know more than policymakers do. Laws will be made and programs launched with or without us, so we might as well contribute what we do have.

However, I did not yet accept that back in 1964, and my scientific side made it difficult to accept the lack of a pilot program. When it became clear there would be none, I insisted that Head Start at least be evaluated so we could have some way of knowing if the program was accomplishing anything and some clues as to what we might do to improve it. The majority of the planners felt we were going to give children health care and some pleasant experiences (all good things), so there really wasn't anything to evaluate. I found an ally in Julius Richmond, the project director, who advised the committee that research and evaluation be added to the planning document. Because I was the one who had made all the noise, he told me to go ahead and develop some measures.

I worked with Edmund Gordon, who became director of Head Start's evaluation component. We only had a little over 2 weeks to decide on what to measure and how. (Some three decades later, I am still indebted to that hardy band of graduate students who labored day and night to help us meet this impossible deadline.) With the little time we had, our instruments were never psychometrically adequate, so the scores were not a bit useful. Their only value was in representing a commitment to evaluation that would take some time to mature—30 years, to be precise. The 1994 Amendments to the Head Start Act began an unprecedented federal commitment to research and evaluation, and I guess I should be proud of my stubbornness in making research part of Head Start.

My next foray in uncharted territory came just a few years after the Planning Committee disbanded, when the Nixon administration asked me to serve as the first director of the Office of Child Development (now the Administration on Children, Youth and Families). The new office would house the Head Start program, the venerable Children's Bureau, and other child-oriented bureaucratic entities. (The full story of my days planning Head Start and in Washington is told in Zigler & Muenchow, 1992.) Although I had doubts about leaving academia to become a bureaucrat, I was attracted by the administration's expressed interest in early childhood. There was also the possibility that I would be able to help shape the child care component of the Family Assistance Plan, which was the president's proposal to help families leave welfare. Finally, no one really understood what this new child development office was supposed to be. It would be up to me to set its course—and thus the course of our nation's response to meeting children's needs. This was more than an opportunity to me. It was an obligation.

The Errant Scholar

My colleagues in academia thought the opposite, that I was not meeting my obligations. I was supposed to be a scientist, but I was sullying the profession by working on practical details, public administration, and politics. I was told so in no uncertain terms by a prominent developmentalist who made a point of scolding me when he came to Yale on business. "Ed," he said, "you have all the makings of a first-rank developmental psychologist, if only you would stop this policy nonsense." His opinion that basic and applied science were at opposite ends of scholarship and that basic researchers were superior to those who worked in application was firmly entrenched in academia at the time.

To illustrate: I vividly recall a meeting of the governing council of the Society for Research in Child Development (SRCD), a professional association dedicated to methodologically rigorous, theory-based studies of developmental phenomena. The time was 1975, when the United States withdrew from the conflict in Vietnam. Fearful of the future, Vietnamese parents were hoping to save their children by putting them on planes bound for the United States, a frantic effort dubbed "Operation Babylift." At the council meeting, I pointed out that our membership had a wealth of expertise that could aid in the resettlement of these children. We knew about the effects of social deprivation, about the potential developmental harm after separation from an attachment figure, about difficulties in adapting to a new environment. I suggested that SRCD write to President Gerald Ford and offer our services. SRCD's president said that he would send a letter offering his personal help, but he argued that the society should not be committed to such applied tasks.

Ironically, the Ford administration turned to me to convene a task force that could make recommendations and give professional leadership to the administration's resettlement effort. The chief staff person helping me in this effort was Sally Styfco, a trusted aide who continues to work with me on the social policy front to this day. In putting together our council of advisors, we again vividly encountered the chasm between social action–oriented developmentalists, who wanted to use the knowledge we had to help the nation deal with the pressing issue of integrating thousands of high-risk children, and the laboratory-oriented developmentalists, who felt there was really nothing to meet about. This latter group's solution to the problem was to get a large amount of money from the federal government so we could conduct a longitudinal study to examine how these displaced children adjust to American homes and society. Without the help of these laboratory types, the selected developmentalists (with input from the Vietnamese community) did a commendable job in meeting the requests that were made of us.

The contrast between the vast knowledge in the scholarly community and the need for knowledge in the policy community had appeared to me before. In my first days in Washington, I was shocked to realize how little I knew about the policymaking process. But I also saw how little policymakers knew of the child development literature. They were very eager to learn. I came to be called "Professor" Zigler, and my staff meetings were known as "lectures." This of course was not academia, and the people who attended were not my staff or my students but very high-ranking officials. They were dedicated public workers who really wanted to hear what research could tell them and to use this information to form better policies.

By the time I returned from Washington to Yale, a growing number of university researchers believed that policy construction could be enriched by developmental science. I shared my firsthand experiences with three leading developmentalists—Urie Bronfenbrenner, Julius Richmond, and Sheldon White—none of whom was afraid to think outside of the box. Soon we approached the Bush Foundation (established by Mr. and Mrs. Archibald Granville Bush of Minnesota) with our ideas. We proposed creating centers for training child development scholars who wanted to work at the intersection of research and social policy. The concept seemed to shake the pillars of traditional academia by melding basic and applied sciences and spanning across disciplines within settings known for departmentalism.

The foundation granted seed money for four of these centers for one decade. Perhaps the philanthropists believed that we were ahead of our time, but that in 10 years (and with the centers' success), multidisciplinary, applied work would become standard fare in higher education. And the centers were successful, drawing professionals as well as traditional students to their unique programs. I still direct the Yale Bush Center in Child Development and Social Policy, which is the only remaining center under the Bush name. It is not that the idea of training students to use scientific knowledge to solve social problems did not catch on. It did, but universities were loathe to use their own endowments to pay for them.

Although there is only one Bush Center left, our original mission has become more acceptable in academic circles. Similar institutes are now operating at many schools. An exemplar is the applied developmental program at Fordham University. There are several reasons why students are being encouraged to take the same steps I was discouraged from taking not that many years ago. One is that government and many private funding sources are most interested in projects that have visible results. Also, the spread of interdisciplinary work has brought psychologists closer to those in fields devoted to practice. Even the bastion of basic research, SRCD, has begun to welcome applied research topics into its semiannual conferences and into the pages of its flagship journal, *Child Development*, joining several journals that encourage articles that bridge developmental thought and social action (Zigler, 1980, 1998). The society also now publishes *Social Policy Report*, the goal being "to promote the application of developmental science so that the social work we do for children and families is the best it can be and to demonstrate the importance of developmental science to the well-being of children and families" (Sherrod, 2000, p. 2). Finally, today's young students are an active-minded generation who want to contribute both to the knowledge base and to humanity.

Thinking back, I attribute my success in having some influence over national social policies, and over my professional field, to my posture as a scientist—the very place where I began. I have always believed that the scientific method is a powerful tool for discerning what drives human behavior and development and, eventually, for improving these facets of human life. It was not hubris that led me to disavow the accepted belief that defective cognitive systems drove the behavior of individuals with mental retardation. It was the data from my empirical work that made me question what I had been taught. And it was not lust for power or fame that led me to contribute to Head Start's planning and administration. It was my belief that my understanding of the knowledge base derived from research in child development was a worthy contribution.

Over the years, I have relied on scientific advances to advance children's well-being. My commitment to guiding the development of Head Start by experimentation, empirical scrutiny, and evaluation has spurred genuine quality improvements. Science convinced me that the poor quality of child care commonly available is harmful to children's development and propelled me, not yet successfully, to promote policies to ensure that all children in out-of-home care have safe, nurturing learning environments (see, e.g., Zigler & Lang, 1991). Empirical evidence highlighting the importance of the first 3 years of life inspired me to promote the Family and Medical Leave Act (1993), which was conceived at the Yale Bush Center (Zigler & Frank, 1988), and to envision Early Head Start (Zigler & Styfco, 1993), which I advised Senator Ted Kennedy (D-MA) and the Clinton administration on in addition to serving on the program's planning committee.

I offer these lists to prove that I am a firm believer in basic science —the same basic science I was accused of degrading by my work in social policy. But I am not a believer in knowledge for its own sake. What we learn from our scientific studies is too valuable to be held in an academic vacuum. I believe the 18 million children and families who have attended Head Start since it began, and the countless number of persons with mental retardation who have had more humane treatment since I insisted that they have personalities too, would whole-heartedly agree.

References

Amendments to the Head Start Act, 42 U.S.C. § 9801 *et seq.* (1994).

Burack, J., Hodapp, R., & Zigler, E. (Eds.). (1998). *Handbook of mental retardation and development.* New York: Cambridge University Press.

Crespi, L. P. (1944). Amount of reinforcement and level of performance. *Psychological Review, 51,* 341–357.

Family and Medical Leave Act, 29 U.S.C. § 2601 *et seq.* (1993).

Sherrod, L. R. (2000). From the editor. *Social Policy Report, 14*(2), 2.

Zeaman, D. (1949). Response latency as a function of the amount of reinforcement. *Journal of Experimental Psychology, 39,* 466–483.

Zigler, E. (1980). Welcoming a new journal. *Journal of Applied Developmental Psychology, 1,* 1–6.

Zigler, E. (1998). A place of value for applied and policy studies. *Child Development, 69,* 532–542.

Zigler, E., & Bennett-Gates, D. (Eds.). (1999). *Personality development in individuals with mental retardation.* New York: Cambridge University Press.

Zigler, E., & Frank, M. (Eds.). (1988). *The parental leave crisis. Toward a national policy.* New Haven, CT: Yale University Press.

Zigler, E., & Lang, M. (1991). *Child care choices: Balancing the needs of children, families, and society.* New York: Free Press.

Zigler, E., & Muenchow, S. (1992). *Head Start: The inside story of America's most successful educational experiment.* New York: Basic Books.

Zigler, E., & Styfco, S. J. (1993). An earlier Head Start: Planning an intervention program for economically disadvantaged families and children ages zero to three. *Zero to Three, 14*(2), 25–28.

Index

About the Editor

Robert J. Sternberg is most well-known for his theory of successful intelligence, investment theory of creativity (developed with Todd Lubart), theory of mental self-government, balance theory of wisdom, and triangular theory of love and theory of love as a story. The focus of his research is intelligence and cognitive development. Dr. Sternberg is the author of over 800 journal articles, book chapters, and books and has received about $15 million in government grants and contracts for his research. He is currently president-elect of the American Psychological Association (APA) and editor of *Contemporary Psychology*. He received his PhD from Stanford University in 1975 and his BA summa cum laude, Phi Beta Kappa, from Yale University in 1972. He has won many awards, including the Early Career Award from APA, Outstanding Book Awards from the American Educational Research Association, the Distinguished Lifetime Contribution to Psychology Award from the Connecticut Psychological Association, the Cattell Award of the Society for Multivariate Experimental Psychology, and the Award for Excellence of the Mensa Education and Research Foundation. He has held a Guggenheim Fellowship as well as Yale University Senior and Junior Faculty Fellowships. He has been president of the Divisions of General Psychology, Educational Psychology, Psychology and the Arts, and Theoretical and Philosophical Psychology of the APA and has served as editor of the *Psychological Bulletin*.